FINDING CHANDRA

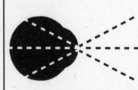

FINDING CHANDRA

A TRUE WASHINGTON MURDER MYSTERY

SCOTT HIGHAM
AND SARI HORWITZ

THORNDIKE PRESS
A part of Gale, Cengage Learning

GALE
CENGAGE Learning

Detroit • New York • San Francisco • New Haven, Conn • Waterville, Maine • London

GALE
CENGAGE Learning™

Copyright © 2010 by Scott Higham and Sari Horwitz.
Photograph credits appear on pages 451-452.
Thorndike Press, a part of Gale, Cengage Learning.

LIBRARY OF CONGRESS CATALOGING-IN-PUBLICATION DATA

Higham, Scott.
   Finding Chandra : a true Washington murder mystery / by
Scott Higham and Sari Horwitz. — Large print ed.
    p. cm.
  Includes bibliographical references.
  ISBN-13: 978-1-4104-2865-3 (hardcover)
  ISBN-10: 1-4104-2865-6 (hardcover)
   1. Levy, Chandra, 1977–2001. 2. Murder—Washington (D.C.)
3. Condit, Gary, 1948– 4. Guandique, Ingmar. 5. Large type
books I. Horwitz, Sari. II. Title.
HV6534.W3H54 2010b
364.152'3092—dc22   2010018556

Published in 2010 by arrangement with Scribner, a division of Simon &
Schuster, Inc.

Printed in the United States of America
1 2 3 4 5 6 7 14 13 12 11 10

For Chandra

CONTENTS

7

CAST OF CHARACTERS

THE LEVY FAMILY
Chandra Levy
Susan Levy, Chandra's mother
Robert Levy, Chandra's father
Adam Levy, Chandra's brother
Linda Zamsky, Chandra's aunt

METROPOLITAN POLICE DEPARTMENT
Police Chief Charles H. Ramsey
Executive Assistant Police Chief Terrance W. Gainer
Chief of Detectives Jack Barrett
Detective Ralph Durant
Detective Lawrence Kennedy
Detective Kenneth "Todd" Williams
Detective Anthony Brigidini
Detective Emilio Martinez
Sergeant Raul Figureas

FEDERAL BUREAU OF INVESTIGATION

Special Agent Brad Garrett
Special Agent Melissa Thomas

U.S. PARK POLICE

Detective Joe Green
Sergeant Dennis Bosak

THE PROFILER

Kim Rossmo, geographic profiler

U.S. ATTORNEY'S OFFICE

Assistant U.S. attorney Barbara Kittay
Assistant U.S. attorney Heidi Pasichow
Assistant U.S. attorney Elisa Poteat
Assistant U.S. attorney Kristina Ament

CONGRESSMAN GARY CONDIT

Carolyn Condit, Condit's wife
Mike Dayton, Condit's chief of staff in Washington
Michael Lynch, Condit's chief of staff in Modesto

THE WOMEN

Anne Marie Smith, United Airlines flight attendant
"Janet," Condit's legislative assistant in Washington

THE LAWYERS AND PRIVATE INVESTIGATORS

Abbe Lowell, Condit's attorney in Washington

Billy Martin, the Levys' attorney

Joseph Cotchett, Condit's attorney in California

Mark Geragos, Condit's attorney in California

J. T. "Joe" McCann, the Levys' private investigator

Dwayne Stanton, the Levys' private investigator

INGMAR ADALID GUANDIQUE AND HIS ASSOCIATES

Iris Portillo, Guandique's girlfriend

Maria Portillo, Guandique's girlfriend's mother

Sheila Phillips Cruz, Guandique's landlord

WOMEN ASSAULTED OR ACCOSTED IN ROCK CREEK PARK

Halle Shilling

Christy Wiegand

Amber Fitzgerald

Karen Mosley

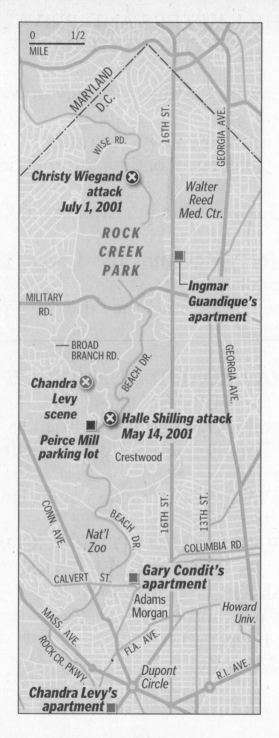

1
THE BONE COLLECTOR

The Crime Scene

On the slope of a steep ravine, deep in the woods of Washington's Rock Creek Park, Philip Palmer spotted an out-of-place object resting on the forest floor. He saw a patch of white, bleached out and barely visible through a thin layer of leaves.

Walking these woods was a ritual for Palmer, an attempt to flee the madness of the city. Each morning, the furniture maker tried to lose himself in the nine-mile-long oasis of forests, fields, and streams twice the size of New York's Central Park that slices through the center of the nation's capital. On this morning, May 22, 2002, the sun filtered through the leaves of the poplar and oak trees shading the hillside off the Western Ridge Trail, a solitary lane that begins near a centuries-old stone mill and winds its way north through the woods to the border of Maryland. Palmer moved closer to the object, his dog Paco by his side. The object, the size of a silver dollar, stood out against the leaves.

Palmer's quest seemed unusual for a man of forty-two who was raised in Chevy Chase, a neighborhood largely reserved for Washington's upper middle class on the northern edge of Rock Creek Park. Thin and wiry, with a mustache, beard, and an earring in his left ear, he looked like someone who belonged in the wilderness of the Colorado Rocky Mountains. He preferred the solace of the park to the bustle and affluence that surrounded him, and he prided himself on knowing every trail and path and glen. As a boy, he would head alone to the woods after school, sift through the dirt and leaves, and look for bits and pieces of animal bones. On good days, he'd find a complete skeleton, a mouse or a rat, a vole, maybe a raccoon, prizes he would keep and cherish. The finest examples of his collection from forgotten places in the park would later be carefully displayed on the shelves that lined the sitting parlor of his Victorian home in one of Washington's trendier neighborhoods, Dupont Circle.

By the spring of 2002, the park had become even more of a refuge for Palmer. Eight months earlier, on September 11, Washington watched as acrid smoke billowed from the Pentagon across the Potomac River. People in the streets looked skyward for the last of the four hijacked planes still trying to reach its Washington target. Rumors coursed through the city. The White House was next, maybe the U.S. Capitol. Since that day, the city had been under siege, awash in fear, prompted by security barricades, color-coded warnings, and police carrying automatic weapons. Congress rushed to create the biggest federal bureaucracy since World War II, the Department of Homeland Security. The nation prepared for war in the Middle East. Washington braced for a second wave of terror: a dirty bomb, another anthrax mailing, a suicide attacker on the National Mall or in the tunnels of the Metro that carried hundreds of thousands to work every day.

All that seemed a world away beneath the dark green canopy of Rock Creek Park. At the northern end of the park was a popular stable, its horses carrying riders along broad, leafy bridle paths. During the day, visitors picnicked in meadows and on tables perched along the creek. At night, children gazed at the stars near the only planetarium in the national park system. Founded in 1890, Rock Creek Park consists of 2,800 acres and is the country's oldest natural urban park. The heart of the park, the original "pleasure ground" approved by Congress, is where Palmer spotted the object, between the National Zoo and the border of Maryland. The park also includes Fort Stevens, the site of the lone Confederate attack on Washington. By the turn of the century, the park on the edge of the growing capital provided a cooling respite for city dwellers. They would ride in horse-drawn carriages, and relax on giant boulders in the middle of the creek. President Theodore Roosevelt took long walks in Rock Creek Park.

The park remained a pleasure ground, but over the years it had come to symbolize something else. Like many other urban parks, it had become the geographic dividing line of a racially polarized city with its vast wealth, abject poverty, corrupt and incompetent local governance, and some of the most abysmal crime statistics in the nation. On the west side were the city's well-to-do, middle-class, and mostly white neighborhoods — the stately foreign embassies along Massachusetts Avenue, the mansions of Georgetown, the soaring Gothic arches of the Washington National Cathedral, and the exclusive enclave of Cleveland Park with its Victorian homes and wraparound porches. "West of the Park" had become a euphemism for good schools and safe streets.

Southeast of the park were the city's museums and Capitol Hill, but some of the neighborhoods were home to the city's most impoverished residents. Not far from where Palmer spotted the object, the cityscape began to change, the street scene growing edgier with each passing block. The transformation started east of Eighteenth Street, a thoroughfare lined with Cuban, Salvadoran, and Ethiopian restaurants and popular nightclubs in a section of the city known as Adams Morgan. Farther east were the largely Latino and African-American neighborhoods of Mount Pleasant, Columbia Heights, and Shaw, the city's nearly all-black public schools, and the dilapidated housing projects of northeast and southeast Washington, where guns and drugs claimed hundreds of lives each year, many of them young black men.

Dupont Circle, where Palmer lived, was a southern gateway to the park. The three-story, turreted brownstone built in 1892 that he shared with his wife, a Washington defense lawyer, stood out among the rows of more traditional homes. Deer antlers and a large peace symbol adorned the façade.

To earn a living, Palmer built and restored furniture in his workshop. He didn't watch television and he refused to take photographs. He wanted to live in the moment, and photographs, he thought, tarnished memories because they could only capture what things looked like, not the smells or sounds or sensations that made them whole. He had a simple philosophy — "We're like animals, we come and go" — and he was childlike in his wonder and fascination with the outdoors. "You never know what you're going to find," he liked to say.

May 22 was one of those mornings that would prove him right. At about 9 A.M., Palmer parked his truck at the top of a hill near the horse corral of Rock Creek Park. He decided to walk near the Western Ridge Trail, which he hadn't been on for nearly five years. He noticed with disgust several beer bottles amid the thorny vines, patches of poison ivy, and mountain laurel that covered the forest floor. As he and Paco trudged farther into the woods, off the trail and down the ravine, he spotted a piece of red clothing. He kept walking and a few moments later came to a shallow depression in the ground. The remote spot was less than one hundred yards down the steep hillside from the top of the trail. He could hear the cars along Broad Branch Road another hundred yards below him.

At first Palmer thought that the bleached-out object he spotted was a turtle shell beneath the leaves. He bent down and swept the leaves aside. Then he abruptly stood up and backed away. He marked the spot with Paco's blue leash, and his dog bounded after him as he scrambled down the hillside toward Broad Branch Road. At the bottom, Palmer hung his sweatshirt over another branch so he could find his way back up. He crossed the creek bed, clambered up the other side, and went to the first house he saw. He knocked on the door. No answer. He went next door to a house that was being renovated and asked a construction worker if he could borrow his phone to call 911. As Palmer waited for the police, his mind raced, the tranquility of the morning shattered by what he had seen: molars, missing front teeth, dental fillings, a human skull.

2
BURN IT TO THE GROUND

In the fall of 2000, a year and a half before Palmer made his discovery, a young woman from an upper-middle-class California family left the West Coast for Washington, D.C., to begin an internship at the Federal Bureau of Prisons. Chandra Ann Levy was not unlike the thousands of college and graduate students who arrive in Washington as interns each year. She wanted to leave the familiar surroundings of her home in the San Joaquin Valley and find her own way in the nation's epicenter of politics and power. At twenty-three, she hoped to become an agent for the FBI or the CIA one day. Seven months after arriving in Washington, Chandra signed off her computer inside her Dupont Circle apartment on a warm spring day and went for a walk in her gym clothes. She was never heard from again.

D.C. detectives investigating her disappearance soon learned that Chandra had been carrying on a months-long affair with a married congressman from her home district in California. At fifty-two, Gary Condit was handsome and charismatic, a conservative Democrat who had been in Congress for eleven years. Word of the affair leaked and the news media became obsessed by the story of sex and suspicion. The coverage was incessant. During the summer of 2001, the story generated sensational headlines in newspapers around the world. The fledgling cable news shows that relied so heavily on fame, crime, and scandal to energize their broadcasts updated the story every twelve minutes or so, and polls showed that nearly two-thirds of the nation was following every turn of the real-life soap opera. When Condit consented to a nationally televised interview late that summer, 24 million Americans tuned in. But nearly three weeks later, when terrorists struck the World Trade Center and the Pentagon, the story about the congressman and the intern became a curiosity of the pre-9/11 world and quickly faded.

In 2007, as two senior editors at the *Washington Post* reviewed their story lists for the upcoming year, they considered including the Chandra Levy case. Six years later, it still endured as Washington's most famous murder mystery. Investigative editors Jeff Leen and Larry Roberts thought a reexamination of the case could perform a public service — and attract thousands of readers. They wondered why the murder had never been solved, whether the homicide investigation had been mishandled, and if anyone would ever stand trial for the crime. Leen and Roberts pitched their idea to one of their reporters, Sari Horwitz, who had worked briefly on the Chandra story years earlier. Her obsession with the unsolved case was no secret — Horwitz seemed to have a fated relationship with the homicide. She had been assigned to cover the story the day before Chandra's remains were discovered in Rock Creek Park in May 2002. A few weeks later, she was with private investigators when they unearthed one of Chandra's bones themselves. And a month after that, she met a source who said something that would haunt her for years: Police had missed the real killer. It wasn't Condit. The source gave her a name and enough details to persuade her that the information was true.

Horwitz, along with two other reporters, threw herself into the investigation and began to make real progress. They published several stories focusing on a suspect other than Condit. The last of these, about a Salvadoran immigrant convicted of assaulting two women in Rock Creek Park, appeared on the front page of the *Post* three days before serial snipers struck the Washington region in 2002. Horwitz was taken off the Levy story and assigned to the sniper attacks, but in the years that followed, she never forgot about the case; she kept a copy of the "Missing" poster of Chandra pinned up at her desk in the cavernous newsroom crowded with hundreds of reporters and editors.

The thought of renewing the investigation thrilled her. She knew how rare it was to get a second chance on something important in life. But she also worried about retracing her steps. She had been covering terrorism, and she wondered about the wisdom of leaving such an important beat.

Horwitz had been at the *Post* for twenty-three years, most of her adult life. Raised in Tucson, Arizona, Horwitz arrived at the *Post* as a summer intern in 1984. Early on, an editor thought she needed a big-city lesson. He dispatched her to the overnight police beat, considered to be a dismal, dead-end shift and a career killer for many reporters. Horwitz sought advice from the man who had hired her, the famous executive editor,

Ben Bradlee. "If you want to write about real life, about love and hate and greed and the human condition," he said, "go on the police beat."

Horwitz wound up falling for the dangerous, unpredictable life on the streets. She had arrived at the beat just as crack cocaine had inundated the inner city and was transforming Washington into the murder capital of the nation. Night after night she found herself in the middle of the grim and gritty drama of a city lost in crime, making strong connections with battle-hardened cops and parents gripped by grief in the moments after their children had been murdered. It was demanding and heartbreaking, but it lived up to every bit of Bradlee's billing. She soon developed a deep network of sources that would serve her well as she went on to cover education, poverty, the FBI, and counterterrorism for the paper. In 2006, Horwitz was named to the paper's investigative staff, a unit founded by legendary *Post* reporter Bob Woodward.

Leen and Roberts knew that the Chandra Levy project would be difficult to pursue and execute. They wanted no less than to find everything the police had found, and everything they had missed, reinterview every suspect and every witness, find out

29

everything there was to know about Chandra and Condit, and travel wherever the leads took them. Start from scratch, fill every hole, burn it to the ground.

The story would be bedeviled by all the difficulties typical of cold cases. People who had been interviewed years earlier would only be more reluctant to talk the second time around, for reasons ranging from forgetfulness to fear that a murderer was still loose, to the memory of getting singed in the media glare. Obviously Condit would be a hard sell, but even the Levys weren't certain to want to cooperate. Why should they reopen painful wounds and subject themselves to another round of exposure and public scrutiny? There was far too much ground to cover for one reporter. Leen and Roberts summoned another reporter from their staff and asked him to join the project, one who they knew would be an asset with his twenty years of experience as a dogged investigator.

The son of a New York City homicide detective who worked in the infamous Fort Apache station house in the South Bronx, Scott Higham had rejected the life of law enforcement. He instead pursued a career as an investigative reporter and made his way through the East Coast newspaper hierarchy with tours in Allentown, Miami, and Baltimore, where he produced investigations that resulted in the expulsion of corrupt public officials and prompted numerous reforms. After joining the *Post* in 2000, his first investigative assignment was an examination of a D.C. judge who had ordered a toddler named Brianna Blackmond removed from her foster home and returned to her mother, who had a history of neglecting her eight children. Brianna was sent to her mother for Christmas, and two weeks later a family friend beat her to death. Higham well knew the reputation of the *Post*'s newsroom: a place of intense competition among reporters who were desperate to stand out. So he had some trepidation about parachuting into the story about Brianna, right on top of the reporter who had already written several key articles — Sari Horwitz.

To his surprise, Horwitz was welcoming instead of hostile, and it was the beginning of a collaboration on an emotionally taxing two-year-long investigation into the death of Brianna and other foster children that cemented a close friendship between the two and would lead them to a Pulitzer Prize in 2002. Higham went on to spend several years examining detainee abuse at Abu

Ghraib and Guantánamo Bay and fraud and abuse in Homeland Security contracts.

Now, in 2007, Horwitz struggled with her mixed feelings about resuming the investigation of the Chandra Levy case. She reached Higham on his cell phone as he was driving back to Washington from a vacation on Chincoteague Island in Virginia.

"Is it the right move?" Horwitz asked.

"Sari," Higham said, "you could solve a murder."

When Leen and Roberts asked Higham if he wanted to join up with his old partner, he didn't hesitate. He had meant what he said to Horwitz, and he knew that this was a rare opportunity. He also saw a chance to follow the passion of his late father by working on an unsolved homicide case for the first time in his career.

By now, Higham and Horwitz knew each other's contrasting reporting styles intimately. They were both driven, and could be relentless. While Horwitz tended to elicit information from sources through her gentle persistance, Higham could sometimes play the bad cop by demanding answers. They had a literal mountain of thousands of newspaper stories, transcripts of television news broadcasts, and Horwitz's own notebooks to read through, as well as sources with firsthand knowledge of the investigation to find and cultivate. Horwitz contacted several sources, including one she had met years earlier. She told the source that the *Post* was embarking on a thorough investigation of the Chandra Levy case and asked for help.

The source was glad the *Post* was back on the case, but had nothing new to offer. Horwitz hadn't expected anything, really. She just knew she needed to start somewhere.

About a week later, Horwitz spoke to the source again.

"I've got something for you," the source said. "Be careful with this."

The source told Horwitz to drive to a side street near the National Mall. She grabbed a notebook, not knowing exactly what kind of information she was about to receive, but she kept thinking about the source's admonishment to "be careful." That suggested secret documents, something nobody outside the investigation had seen. It was around seven in the evening when she pulled up to the curb at the meeting point. The source walked over, opened her door, slipped inside, and handed her a thick manila envelope. "This should get you started," the source said before stepping from the car and disappearing down the street.

Horwitz waited until she returned to the newsroom before opening the envelope. Inside were dozens of confidential documents from the homicide investigation. Over the course of several months, Horwitz would meet the source outside parks, museums, and restaurants across the city. The source grew increasingly cautious; the meetings lasted only a few minutes and they became less frequent. Several other sources would ultimately deliver thousands of documents, providing the reporters with nearly every piece of evidence known to investigators. As Horwitz and Higham examined the documents and interviewed witnesses on both coasts of the country, they caught tantalizing glimpses of the truth and began to understand the extent to which the criminal investigation had been bungled. To conduct their own investigation and to tell the story, they knew they had to go back to the beginning.

3
SUDDENLY, GONE

Chandra Ann Levy

Any moment now, Robert Levy hoped, his only daughter would step through the front door of the California home he shared with his wife, Susan, and set her bags down at the entrance to the great room, with its panes of stained glass casting colorful streaks of sunlight across the floor. He hadn't heard from Chandra Ann for several days and he was losing patience. Why wasn't she returning his calls to her cell phone or her apartment in Washington? By now, the first week of May 2001, she should be home.

A week before, Chandra had told her father she was leaving Washington. She adored the city, but her brush with the world's center of political power as an intern for the federal government was over. She planned to head home to pick up her diploma from the University of Southern California within the week, and she wasn't sure what she would do next. Levy waited for his daughter to call with a flight number, possibly an arrival time on the California Zephyr, a transcontinental train that has carried travelers across the Rockies and over the Sierra Nevada since 1949. Chandra, a twenty-four-year-old with a penchant for adventure, had always wanted to take that trip. Maybe she was sitting in the observation car as it clicked across the achingly beautiful Colorado landscape, watching the mountains slide by and listening to Frank Sinatra on her portable cassette player. Robert and Susan Levy knew their daughter could be independent, not checking in for days at a time. But with so many travel plans left undone, and Chandra's college graduation less than a week away, they thought their daughter would at least return their calls, and they were becoming increasingly worried.

Robert Levy tried not to panic. As an oncologist in Modesto, he was able to traverse tough situations with an inner calm and a gentle soul. He also drew strength from a spiritual view of the world that placed people and events in a larger metaphysical context: Everything happens for a reason. He genuinely believed that the patients he lost to cancer passed into a more permanent, peaceful place. This belief consoled him and steeled him for the all-too-regular task of delivering heartbreaking news to the families of his patients at the Memorial Medical Center in Modesto.

Susan Levy, a whimsical woman with a raucous laugh, had turned somber and reticent. Why was Chandra not sharing her travel plans? Susan had also placed several calls to her daughter, leaving anxious messages on the answering machine in Chandra's apartment. When no response came, Robert Levy gave his daughter another try. Her answering machine picked up yet again. "Damn it, Chandra," he snapped. "Call me."

Chandra's graduation plans were proceeding without her. Her eighty-four-year-old grandmother had made the journey to Modesto from her home in Fort Lauderdale, Florida. The Levys needed to make arrangements for the 290-mile trip to the USC campus in Los Angeles. Was Chandra planning to meet them in L.A.? Was she coming to Modesto first? To distract himself, Robert Levy tried to focus on his routine. He spent long hours at his medical office, which was decorated with art from around the world and cluttered with white lab coats hung on a portable rack, and papers and reports scattered about his desk.

His work was far more important than the mess. He was known in Modesto as "Last Chance Bob" for his aggressive yet holistic approach to treating cancer. He visited his patients late into the night and mourned for the ones he lost.

Levy understood how horror could hit a family. Though his parents escaped the Holocaust, by fleeing Germany on French visas in 1939, many of his relatives perished under Nazi rule. His wife, too, knew family tragedy. Her father, Bernard Katz, was a real estate man and car dealer in New Mexico. He fell behind on his bills and became consumed by depression. Susan was fifteen when she found his suicide note, telling the family they would be better off without him. A short time later, she found him slumped behind the wheel of his car. He had asphyxiated himself in the garage of the family home.

Robert and Susan met at a dance in 1968 while they were students at Ohio State University. He was an aspiring doctor; she was an art education major who wanted to join the Peace Corps. They were kindred spirits, sharing a love of philosophy and an openness to exploring the beliefs of different religions — Buddhism, Pentecostal Christianity, and Hinduism — borrowing bits and pieces from each and blending them with their own faith, Judaism. They married four years later and soon afterward had a little girl they named after a Hindu demigod: Chandra, from the Sanskrit word for "moon."

After medical school, Robert trained at Mt. Sinai Hospital in Cleveland and the Virginia Commonwealth University in Richmond. The couple wanted to make a move and they began to look for a place where oncologists were in high demand and they could raise a family. They left the precise location to fate. They jotted down the names of several cities that met the criteria — Zanesville, Ohio; Council Bluffs, Iowa; Las Cruces, New Mexico; and Modesto — and put the pieces of paper in a baseball hat. Reaching inside, they drew their destiny and began to pack for Modesto, a small, sunbaked city at the center of the San Joaquin Valley, one of the richest agricultural regions of the country. Vast groves of almonds and walnuts surrounded the city. Orchards of blossoming peach trees filled the air with their sweet scent. In 1870, citizens wanted to name the city after its founder, San Francisco banker William Ralston. When he declined, they decided to name it for what they believed to

41

be his modesty, using the Spanish word *modesto,* though some theorized that Ralston didn't want his name to be associated with a tiny town in the middle of nowhere. Its motto was emblazoned in 668 lights on a steel archway that stretches seventy-five feet over a downtown street near the city's Southern Pacific rail depot: "Water Wealth Contentment Health." Because its climate and soil were perfect for grape production, Modesto became home to the E.&J. Gallo Winery, the largest family-owned winemaker in the world. The town was also home to George Lucas, the Hollywood writer and director. Before he became internationally famous for creating *Star Wars,* Lucas put Modesto on the national map by using the main drag as the inspiration for the movie *American Graffiti.* The Levys moved into their California ranch house in a Modesto subdivision known as Golden Estate Acres. The house had a pool and a one-acre paddock out back where Susan, who loved to ride, could keep her horses.

As the days passed without word from Chandra, the Levys' impatience gave way to fear, something they had been trying to suppress all week. After work, Robert would sink into his favorite sofa in front of the stone fireplace and stare out at the paddock. Susan took long rides on her horse in the groves while her husband grew increasingly worried. Where could Chandra be? Maybe she *couldn't* call him back. Something must have happened to her. Something terrible. It was unbearable to imagine. All around the house were images from the past. Chandra as a baby, wearing a pink jumper and white lace shoes, sitting in Robert's lap as his wife blew bubbles about the room. Chandra as a toddler running through a field of flowers, her arms stretched wide, tilting from side to side as she pretended to fly above the petals. Chandra as a shy and slightly awkward teenager, raising her hand to her face, imploring her father to stop trying to take her picture.

During Chandra's childhood, Levy and his wife sought to expose their daughter and her brother, Adam, four years younger, to the world. They trekked to places pulled from the pages of *National Geographic:* the ruins of Machu Picchu, the wildlife preserves of Tanzania, the old city of Jerusalem, the volcanoes and rain forests of Costa Rica. During each journey, they collected artifacts and artwork, and they transformed their sprawling split-level house into a mini-museum, a testament to their passion for the cultures and wildlife of the world. A statue of Buddha greeted visitors at the front door; an African spear rested against a bathroom wall; photographs of elephants and giraffes were all around.

During these trips, Chandra's personality began to emerge. In grade school, she was far less adventurous than her parents. When the family went camping in Yosemite National Park, Chandra slept in the car, fearing a bear attack. Another time, Susan took the family on a side trip to visit a Rastafarian poet in the mountains of Jamaica, despite warnings from beach resort managers. Chandra stayed in the taxi the entire time.

Her parents were determined to instill confidence in Chandra. As a young girl, they brought her to the mountains near their home and taught her to ski. She eventually abandoned her parents' sport in favor of a hipper pursuit, snowboarding. One year, Susan took Chandra out of junior high school for a whitewater trip down the Merced River, a ninety-minute drive from their home. The Merced contained a class IV rapid, with four-to-five-foot-high waves and difficult passages that required steady nerves and precise maneuvering. Chandra didn't want to go, but by the end she treasured the trip, excited by the power of the river and her ability to conquer the rapids. As Chandra grew older, she became more independent — and stubborn. One summer, she refused to go to camp. Susan, not wanting her daughter to sit around doing nothing, made her take a ten-day rock-climbing course. The seventh-grader resisted but ultimately relented in the face of her mother's will. Chandra was one of a handful of girls, and the boys taunted her incessantly. When the course was over, five boys had dropped out; Chandra was the only girl to make it through.

At Davis High School, her guidance counselor, Julie Danielson, was struck by how Chandra stood out from the other students. She was a petite, pretty girl with unruly curls and an unmistakable giggle. She didn't care about makeup, getting her nails done, or who was going to ask her to the prom. She wasn't a party girl and she wasn't concerned if she was having a bad-hair day. She loved sports, especially baseball and her favorite team, the San Francisco Giants. Unlike many students her age, Chandra set goals for her next step in life and she seemed certain of her future. She had an upbeat way about her, and was always in a good mood, a trait that drew people into her circle of friends.

She began spending time in high school at the Modesto Police Department, where she volunteered as a Police Explorer. She answered phones, delivered mail, and issued tickets for expired dog licenses, but she also went on ride-alongs with police officers. Law enforcement excited her and she saw it as a public service. She proudly wore her department-issued Police Explorer uniform nearly everywhere she went, even to school. She didn't care if it was blazing hot or if the other kids teased her as she strode down the halls of Davis High.

Her pull toward a conservative and traditional career with the police department was a push away from her parents' free-spirited California lifestyle. She wasn't interested in her mother's passions — horses, painting, sculpting, and singing — and she jokingly called her mother "Flaky Sue." Chandra gravitated toward a more practical view of the world. She also developed an ability to listen and demonstrated deep empathy toward other people. Danielson asked Chandra to become one of her conflict mediators and called upon her to help settle disputes between students in a school that teemed with competing kids and cultures. Racial lines divided Davis High and emotions erupted between whites and blacks, Hispanics and a growing number of Cambodians, whose parents had fled the terror of the Khmer Rouge in 1975 for the safety of the San Joaquin Valley. Fitting in was not easy in Modesto, and Chandra's world travels helped her to move easily across the cultural lines.

Chandra's days working at the Modesto Police Department also exposed her to colleagues more mature and streetwise than her high school friends. She became close to several of the officers on the force and showed little interest in the boys in her class. She sighed over movie stars like Harrison Ford, who played a police detective in one of her favorite movies, *Witness,* and Brad Pitt, a drop-dead-handsome drifter in *Thelma & Louise.*

She shared her interest in older men with a close high school friend, Channaly Oum. As their senior year drew to a close, Oum wrote on the back of her graduation photograph:

Older guys are better! I mean, so what if Harrison F. is in his mid fifties? We'll probably like younger guys as we get older ourselves. It's really been a lot of fun giggling together; you've got to promise to keep in touch when we go our separate ways. Till then — Viva Brad! . . . Viva older men!

Love,
Channaly

By the time Chandra arrived at San Francisco State University, she had flirted briefly with becoming a journalist and had worked in the sports department of her hometown newspaper, the *Modesto Bee.* Her other goal of becoming a police officer was giving way to a bigger ambition. After earning a bachelor's degree in criminal justice, she dreamed of leaving small-town Modesto to join the FBI or CIA. She could travel the country, perhaps the world, be on her own, and have someone other than her parents pay her way. She applied to graduate school at one of the top programs in the nation for students considering careers in public service, USC's School of Policy, Planning, and Development.

At USC, Chandra was seen as gregarious, a graduate student who was eager to learn and outspoken in class. David Grazman, one of her professors, liked her warmth, her sense of humor, her easy laugh and sarcasm. She reminded him of the girls he knew when he attended Jewish summer camp as a kid growing up in the Midwest — friendly and fun with no pretense. She was a B-plus student who didn't wear makeup and dressed in jeans and an oversized USC sweatshirt. She was like the girl next door, carefree and optimistic.

In her first year in the school's master's program, Chandra interned for Richard Riordan, the mayor of Los Angeles. Next she went to Sacramento as an intern for Governor Gray Davis. She was enamored with the capital city. The statehouse is impressive, its rotunda towering over the chambers of the State Senate and the State Assembly, its 120 members making up the largest state legislature in the nation. Each day, hundreds of lawmakers, lobbyists, and legislative aides rushed across its marble mosaic floor. Davis's office stood at the center of the action and the behind-the-scenes deal making. Chandra was inspired to be part of something important, thrilled by her proximity to raw political power. She had visited Folsom State Prison, twenty miles outside the capital city, and attended a parole hearing during her tour. She was fascinated by the experience, far from the sheltered world of Golden Estate Acres. During the summer of 2000, Chandra announced that she would be heading east to live in Washington, nearly 2,300 miles away from Modesto. She had lined up an internship that fall with the Federal Bureau of Prisons for her final USC semester, a logical step in her pursuit of a career in law enforcement.

Chandra was hired to work in the bureau's public affairs office. Although her supervisor, Bureau of Prisons spokesman Dan Dunne, had interviewed and hired Chandra over the phone, the paperwork approving her job continued to languish in the bureaucracy of the Justice Department, which was responsible for managing the federal prison system and its nearly two hundred thousand inmates. When Chandra arrived in Washington that fall, Dunne told her she couldn't start for several weeks. Frustrated, she showed up at the office near Capitol Hill anyway, pleading with Dunne to let her start. She told him she needed to work right away, mentioning that she needed the money, but he told her that unfortunately, everyone had to be screened and the paperwork needed to be completed. Washington was a bureaucratic town, Dunne explained, and she had to wait along with everyone else.

Once Chandra started, Dunne was impressed. She was smart and personable, a pleasure to be around. Her job was not particularly glamorous, but she followed instructions and she never complained. Like most Washington interns, Chandra was a glorified gofer. She answered phones and did whatever she could to ease the burden on the full-time employees in the office. One of Chandra's main responsibilities was handling queries from the public; she responded to general information requests and passed media calls along to Dunne. In the spring of 2001, a crush of calls came into the office because of the pending June execution of Timothy McVeigh, who had been convicted of bombing the Alfred P. Murrah Building in Oklahoma City six years earlier, on April 19, 1995. Chandra fielded those calls and helped escort reporters into a press conference held during the run-up to McVeigh's execution for the murder of the 168 people who died in the blast.

On April 28, 2001, Chandra e-mailed her landlord. The message raised more questions than it answered.

It looks like my plans have suddenly changed. I was just informed this week that my job appointment time is up, so I am out of work now. I am going back to California for my graduation during the week of May 8 and [I'll be] moving back there for good. I haven't heard from the other jobs that I applied for yet and I have a feeling that it will be at least a few weeks for me to hear back from any of them. I don't really think it would be worth it for me to stay in D.C. now since I have no job or school to keep me busy here. I would like to vacate the apartment on May 5 or 6 if possible . . . I really hate giving up the apartment but I think I need to be in California for a while to figure out what my next move is.

Three days later, on May 1, Chandra booted up her blue Sony Vaio laptop on a makeshift desk in a hallway nook of her studio apartment and began to make her final travel plans. She had fallen in love with Washington and her Dupont Circle neighborhood. Her apartment was three blocks off Connecticut Avenue, a wide boulevard lined with fine shops, restaurants, and famous hotels such as the Mayflower and the Washington Hilton, where one of Chandra's political inspirations, Ronald Reagan, had been shot by would-be assassin John

Hinckley twenty years earlier. The elegant avenue begins near the White House and runs through Dupont Circle, past the National Zoo, Rock Creek Park, and block after block of splendid art-deco apartment buildings, across the border of Maryland, and beyond the Capital Beltway. Along the way, the avenue provides passage into some of the most desirable neighborhoods of the city in northwest Washington.

Chandra signed on to the Internet at 10:27 that morning and bounced from site to site. She went to the Drudge Report and *National Geographic,* Amtrak and Southwest Airlines. At 10:45 A.M., she sent an e-mail to her mother, listing some Southwest fares. At 11:26, she visited washingtonpost.com and clicked on the weather report. It called for fair skies and warm temperatures, a picture-perfect spring afternoon in Washington when pollen from millions of blossoms casts a dreamlike haze of soft green powder across the city. At 11:33, Chandra clicked on a washingtonpost.com "Entertainment Guide" to Rock Creek Park. At the top of the page was the address for the administrative office of the park at the Klingle Mansion, a Pennsylvania Dutch–style home not far from the zoo. One minute later, she clicked on a link for a map of hiking trails that traversed the park's hills and ravines. The page gave her details about horseback riding; the Peirce Mill, a stone shrine to nineteenth-century industry and the last of eight mills that churned along Rock Creek; and the Nature Center and Planetarium, just off the park's Western Ridge Trail. At 12:24 P.M., she signed off her computer.

And then she disappeared.

A week had passed since Chandra e-mailed her mother. On Sunday, May 6, Robert decided he had no place left to turn; he picked up the phone and dialed the police in Washington to report his daughter missing. The officer who handled the call sent a squad car to her apartment in the Newport Condominium on Twenty-first Street. The manager opened the door and the officer peeked inside. The modern, third-floor studio was neatly furnished with a futon, sleek stainless-steel chairs, and a glass coffee table. Two open suitcases rested on the floor. He could see a wallet and other personal items scattered around the studio.

Robert Levy frantically placed other phone calls. He called the Bureau of Prisons and the FBI. Nothing. Then he tried hospitals in Washington, checking for incapacitated patients and accident victims. Nothing. There was no sign of Chandra. He and his wife began to sift through their daughter's cell phone bills, which they paid each month. They spotted several unfamiliar, recurring Washington numbers. Susan Levy dialed one of them and the call rolled into an answering machine that played soft background music. Susan dialed the next number. An answering machine picked up and announced she had reached the office of Congressman Gary Condit, a Democrat who represented Modesto.

The recording struck Susan like a minor chord in a horror movie. She immediately suspected that her daughter's disappearance might have something to do with Condit. Three weeks earlier, Susan had learned something disturbing, something she had not told her husband. It appeared that their daughter had been having an affair with the congressman.

Her suspicions began during an unusual conversation with a Pentecostal minister named Otis Thomas. He had parlayed his groundskeeping chores at his Modesto church into a freelance gardening business and he had been working for the Levys for four years as a handyman. In mid-April, Thomas had been tending roses in the Levys' backyard when he struck up a conversation. The two often shared stories about their children, and Thomas asked about how Chandra was faring in Washington. Susan said her daughter was doing well. She said she had recently spoken to her sister-in-law, who lived near Washington and was close to Chandra, and heard that her daughter had become friends with a congressman.

Thomas paused. He had a story to tell Susan. Thomas said his daughter had come to him for advice about seven years earlier. His then eighteen-year-old daughter told him she had been dating the congressman who represented Modesto, Gary Condit. She had met him at a political rally in the area.

"Lord have mercy, I told her she has to be around men her own age," Thomas told Susan.

He told Susan he urged his daughter to call it off and the affair ended badly. Thomas said his daughter had been warned to keep the relationship confidential and she went into hiding because she was concerned for her safety.

Susan grew worried. She wondered whether Condit was her daughter's "friend" in Congress. Susan told Thomas her suspicions, and he advised her to tell Chandra to end the affair immediately. Susan strode into her home and called her daughter. Chandra picked up.

"Are you involved in a relationship with Gary Condit?" she asked.

"How did you know?" Chandra said.

Susan recounted Thomas's tale and said, "Chandra, I'm concerned for your safety."

The conversation turned tense. Chandra told her mother that she should mind her own business. She said she was a grown woman and could make her own decisions about whom to date. Chandra added that no one was supposed to know about the relationship, and she ordered her mother not to say a word.

Susan responded: "Be careful, you could get hurt."

Susan obeyed Chandra's request. She didn't tell anyone, including her husband. About a week later, she and Robert traveled to Hershey, Pennsylvania, where they met Chandra to celebrate her twenty-fourth birthday on April 14. During the visit, Chandra told her mother that she had spoken to Condit about Thomas's story and he "explained it all." Chandra declined to be more specific or say anything else about her relationship with Condit.

Back in California, with Chandra's graduation day, May 11, 2001, less than a week away, Robert and Susan Levy were sickened by their inability to reach their daughter. Chandra's answering machine was no longer taking messages; it was full with twenty-five calls. Susan worried that Chandra's silence was somehow connected to Condit. She wondered what the congressman had "explained" to her daughter. Maybe Chandra had angered Condit by confronting him with the Thomas story. Susan's mind raced. She decided it was time to break her promise to Chandra and tell her husband that their daughter had been having an affair with Condit.

Robert Levy pulled out a phone book. He flipped through the pages until he found a home number for Condit in the Central Valley. When he was not in Washington, the congressman lived with his wife, Carolyn, in Ceres, a small town that straddles California Highway 99 about five miles south of Modesto. Carolyn Condit picked up the phone. Levy told her that his daughter was missing and he needed help from the congressman. She said her husband wasn't home but she would be happy to pass along the message and have him call back.

Soon after, the Levys' phone rang. It was Condit.

"I'm the father of Chandra Levy, an intern

in Washington," Levy told the congressman. His voice trembled; he was having a hard time catching his breath as he spoke. He explained that he was calling because Condit's number showed up on his daughter's cell phone bills. "She's missing. Can you help?"

Levy said the police in Washington had told him that his daughter's luggage was still in her apartment, along with her wallet and her identification. "Do you know my daughter? Where is she? Do you know where she went?"

Condit told Levy that he knew Chandra, but not well. He said he met her in Washington during her internship, that she had visited his congressional office, and that he had given her some career advice. The congressman said he would make some calls to the police. He was sorry he couldn't be more helpful, but he had no idea where Chandra could be. Robert Levy was upset by the call, but his wife was furious. She knew Condit wasn't being forthcoming about his relationship with their daughter. She wondered what else the congressman was hiding.

4
CONDIT COUNTRY

Gary Adrian Condit

In the spring of 2001, as Chandra Levy began to pack her few possessions scattered about her studio apartment and surf the Web for bargain airfares back to California, Gary Adrian Condit arrived at Washington's inner sanctum. Secret Service agents checked his credentials at the White House gate and the congressman from California with graying blond hair and sky-blue eyes strolled onto the lawn just outside the Oval Office. The Rose Garden, reserved for official Washington's elite, lay before him, its expanse of flawlessly manicured lawn framed by crab apple trees and flower beds.

George W. Bush invited Condit here to be by his side during a luncheon to mark his first hundred days as president. Condit's presence was a testament to his willingness to cross the political aisle, his increasing star power on Capitol Hill, and the promise of the heights he could reach if he continued on his current path. After listening to Bush speak for two minutes, Condit and 192 other members of Congress left the Rose Garden and filed into the East Room for the luncheon. The largest room in the White House — a place for receptions, concerts, and important presidential press conferences — it has been the setting for some of the nation's most somber occasions; Presidents Lincoln and Kennedy had lain in state here. The East Room has also accommodated the more prosaic and whimsical needs of the first families — a playroom for the children of President Theodore Roosevelt; a roller rink for President Carter's daughter, Amy.

On this day, April 30, 2001, President Bush invited a spectrum of people — from political critics to steadfast loyalists — to the celebratory luncheon, where he proclaimed his administration to be at the dawn of a new era of bipartisanship in Washington. The members of the House and Senate took their places at immaculately set tables arranged beneath the frescoed ceiling and opulent chandeliers. Condit veered away from his colleagues, taking a seat at Bush's table. Two of the Republican Party's most important men joined them: Senate Majority Leader Trent Lott of Mississippi and

House Majority Leader Dick Armey of Texas. To the uninitiated, the seating arrangement had the air of political heresy, a turncoat Democrat consorting with the enemy. A mere 50 of the 261 Democrats on Capitol Hill had accepted Bush's invitation. The leaders of Condit's party, Senator Tom Daschle of South Dakota and Representative Richard Gephardt of Missouri, had curtly declined to attend.

Condit's seat in the East Room made perfect sense; playing the role of the outsider and rebellious member of his party had been a hallmark of his career. In Washington, the White House, Senate, and House were under the control of the GOP for the first time in four decades. Condit had cemented his standing with the newly elected Republican triumvirate and had solidified his position as the leader of the right-leaning Blue Dog faction of the Democratic Party. The Republicans courted Condit and urged him to split with his party to help push through pieces of conservative legislation. In return, Condit could win contracts and grants and government projects for his congressional district. Condit had just broken from his party to help pass Bush's budget and $1.6 trillion tax cut package. That step, taken by just two other Democrats, helped to earn him a place at Bush's table. Condit took the opportunity to talk to the president about the energy shortfalls that were plaguing his state and the export barriers that were hurting California's agribusiness, the core of his constituency. Condit saw the luncheon as a win-win for his career: He left with an invitation from Bush to speak to Vice President Dick Cheney the following day, May 1, 2001, about his state's energy woes, and his appearance next to the president played well with the California media and the voters in his rural, conservative district.

Condit's past had prepared him to seize these kinds of opportunities. He understood that they were rare, often fleeting. Condit grew up as a teenager in Tulsa, Oklahoma, during the 1960s, a time when the dry and desolate land was again losing its people to the promise of places like California. As a child, he tagged along with his father, Adrian, a Baptist preacher, to tent revivals around the Bible Belt state. By the time he reached high school, Condit began to work the oil fields, sometimes as a roughneck on the rigs, other times as a welder or behind the wheel of a backhoe. There were frequent fights on the oil-soaked ground, workers in their coveralls cheering for one side or the other, rooting for an old-fashioned, bloody brawl. Condit learned how to use his fists on those fields.

A handsome, daredevil teenager, Condit was drawn to fast cars and a fast crowd but fell for a straitlaced girl named Carolyn Berry. She was petite and blond with a kind voice that didn't seem capable of speaking a harsh word. Berry came from as far away from the oil fields as a Tulsa girl could get. Her father owned a discount designer shop called Spot Bargain and he raised his family on the better side of town. Berry, who drove a Dodge Dart convertible — a sixteenth-birthday present from her parents — was one of the best dressed and most popular girls at Nathan Hale High School. She could have dated anyone she wanted. During her junior year, she chose to date Condit, also a junior.

Just one year out of high school, on January 18, 1967, the two were married. Their first child, Chad, was born that summer. A daughter, Cadee, would follow. The newly-weds traced Condit's father's steps to Ceres, California, named after the Roman goddess of agriculture. A suburb of Modesto, it was dry and dusty and home to legions of field-workers who tended to the farms and vineyards of the Central Valley. A tall, silver metal water tower stood over the town, the paint peeling from an American flag stenciled on its side.

During the day, Condit attended California State University, Stanislaus, a small college in Turlock, a thirteen-mile drive from Ceres. In the afternoons, he worked for Norris Industries, a munitions factory that had perfected steel bullet casings for World War II and now was making mortar shells for the Vietnam War. As Condit became increasingly opposed to the war, he decided to run for political office as a local city councilman. The college senior could rely on his charm and his way with words. His style wasn't fancy, but he thought he might be able to convince others of his beliefs, most of them lining up with the less-government, fewer-taxes voters of Ceres. Condit won the seat, to the surprise of everyone, including himself, and two years later, at the age of twenty-six, he became the mayor of Ceres. His ascent was steady: at twenty-eight a member of the Stanislaus County Board of Supervisors, and at thirty-five a California state assemblyman, standing in the marbled corridors of power in Sacramento.

In a liberal-leaning state, Condit arrived as one of the capitol's more conservative members. He gravitated toward other like-minded legislators, and he and four other Democrats formed a political and social rat pack that statehouse lawmakers and reporters nicknamed the "Gang of Five." Condit learned the value of camaraderie — and the price that accompanied high-stakes political gamesmanship.

In 1988, Condit and his allies formed a block of swing votes in the State Assembly and tried to use their power to unseat the longest-serving speaker in California history, Willie Brown of San Francisco. The lawmakers thought he was too liberal to lead and they confronted him in his statehouse office. They were cocky, convinced they had the votes to topple Brown from his perch and move the assembly in a more conservative direction with a new speaker. Condit took the lead, with an approach reminiscent of his days as a roughneck on the drilling platform.

"We think it's time for you to give us your exit date," he told Brown.

Brown, an old-school politician partial to dapper hats and colorful silk pocket handkerchiefs, kept his cool. "Each of you is the chair of a major committee, each of you holds an important position, so when people like you say something like this, I have to listen. But, oh boy, this is not something we can decide easily — there are a lot of ramifications."

After the meeting, behind the scenes, Brown quietly sharpened his sword and prepared for revenge. He lined up political supporters until he had the votes he needed to quash the attempted coup. Then he began to politically eviscerate the men he deemed as traitors. He stripped each of them of their committee chairmanships. He ordered them evicted from their offices, their furniture shoved into the hallways of the statehouse like deadbeats. He directed that their committee staff members be fired, and in a final flourish, Brown leaked word of what he had done to the Sacramento press corps without speaking to the Gang of Five. Reporters set upon Condit and his co-conspirators like a pack of dogs. It was front-page political drama. The reporters hounded the legislators to explain what had happened, asking them how it felt to lose their coveted committee chairmanships, possibly their careers.

When it was over, Condit received a call. Brown, the consummate politician, keeping friends close, his enemies closer, invited him to lunch. Condit accepted.

"Look, Gary, we need to bury the hatchet.

We need to be friends," the speaker told him.

Condit replied coolly, in his mild Oklahoma twang: "Willie, we're not going to run around together again. We're not going to be friends."

Condit left the luncheon, badly beaten — but back in the San Joaquin Valley, voters embraced him as a conservative folk hero, a brave brawler who sacrificed his career in the face of unchecked political power. Condit watched his flagging career gather new momentum, and soon he saw the biggest opportunity of his political life.

In 1989, Tony Coelho, the House majority whip in Washington, a formidable force in national politics, and the congressman from Condit's hometown district, became embroiled in a financial scandal. He made a hundred-thousand-dollar investment in high-yield junk bonds issued by Drexel Burnham Lambert. The bonds were generally available only to institutional investors and regular customers of the Wall Street banking firm. Coelho couldn't survive the ensuing firestorm. The third-highest-ranking Democrat in the House resigned his seat, setting off an inside-the-Beltway guessing game of who might fill the vacuum on Capitol Hill. Condit viewed Coelho's fall as his ticket to rise from Sacramento, clearing a path to the national stage and the biggest political show in the world. In Washington, he would not make the mistakes he had made in Sacramento. He had learned his lesson, and this time he would be more patient and wait for his openings.

Condit won a special election to fill Coelho's seat, and he bought a condominium in the Adams Morgan section of Washington. Condit flew home most weekends when the House of Representatives was in session. His constituents called him "Gary." He sent flowers to his voters when they married, condolences and more flowers when they died. He was well regarded by the local news media, and the television cameras favored him. With his fit frame, confident swagger, and passion for horses and the outdoors, he came across like a telegenic Marlboro Man, even though he would never touch a cigarette or take a drink. The editorial board of the biggest newspaper in the valley, the *Modesto Bee,* endorsed him each time he ran for reelection — his seat in the 18th Congressional District became so secure that his Republican opponent complained during one race that he couldn't convince the local GOP political machine to back his bid. He also had powerful financial backing. Agricultural companies in his district were among the largest contributors to his campaign. They included E.&J. Gallo Winery and Blue Diamond Growers. The congressman's swath of the San Joaquin Valley was now simply known as "Condit Country."

In Washington, Condit carved out a niche as a conservative member of his party, just as he had in Sacramento. He often disagreed with his colleagues and he voted against President Clinton nearly half the time. In 1993, he broke ranks to vote against Clinton's stimulus package, which had been designed to jumpstart the weak economy. Opting for a lower profile, he mostly steered clear of the spotlight — but not for long. In 1994, a political revolution turned Washington on its head. The Republican Party swept to power and took control of Congress for the first time in forty years by ousting thirty-four Democrats in the midterm election. The GOP had campaigned under the banner of a "Contract With America," a legislative plan that promised to balance the budget, cut taxes, and do away with numerous social programs favored by the Democrats. The Republicans picked Representative Newt Gingrich of Georgia as their leader to replace Democrat Tom Foley of

Washington, the first Speaker of the House to lose reelection to Congress since the Civil War. The realignment of the political fortunes was a disaster for most Democrats on the Hill. They lost their positions of power on the congressional committees that oversaw the nation's finances and industries, and more important, they lost their access to campaign contributions because the corporations and trade groups had shifted their allegiances and their largess to the party in power.

Condit made the most of the Republican Revolution. The pledge to spend less and reduce taxes had been his mantra for years. The lawmaker subsequently crafted a way to raise his profile among the 435 congressmen on Capitol Hill, resurrecting the concept of the Gang of Five and assembling a group of like-minded Democrats. He helped to organize the "Blue Dogs," fiscal conservatives who would foil the tax-and-spend liberals with their block of votes. The name lampooned the Yellow Dog Democrats of the early 1900s, a group of left-leaning politicians so nicknamed because they would vote for anything, even a yellow dog, over a Republican. Condit hung a mural of a giant blue dog on the wall of his congressional office along with a portrait of Speaker

Gingrich. Not only had Condit won the respect of prominent Republicans, he was gaining ground with the more conservative members of his own party, many of them clinging to their seats in the uncertain political climate. He didn't care what the members of the East Coast liberal wing of his party thought; they weren't his people.

For Condit, President Bush's East Room invitation was confirmation that he had arrived. Washington was a city that rewarded power and success with lavish lunches and expense-paid trips but could just as quickly pounce on failure. Condit knew that politicians came and went. So did the people who depended on them — the thousands of staff members and political appointees, and the ambitious young interns who overtook the city during the stifling summers as the rulers of official Washington fled for the beaches of Rehoboth, Bethany, Cape Cod, and Martha's Vineyard. In a town full of transients, Condit had finally found permanence.

Though Condit projected an easy air of confidence in public, his personal life was likely far less comfortable. Two days before the White House luncheon, on Saturday, April 28, Carolyn Condit had flown to Washington. She had been invited to a luncheon for congressional spouses hosted by First Lady Laura Bush and she planned to stay with her husband at their Adams Morgan condominium for the next five days. From all appearances, the Condits seemed to be the perfect couple. They doted on each other in public, holding hands and speaking lovingly about their marriage and the importance of family and faith. She was the consummate politician's wife, an attractive woman who stayed in the background and spent time with her husband's constituents in the Central Valley. For Carolyn, it was a rare visit to Washington, and during her stay, Condit could not risk being seen with the woman he had been secretly dating for the previous five months: Chandra Levy.

The affair began in the fall of 2000 when Chandra arrived in the city as a bright, ambitious intern for the Federal Bureau of Prisons. In her world, with its own pecking order and star system, she found herself someplace in the middle of the twenty-something intern power structure. She wasn't working at the White House or the FBI or inside an office of political leadership on Capitol Hill, but she was close enough to where she wanted to be, at the brink of a career in federal law enforcement. She was awestruck by her surroundings and the Capra-esque qualities of the city — the wide boulevards, the temples of the federal government that lined them, and the marbled monuments to the architects of American democracy that rose above the low-slung skyline. She couldn't wait to visit one of the world's centers of political power, the U.S. Capitol.

One day that October, Chandra went to the Hill with a friend she had met at the USC public policy graduate program, Jennifer Baker. At twenty-four, Baker was a year older than Chandra and still looking for an internship to complete her degree. To find a job, Baker had suggested that they try to meet their representatives from California. They brimmed with optimism as they strolled down the polished hallways of the Rayburn House Office Building and made their way to the office of Congressman Gary Condit. They expected to meet a low-ranking staff member. Instead Condit stepped into the reception area of his office to greet them. With his charming smile and carefully coiffed hair, he reminded Chandra of her longtime matinee idol: Harrison Ford. The congressman offered them white grape juice and showed the pair around, eventually escorting them to the gallery of the U.S. Capitol's historic House chamber.

Chandra was intoxicated by the moment. She was young, idealistic, aspiring, and before her stood a handsome politician at the height of his career. They both came from the same place, and they shared a certain sensibility, but they were worlds apart. Condit occupied the center of the Washington universe; Chandra clung to its outermost ring. Interns were in Washington to serve: fetch mail, answer phones, photocopy press releases, give tours of the U.S. Capitol to constituents.

Each summer, as many as twenty thousand interns descended on Washington to work on the Hill and in the federal agencies, nonprofits, and think tanks scattered across the city. Congressmen sometimes gave the interns an important-sounding title: staff assistant. Around town, they were sometimes referred to as "staff ass." Some were paid, many were not, but over the years Washington internships had become a rite of passage for hundreds of thousands of college students and recent graduates. They crammed into group homes and logged ten-to-twelve-hour days. For dinner they raided hotel happy hour buffets and spent their nights drinking cosmopolitans, Long Island iced teas, and bottles of Budweiser at bars like the Hawk 'n' Dove, on Capitol Hill; the

Spot, near Ford's Theatre; or Tryst, in Adams Morgan. They injected youthful exuberance into the staid, buttoned-down town, an idealism and vitality that some men — and women — in positions of power found irresistible.

As Condit gave the two young women from his home state a tour of the Capitol, Baker told him she was looking for an internship and wondered if he could help. The congressman offered her a job on the spot. Before leaving that day, Baker asked Condit if he would pose for a picture. Condit draped his arms over the shoulders of the two women as they stood before the mural of the big blue dog.

A few days later, Chandra stopped by Condit's office to see Baker. She ran into the congressman, and after some small talk, they exchanged phone numbers and e-mail addresses. Several days went by before Chandra called Condit. The conversation bounced from topic to topic. She told him she wanted to work in the federal government, possibly as an FBI or CIA agent. Did he have any career advice? Condit told her that learning a foreign language might help. They shared stories about Modesto and Ceres. They talked about Israel; she told him she was pro-Israel but not a practicing

Jew. She asked a few questions about the inner workings of the federal government, and at the end of the conversation Condit gave her his private phone number.

The affair began a few weeks later, shortly before Thanksgiving. Chandra called Condit and he invited her over one night after work to his one-bedroom condominium in Adams Morgan, an urban, chic northwest D.C. neighborhood of eclectic restaurants and jam-packed nightclubs. It was not the typical neighborhood for a conservative congressman from a right-leaning agricultural district. His turn-of-the-century building was perched on a hill above Rock Creek Park, so close to the National Zoo that residents could hear the lions roar in the early morning hours. The fourth-floor apartment had wall-to-wall white carpeting. A black leather sofa and a glass coffee table stood at the center of the living room. A black-and-white comforter covered the bed, and full-length mirrors adorned a wooden wardrobe and the bedroom closet.

Condit saw Chandra as savvy for her age, happy and focused on her career. Soon they settled into something of a routine. After working out at the Washington Sports Club, Chandra would take the Metro one stop from Dupont Circle to the Woodley Park-

Zoo station. From there she would walk across the Duke Ellington Bridge, which arches over Rock Creek Park, and make her way to Condit's condominium. Chandra typically spent the night, twice, sometimes three times a week. They rarely went out in public. They ordered take-out from Condit's favorite restaurant, Pasta Mia, and watched movies on HBO. On her cell phone, Chandra listed "Gary" as speed dial number seven. She programmed speed dial number eight for his Capitol Hill office number.

Condit was playing a high-risk game. Any misstep, any leak to the press, if Chandra told anyone and word of the relationship got out, his career could be over. Chandra didn't tell Baker or her friends back in California about the affair. She dodged Baker's invitations to go out, telling her she had started dating an FBI agent. Early on, Chandra confided in just one person, her aunt, Linda Zamsky, who lived a train ride away in Chesapeake City, Maryland. She told Zamsky that the relationship had to stay a secret, that she had to wear a ball cap when she visited Condit's apartment and always make sure no one saw her get off the elevator on his floor. Chandra told her aunt she was in love with "her man," a Harrison Ford look-alike who promised to leave his wife, give up his seat in Congress, and start a family with Chandra one day. Zamsky agreed to be Chandra's confidante and keep the affair a secret.

The affair carried on through the winter and into the spring of 2001. Condit saw Chandra on Tuesday, April 24, four days before his wife's plane touched down in Washington for the Laura Bush luncheon. Chandra told him that she had lost her internship; she had completed her USC coursework the previous semester and was no longer eligible for the Bureau of Prisons post. She said that she was looking forward to returning to California and picking up her diploma at the graduation ceremony at USC on May 11. She was thinking about taking a train across the country, a four-day trip. After her visit to California, she wanted to return to Washington.

When Carolyn Condit arrived on April 28, Chandra — who had turned twenty-four two weeks earlier — knew she had to stay away from the congressman. Still, she and Condit spoke on the phone several times, the final conversation on April 29. When he didn't hear from her over the next few days, Condit left two messages on her home answering machine. In the last one, on May

3, he asked Chandra if she had left town and he asked her to call when she arrived in California.

By the time Condit received the phone call from Robert Levy on May 6, he hadn't heard from Chandra for nearly a week. The call shook Condit. The last person he would have wanted to hear on the other end of the phone line was the father of his secret twenty-four-year-old girlfriend. Did Levy suspect the truth? Anything connecting him with Chandra was a potential disaster, and the fact that she was missing made matters so much worse. He was a married man at the apex of his career. For months he had managed to keep the romance hidden, but now the girl's father was calling him at home. At the very least, this was messy, and for a man in Condit's position in Washington, mess was dangerous.

The following day, Condit received another troubling call, this one from the Metropolitan Police Department in Washington. The detective left a polite message asking if he could speak to the congressman. He knew Condit was an important man with a busy schedule, but he had a few questions about a missing intern from California named Chandra Levy.

5
An Explosive Case

Jack Barrett

Jack Barrett bounded up the steps of the Metropolitan Police Department headquarters, an imposing limestone building just off Pennsylvania Avenue and located near citadels of government power: the Justice Department, the Federal Trade Commission, the headquarters for the Federal Bureau of Investigation.

Barrett, a tall man with an unflinching stare and a ruddy complexion framed by short, silver-gray hair, exuded the no-nonsense confidence of an FBI agent who had spent his entire career capturing criminals. In his nearly three decades with the bureau, Barrett built an impressive résumé of casework ranging from organized crime in Newark to drug trafficking in Miami; police corruption in Washington, D.C., to labor rackets in New York City.

Now, back in Washington, lured out of retirement at fifty-five, Barrett felt slightly out of place. It was the beginning of May 2001 and he was starting over as the District of Columbia's police superintendent of detectives. He didn't know many of the detectives under his command. He didn't have a desk, and he didn't have an office, but he did have a potentially explosive investigation into the disappearance of a government intern and her connection to a California congressman. Like much of what he had seen in his first weeks on the job, Barrett didn't quite know what to make of the case.

He passed through the metal detectors of police headquarters and stepped into the old, sluggish elevator. Headquarters was named "The Henry J. Daly Building" after Hank Daly, a popular homicide sergeant. The metal detectors were installed after a deranged criminal, Bennie Lee Lawson Jr., slipped into the building with an assault pistol two days before Thanksgiving in 1994. Angry that police had questioned him in connection with a triple murder, he made his way to a homicide task force on the third floor and opened fire, killing Daly and two FBI agents. Barrett had been inside this building countless times to meet with police officers and detectives when he was one of the special agents in charge at the FBI's

Washington field office. Judiciary Square, the neighborhood surrounding police headquarters and the FBI's field office, bustled with special agents and police officers, defense lawyers and prosecutors hurrying to attend hearings, arraignments, and trials at the D.C. Superior Court and the nearby federal courthouse.

Barrett tried to hold the new missing persons case in its proper context amid the broad spectrum of D.C. crime. Washington had long been one of the nation's most violent cities, and "missing" people were hardly a rare occurrence: an elderly man, a runaway girl, someone trying to avoid an abusive spouse. They always seemed to turn up, but this case seemed different. From what Barrett was hearing, Chandra Levy was a responsible, ambitious, twenty-four-year-old woman who had been working as an intern at the Federal Bureau of Prisons since the fall. She hoped to be an FBI agent like Barrett and was set to go home to California to pick up her graduate degree in public administration.

Barrett also knew this case could provide white-hot material for the Washington press corps. His detectives had told him that there appeared to be some involvement between Chandra and a congressman, Gary Condit.

If the congressman had anything to do with her disappearance, Barrett knew the investigation could quickly spin out of control. He didn't want to make a mistake, and he didn't want to embarrass the department or his friend Chuck Ramsey.

D.C. police chief Charles H. Ramsey was a cop's cop, a stocky, broad-shouldered man from the South Side of Chicago. He hired Barrett to help shield the department from further ridicule. Months earlier, Ramsey's officers had botched the case of a student who had been beaten to death in his room at Gallaudet University, the world-renowned college for the deaf in Washington. His officers wrongly arrested a freshman student, and the true killer murdered a second student. Ramsey needed a respected manager, someone like Barrett from the FBI, to restore professionalism and credibility to his department.

Local police departments across the country are often wary of the FBI, and these tensions are more pronounced in Washington, where federal and local law enforcement lines are frequently blurred. To the local police officers, it seems that the FBI leaves the dirty work to them, and the bureau's special agents show up to assume control of the big cases and take the credit before the television cameras. When Barrett worked at the FBI's Washington field office, he tried to be more sensitive to the street cops and he forged a strong bond with Ramsey, keeping him apprised of the FBI's cases. Barrett retired in 1999 and Ramsey tried to hire him at the police department. Barrett chose instead to become a consultant for the Justice Department before taking a security job with American Airlines in Miami. But he quickly tired of the constant travel from his Northern Virginia home, where his wife wanted to stay near their children, and he missed the intense action of law enforcement. When Ramsey again asked him to join the department two years later, Barrett accepted. In late April 2001, he stepped into a new post Ramsey had created for him. Barrett would eventually oversee four hundred detectives based downtown and scattered across the city's seven police precincts.

Barrett knew he was taking a chance. The Gallaudet case was just one in a series of embarrassments for the once-illustrious police force founded by President Lincoln in 1861. Four years after its creation, members of the force joined the War Department's manhunt for John Wilkes Booth. In 1881, a Washington police officer seized President James A. Garfield's assassin at a railroad depot. More than one hundred years later, in 1978, a congressional committee turned to the department's nationally recognized firearms laboratory to help conduct tests on the rifle Lee Harvey Oswald used to shoot President John F. Kennedy in 1963.

But in the two decades before Barrett's arrival, the reputation of the department plummeted, particularly during the era of D.C. mayor Marion Barry. In the late 1980s, the city lowered its hiring standards to flood the streets with new police officers, part of a concerted effort to end a crack-cocaine-fueled crime wave. Seventy-eight of those officers were soon prosecuted themselves for drug trafficking and other crimes. By 1998, the number of police officers arrested, convicted, or under investigation topped four hundred, and Ramsey's predecessor resigned in disgrace.

By the time Ramsey arrived in Washington that same year — the first outsider in thirty years to take the helm of the 3,555-member police force — morale was at an all-time low. The department's reputation was badly tarnished by corruption, misconduct, and the mishandling of homicide cases. Fifteen hundred homicides went unsolved during the 1990s, and nearly two-thirds of the murders that occurred in 1999 remained unsolved by the end of that year. The department's closure rate for homicides was lower than those of Los Angeles, New York, Philadelphia, and St. Louis.

Soaring violent crime rates drove residents and businesses from the city and into the prosperous suburbs of Maryland and Northern Virginia. Washington had the highest homicide rate among major American cities — a trend that peaked in 1991, when 479 people were slain in the city. Police managers permitted the 911 emergency system to deteriorate. Resources were scarce. In some police precincts, officers routinely bought their own patrol bicycles, office supplies, even toilet paper. A few months after Ramsey's arrival, the *Washington Post* published an investigative series documenting that officers in Washington during the 1990s shot and killed more people per resident than officers in any other large U.S. city. Washington's officers fired their weapons at more than double the rate of police in New York, Los Angeles, Chicago, or Miami.

Ramsey candidly shared his thoughts about the state of the police force with the public. "I have never seen a place with so much wrong," he said upon his arrival. With so many failures within the department, he likened his role to that of a doctor treating a cancer patient: "But then the patient gets shot in the chest. So now you have to treat the bleeding, stop it first, before you can even address the cancer."

Barrett sat down at a desk and pulled out the Chandra Levy case file. The investigation had gone to Ralph Durant, a detective assigned to the city's second police district, which covered Chandra's Dupont Circle neighborhood. Known as "2D," it was one of Washington's quieter precincts. The district was so placid that some officers who worked in the tougher neighborhoods east of Rock Creek Park and in southeast Washington sometimes jokingly referred to cops there as "squirrel chasers." Durant's stationhouse, set behind a Giant supermarket off Wisconsin Avenue near the Washington National Cathedral, served the tranquil, well-off neighborhoods west of Rock Creek Park. Places like Georgetown and Chevy Chase, Cleveland Park and Spring Valley. The threats were mostly drunks, burglars, and petty thieves.

Barrett was familiar with 2D. Although murders were rare there, he had helped to supervise a sensational homicide case in the district a few years earlier when he was with the FBI. The two faces of Washington violently clashed inside a Starbucks in Georgetown in 1997 when a robber burst into the shop after hours and executed three employees in a back office. One employee was shot four times in the head. Another employee was shot three times, twice in the head; the third employee was shot once. Two years later, the case was solved by a D.C. homicide detective along with one of the FBI's best agents, Brad Garrett. They arrested Carl Derek Cooper, a twenty-nine-year-old man who had also been suspected of shooting a Prince George's County, Maryland, police officer. He murdered the three Starbucks employees during a botched robbery attempt.

As Barrett reviewed the Levy case file, he realized that Durant didn't have much to go on. Barrett read Durant's "251," a department incident report. The detective reported that he received a call from Chandra's father, Robert Levy, at about four in the afternoon on Sunday, May 6. The report had a matter-of-fact tone: "The reporting person reports that he has not heard from his daughter since May 1st, 2001." Barrett read that Levy hadn't been able to reach his daughter for nearly a week. She was supposed to be home by May 9 for her graduation from the University of Southern California two days later, and it was unlike her to be out of touch for so long. The report stated that Durant sent an officer to Chandra's third-floor apartment in Dupont Circle and no one answered the door. The officer asked a condominium manager to open the apartment.

Durant was a journeyman detective who had spent thirty-three years on the force, the vast majority of them in 2D. He wasn't a star in the department and had little homicide experience; but the disappearance of Chandra was a missing persons case and Barrett heard that Durant had a good reputation as a reliable investigator.

Durant didn't look like a typical detective. He was tall and bespectacled with long, dark hair pulled into a ponytail and the air of an urban cowboy as he worked the streets in his cargo pants and pointy boots. He was an African-American officer in a department with a long history of racial division. For years, black officers could not rise through the ranks to top positions in the paramilitary organization. They could not patrol the city's white neighborhoods and they were not permitted to ride in squad cars. The first black chief of police was not named until 1978. A decade later, in 1989,

Isaac Fulwood became the department's third black police chief. In the '60s, he had hesitated to join the force. He rarely saw black officers on the street back then, and the officers he did see routinely called blacks "niggers." Throughout the years, African-Americans complained to each other that the department placed a higher priority on white lives and property in northwest Washington than it did on the mostly black and Hispanic populations to the east of Rock Creek Park and on the other side of the Anacostia River.

Barrett scanned the Levy case file for something he might have missed. The first twenty-four hours were critical in a homicide case, and with Chandra missing for more than a week, if this was a homicide, it didn't look good. The first officer who went to her apartment on May 6 found no indications of foul play, no evidence of a struggle or a break-in. Chandra's refrigerator was empty except for some leftover pasta and Reese's Peanut Butter Cups. Her suitcases were on the floor, half packed with a few items of clothing, and some of her outfits hung in the closet. The officer left a business card for Chandra, directing her to contact Durant.

Barrett also knew that Chandra had called

Condit in the weeks before on her cell phone, and Robert Levy had told Durant that he thought that his daughter was having an affair with the lawmaker. Durant dialed Condit's Capitol office and left a message on May 7. The next day the congressman returned the call.

The relationship between members of Congress and city government officials has historically been rocky. District leaders have long resented Congress because it controls the city's budget, and D.C. citizens cannot vote for their own member of Congress because Washington is not considered to be a state under the U.S. Constitution. These tensions have been exacerbated by city activists who likened the role played by a mostly white Congress to that of plantation owners overseeing a majority-black city. Of the 535 members of Congress, just 38 were African-American, and not one was a U.S. senator.

Barrett continued to read the file. Durant had asked Condit if he knew Chandra, and he told the congressman that she was missing. Did he know where she might be? Condit said he had already spoken to Chandra's father, that he didn't know Chandra well, but she called him occasionally for career advice. That was the only contact he had with her, he said. Condit told Durant that he hadn't heard from Chandra for about a week, since May 1 or 2. Durant asked Condit if he could take a formal statement from him, and they scheduled a face-to-face interview at the congressman's fourth-floor condominium in Adams Morgan on May 9.

Before the meeting, Durant received a call from Linda Zamsky, Chandra's forty-year-old aunt, who lived about eighty miles north of Washington near the Elk River in Chesapeake City, Maryland. She said her niece had confided to her that she had been having an affair with Condit for the past six months; Chandra told Zamsky that the congressman had promised to leave his wife in five years and marry her one day.

The contents of the case file were puzzling. Did the congressman mislead Barrett's detective? Could Condit have had something to do with her disappearance?

Barrett read on: On May 9 at 9:55 P.M., three days after learning that Chandra was missing, Durant and D.C. police sergeant Ronald Wyatt arrived at Condit's condominium. Condit repeated what he had told Durant over the phone. He added a few fresh details: He said he and Chandra had met in the fall of 2000, when she came to his Capitol Hill office with a friend who was looking for a job as an intern. He said he hired Chandra's friend and he and Chandra had soon become friends. He said she didn't appear to be upset the last time he had seen her. Durant and Wyatt pressed the congressman for more details, and Condit told them that she had visited his apartment, spending the night on a few occasions.

"Did you have an intimate relationship with Ms. Levy?" Wyatt asked.

Condit replied: "I don't think we need to go there, and you can infer what you want with that."

Barrett then read a May 10 search warrant affidavit and the inventory of what was found inside Chandra's apartment. He scanned the list of belongings: a cell phone, credit cards and a driver's license in a purse, dirty dishes in the sink, a blue Sony Vaio laptop computer, assorted papers, and pocketbooks. Also listed: thirty-one dollars and fifty cents, sheets and toiletries, a receipt for the cancellation of her membership at the Washington Sports Club on Connecticut Avenue in Dupont Circle, five sets of earrings, two wristwatches, an ankle bracelet, a necklace with a pendant, and a Williams-Sonoma bag on the breakfast countertop containing dirty laundry: blue jeans, socks, and underwear. Her answering machine was full, with twenty-five messages.

The detectives overlooked one important clue, a potential piece of evidence. Chandra's apartment building had multiple surveillance cameras, each feeding into a video recorder. The videotape was recorded over every seven days. If Chandra last left the building on May 1, the tape of that would have been erased on the 8th. Durant sent the first officer to the apartment on May 6. An officer went again on the 7th and the 8th. Each time they neglected to ask for the tape. By the time they did, it had been erased. Gone were answers to several key questions: What time did Chandra leave? What was she wearing? Was she alone, or did she leave with someone? Without the tape, police were left to speculate. Maybe she had been kidnapped. Maybe one of Condit's aides had picked her up at the apartment. Maybe she had been murdered in her apartment and carried out of the building. The detectives didn't have a clue.

The police made another critical mistake. Chandra had left her Sony laptop open on a makeshift desk in the hallway of her apartment. Sergeant Wyatt turned it on and tried to retrace her last Internet searches. Barrett didn't understand the intricacies of computers, and he wasn't sure exactly what Wyatt did — but he knew one thing: Wyatt shouldn't have touched the laptop. The sergeant wasn't a trained computer technician, and by fooling around with Chandra's laptop, he had accidentally corrupted its hard drive. The detectives couldn't accurately determine which websites she had last visited, and it would be weeks before federal agents could analyze the laptop. With no other leads, the detectives had few investigative paths to follow, aside from Condit. Was he being completely forthcoming? Was he trying to cover up an affair, or was there something else? Barrett had a lot of questions for the congressman.

Barrett reviewed copies of a few stories published by the *Washington Post.* The first, on May 11, running just 319 words, was buried deep inside the paper on page 3 of the Metro section. NW WOMAN MISSING FOR A WEEK, the headline read. The story mentioned that officers had found Chandra's suitcases in her apartment, and Wyatt was quoted as saying the circumstances of her disappearance were noteworthy: "When somebody is expected to travel back to their home state and gave indication to their family that they would be there for their graduation ceremony, only to drop out of sight — we consider that to be unusual." The seven-paragraph story ended with a police phone number and a request for anyone with information to call detectives at 2D. The department also issued a press release with a photo of Chandra, wearing tight jeans and a sweater and striking a sexy pose. It didn't quite square with the image Barrett had of an intern at the Bureau of Prisons who hoped to become an FBI agent one day. Chandra had posed for the picture during an artistic photo shoot while she was in high school. In her haste, Susan Levy provided the photo to police and reporters without thinking about the image it would convey. But the photo didn't come close to capturing the woman Chandra had become.

The story did not mention what the detectives were hearing — that Condit had been having an affair with Chandra. In a city that thrives on press leaks, Barrett wondered how long it would be before one of the hundreds of reporters covering Washington received a tip from a source or a call from someone like Zamsky, Chandra's aunt. He braced himself, knowing that his department was about to be in the glare of a national news story.

The second *Washington Post* story, published five days later, reported that Condit had added $10,000 to a reward fund to help find his missing constituent, but again there was no mention of a relationship. It quoted the congressman: "Chandra is a great person and a good friend. We hope she is found safe and sound."

On May 16, reporters picked up the first hint of a scandal from their sources inside the police department, and the next day they published the first stories linking Condit to Chandra. The *Washington Post* reported that Condit's chief of staff in Modesto, Michael Lynch, had been fielding calls all day from reporters who wanted to know whether Condit was having an affair with Chandra. Lynch was adamant: "Totally did not occur. It's really distressing that a lot of people are focusing on that issue when the focus should be on finding where Chandra is."

The May 17 story in the *Washington Post* puzzled Barrett. Why would Lynch issue a public denial when Condit had already told his detectives privately that Chandra had spent the night at his apartment? Did Condit lie to his chief of staff? Did he order his top aide to lie? Was the congressman keeping something from his detectives? To

Barrett, it looked like the beginning of a classic Washington cover-up.

6
THE IMMIGRANT

Ingmar Adalid Guandique

On May 1, the day Chandra disappeared, Amber Fitzgerald was walking along a heavily wooded hiking path in Rock Creek Park, just south of the Peirce Mill at about 2 P.M. The young lawyer with long blond hair sensed someone watching her from the hillside above. As she reached a remote part of the trail, she looked to her right. Above, on a wooded ridge, parallel to her path, a young man was trudging through the underbrush. She wondered why he wasn't on the trail if he was a jogger. Why was he in the woods, coming increasingly closer?

Fitzgerald slowed, hoping the man would pass. Instead he disappeared behind a bend. Fitzgerald continued her pace. Within a minute or so, she sensed someone approaching. She turned to see the same man, standing less than ten feet away, blocking her path. He was Hispanic, medium height, wearing baggy shorts and a ball cap pulled down over his short dark hair. She ran off the path and down a hill, her heart pounding. She jumped over a fallen tree and sprinted until she was out of the woods. When she reached a footbridge near Beach Drive, a heavily traveled commuter shortcut to downtown Washington, she stopped to catch her breath. She was rattled by what had happened. Over dinner that night, she told her boyfriend about the encounter. She wondered whether she imagined that the man was stalking her. She felt threatened, but perhaps she overreacted. After all, the man hadn't said or done anything. Maybe she had misjudged his intentions. She decided to let it go and not call the police.

The young man with the broad forehead, flat nose, and dark brown eyes that Amber saw that day looked like Ingmar Adalid Guandique, a nineteen-year-old immigrant from El Salvador. He was five foot seven, 130 pounds, lean and strong from his days working on construction crews. Guandique had come to the United States a little more than a year before with big dreams of starting a new life. He came from a hardscrabble hamlet in El Salvador called Cooperativa San Jacinto, about six miles outside the city of San Miguel. The peasants who lived there grew cotton, rice, and corn. Guandique was born in 1981, out of wedlock, to Miriam Blanco. He was the second of her seven children; each of them had a different father.

Blanco always believed her boy had terrible luck. "Even in the womb before he was born," she said. While Blanco was three months pregnant, guerrillas kidnapped Guandique's father, Samuel Cabrera Alvarenga, in the early years of the Salvadoran civil war. More than seventy-five thousand people died during the war that raged from 1980 to 1992 between an anticommunist military junta backed by the Reagan administration and the Farabundo Martí National Liberation Front, a coalition of leftwing guerrilla groups known by the acronym FMLN. The people of San Jacinto found themselves caught in a conflict zone. The guerrillas took young men out of rural towns and forced them to fight against the government, which had killed nearly forty thousand people in the first five years of the war, most of them peasants. Military death squads routinely dumped mutilated corpses in public places to terrorize local populations. One of the squads captured Guandique's father from the guerrillas, executed him, and tossed his body along a rural road.

Guandique's relatives were peasants who lived in poverty. He grew up in an adobe house with a roof made of tree branches, a dirt floor, and an open pit for cooking meals. The home was decorated with family photos and pictures of Jesus and the Virgin Mary taped to pink and white sheets of plastic that served as wallpaper. After the death of his father, his mother returned to the father of her first child. Guandique's stepfather and his mother beat him mercilessly.

Guandique struggled in school with learning disabilities; he was held back in the first and second grades. Gangs harassed him. In the seventh grade, he dropped out and moved in with his paternal grandmother. At fourteen, he moved back in with his mother. His grandfather had high hopes for Guandique. He thought his grandson's hard work in the fields could help his family get ahead one day, but Guandique had other plans. Like many other Salvadorans, he wanted a fresh start in America. During the civil war, more than a million Salvadorans fled the misery and violence, many of them entering the United States illegally. Tens of thousands found their way to Washington. A friend of the Guandique family, Adan Flores, was already living in a growing Salvadoran community in Washington. Flores's family loaned Guandique $5,100 to pay a "coyote" to smuggle him across the Texas border along with more than fifty other Salvadorans, Guatemalans, Hondurans, and Mexicans. The routes over the mountains and across the borders into Texas and the Arizona desert were dangerous; each year thousands were caught and sent back to their home countries. Many died along the way.

On January 13, 2000, Guandique left San Jacinto. Guandique's family paid half of the money to the coyote up front; the rest was due after he arrived safely in Washington. He took a bus with the others into Mexico, swam across the Rio Grande, and slipped over the border near Piedras Negras into Texas. In March 2000, Guandique arrived in Houston. From there he took a bus to Washington and joined his half brother, Huber, who had come from Salvador the year before. By the time Guandique arrived in the capital, Washington was experiencing a historic wave of immigration. Officially, 135,000 Salvadorans were living in the region, the second-largest population of Salvadorans in the nation after Los Angeles, but the embassy of El Salvador put the number closer to 400,000. More than any other major U.S. urban area, Washington and its suburbs had been steadily drawing immigrants from across Latin America. Hispanic migration to Washington began after World War II when Latin American embassies and international organizations opened in the city, followed by domestic workers who sent word home that Washington was a place of prosperity. By 2000, nearly 60 percent of Latino immigrants in the Washington area identified themselves as natives of Central America. The Washington-backed war had an unintended consequence: Two in five immigrants described themselves as Salvadorans, constituting the largest community in the region's Hispanic mosaic.

In the spring of 2000, Guandique moved into a red-brick apartment building on Somerset Place in Washington's Brightwood neighborhood, near Rock Creek Park. Huber lived there with Flores, the man who had helped Guandique make his way to the United States. One of Flores's relatives also helped Guandique obtain a temporary job as a landscaper, cutting grass, planting trees, and picking up dead leaves and broken branches. Guandique found other jobs as a carpenter's apprentice, a maintenance man, and a construction worker. He made $7.50 an hour, sent small amounts of money home, and tried to repay the Flores family.

He had another financial obligation as well: his ex-girlfriend, Sonia, who was still in Salvador and pregnant with Guandique's baby. After she gave birth to a boy, she began to demand child support payments. Guandique started to send $140 a month to his family and $20 to Sonia, but she fumed that he wasn't sending more. She threatened to put a hex on Guandique if he didn't pay. In rural El Salvador, where some peasants believe in the power of spells, Guandique's grandfather visited a psychic three times in an attempt to ward off Sonia's threatened hex.

By the fall of 2000, Guandique had fallen for another Salvadoran woman, Iris Portillo. They met one October day in front of her apartment on Somerset Place. Even though she was a year older than Guandique, she looked like she was thirteen, tiny with an innocent smile and the face of child. She, too, had big dreams and was determined to improve her life; by day she worked at a Mexican restaurant in Washington called Cactus Cantina; at night she cleaned office buildings and took GED classes to earn her high school diploma. Soon Guandique moved in with Portillo and her mother, Maria. Guandique and his new girlfriend took walks near the National Zoo and picnicked in Rock Creek Park. They adored the park, its groves of trees and miles of hiking paths offering plenty of privacy. They snapped photos of each other, standing on the rocks of the creek, lounging on the grass. In one picture, Guandique smiled broadly as he clutched a teddy bear with long furry arms, a red bow fastened to its head. Guandique drew cartoon figures for Portillo and bought her a ring from a nearby pawnshop.

But life was becoming increasingly difficult for Guandique. He had a hard time adjusting to his place near the bottom of the American labor force. He barely spoke English and he didn't like the routine: waking up at dawn, traveling to different job sites, spending the day toiling at backbreaking jobs for little pay. Holding on to work was difficult; he didn't have a work permit and he started to drift from job to job. He struggled to send money home. He still owed the Flores family for his passage to America and he had little cash left over. Portillo was starting to demand that he spend more on her. His half brother, Huber, wrote to his grandfather in Salvador, telling him that he didn't know what Guandique was doing with his money. More worrisome, he noted that Guandique had started to drink. Several of his uncles in Salvador, along with his mother's father, had struggled with alcoholism and now Guandique was drinking heavily, two six-packs of beer and more, sometimes to the point of passing out. He also started to smoke marijuana and snort cocaine that he got from his friends or bought using whatever money he had left. He felt alone and disconnected, mired in the bad luck that had followed him throughout his life.

In early spring 2001, Guandique began to spend time in Rock Creek Park and he became increasingly obsessed with Portillo. One night, after finding letters from an old boyfriend from Salvador, Guandique struck Portillo. Another time, he bit her hard above her breast, creating a wound that left a scar. He warned her not to stray. In a rage one night, he kicked in the bedroom door, splintering the wood. He slammed his head against the bathroom wall, making a hole in the plaster. He hit Portillo in the face and held his hands to her throat. If he couldn't have her, he warned, no one could. Without explanation, Guandique began to carry a six-inch-long knife, wrapped in a red cloth.

Portillo's mother, Maria, had seen enough. She told Guandique to leave her apartment and stay away from her daughter. Guandique, who alternated between anger and contrition, didn't put up a fight. Sporadically, he lived with the landlady of the Somerset apartments, Sheila Phillips Cruz. On May 1, Guandique failed to show for a day job he had on a construction site. Later, Guandique ran into Cruz in his old neighborhood. She was struck by his appearance — he had a fat lip, a bloody blemish in his eye, and scratches around his throat. She asked him what had happened. He told her he had been in a fight with Portillo and she struck him. Cruz doubted the story; she knew Guandique and Portillo were no longer dating, and Portillo was a waif of a woman — it seemed impossible that she could inflict so much damage. To Cruz, he looked like he had been in a bad fight with someone who fought back, hard.

7
JANET

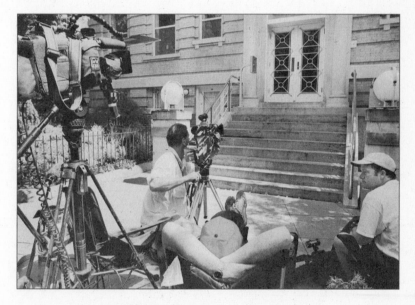

Gary Condit's Condominium

Robert and Susan Levy didn't know what to do or where to turn. They sought help from the Carole Sund/Carrington Memorial Reward Foundation, a nonprofit group based in Modesto that was created after a triple murder near Yosemite National Park in 1999. Organizers of the group told the Levys that their best chance of finding their daughter was to keep the story in the national spotlight. They knew the media had an insatiable appetite for breaking news and the scent of scandal. More stories and more readers and more viewers would increase the pressure on the police to keep the case a priority and not let it fade away.

On Monday, May 14, 2001, with the help of the group, Susan Levy appeared on ABC's *Good Morning America* and organized a news conference at the Sund/Carrington headquarters. The next night the group held a candlelight vigil. Volunteers handed out candles and yellow ribbons and packages of Chandra's favorite candy, Reese's Peanut Butter Cups. "The message tonight is simple and clear," said Chandra's friend Jennifer Baker. "Get the word out about Chandra Levy." On Wednesday, May 16, the Levys flew to Washington, and television camera crews trailed them the next day as they visited Capitol Hill to see their home-state senators, Barbara Boxer and Dianne Feinstein. They also met with D.C. police officials. The Levys told one of those officials, Jack Barrett, that they were concerned the investigation could be compromised because it involved a member of Congress. He told the couple that he had worked sensitive cases before and assured them that he would never permit politics to influence any investigation. At a May 17 news conference at the Key Bridge Marriott in Arlington, Virginia, Susan Levy tried to be strong before the phalanx of reporters and cameras; Robert buried his head in his wife's shoulder and wept. Newspapers around the nation picked up the story. So did CNN and NBC's *Dateline*.

Across the country, in San Francisco, a young woman was following the news coverage. It forced her to confront a secret, something she had kept hidden from nearly everyone she knew, a secret from a part of her life that had made her feel trapped, controlled, even suicidal. After all these years, she felt compelled to call the FBI on May 17 and confide in an agent on the other end of the phone line in the bureau's San Francisco field office.

She didn't want anyone to know her real name. She told the agent he could call her "Janet." She said she feared for the missing intern she had heard about on the news that day. It all seemed so surreal, as though her own past was being repeated in the life of another young woman from California. Janet said that she didn't know Chandra Levy, but she had secretly dated the same congressman, Gary Condit, for nearly three years. The affair began in Los Angeles, continued in Washington, and ended in San Francisco. She told the agent she didn't believe the statements issued by the congressman's chief of staff, denying the existence of a relationship between Condit and Chandra.

Janet said the news reports made her wonder what might have happened to Chandra. She told the FBI agent that she thought Chandra might have committed suicide, or maybe she was in hiding, hoping her disappearance would somehow bring the secret affair to light. Janet thought that the affair might have had something to do with what happened to Chandra.

Chandra had been missing for sixteen days, and the FBI agent wanted to hear more. He urged Janet to come to the bureau's field office on Golden Gate Avenue for a face-to-face interview. At first Janet was reluctant to meet with the agent, but he told her it was critically important for her to tell her story to the FBI in person.

Janet arrived at nine that night, her husband by her side. Two FBI agents, Margaret Eason and Derek Price, escorted her to an interview room. They took careful notes as Janet, an attractive, petite brunette, began to tell her story: She grew up in the San Joaquin Valley and was familiar with Condit's name from an early age because of his political popularity; she remembered first seeing him at a community pancake breakfast when she was twelve years old. She was introduced to him ten years later, in 1992, by her boyfriend, Mike Dayton, who was working as an aide to the congressman at the time. Janet was twenty-two, a college student, and Condit was forty-four, a second-term congressman. Soon after their introduction, Condit asked Janet and Dayton to join him for dinner. After the dinner,

Janet and Condit had no contact for about a year, until the fall of 1993. Dayton, who was still working for Condit but no longer Janet's boyfriend, called her to say that the congressman needed a ride to a fund-raiser in Los Angeles, where she was attending college. Janet agreed to pick him up. After the fund-raiser, she had what she described to the FBI agents as a "physical encounter" with the congressman. At the end of the night, Janet felt uneasy about what she had done; Condit was married, he had two children, and he was highly visible in her hometown. She said the congressman repeatedly called her, inviting her to come to Washington. She resisted, but by October 1993, she relented. She described Condit as charismatic and persuasive. She accepted a United Airlines frequent-flier voucher from Condit and boarded a plane for the nation's capital. The two became a secret couple and saw each other several times over the next few months. She used his vouchers to fly between California and Washington.

In January 1994, as Janet was preparing to graduate from college, Condit asked her if she wanted to work in his Capitol Hill office. He offered her a job as a legislative assistant and a place to stay: his condominium in Adams Morgan. Janet accepted both. She had her own phone line, her own closet, and her own bathroom in the fourth-floor apartment. To maintain appearances, she also rented an apartment on Biltmore Street, a three-block walk from Condit's condominium on Adams Mill Road, but she spent little time there.

Janet felt that she was in a serious romantic relationship. She told the FBI agents that she and Condit exchanged gifts; he bought her clothing, perfume, pearls, an emerald-and-diamond ring and a watch from Neiman Marcus; she bought him a brushed-steel TAG Heuer watch and a red Trek mountain bike. He told her he was considering leaving Congress and talked about their moving in together one day; they'd find a cabin in a small community where he didn't have to work, and she could be a school-teacher if she wanted. But the situation soon became problematic. She said Condit refused to permit her to be around other men. He lectured her about her "loyalty" to him and ordered her not to tell anyone about their affair. He was never physically abusive, but he had rules for the relationship: She was to ensure they were never seen together so no one could take a photograph. If she was confronted about the affair, she was to deny it; there was no way anyone could refute her assertion. He warned that if anyone found out, it would "ruin" everything. Though they eventually did go out in public together — to football games, a few concerts, and occasionally to dinner at Pasta Mia near Condit's condo — Janet had to wear a ball cap. If they bumped into someone, they would say they were friends who knew each other through work. Janet complied with Condit's rules, but she had a hard time masking her misgivings and she sometimes cried at work. She and Condit concocted a cover story for this as well: She was to tell her co-workers that she was upset over a recent breakup.

In July 1994, Janet said Condit's daughter, Cadee, came to town for a summer internship. The congressman told Janet she had to move to the apartment on Biltmore Street. Sometimes, Janet said, she felt she had betrayed herself by continuing the affair; other times she was "pissed off" because Cadee's arrival meant that Janet could no longer spend time alone with Condit. The situation worsened when Cadee began to befriend her. Cadee frequently stopped by her father's office and the two young women would "hang out." Janet never confided the affair to Cadee, but her feelings of guilt mounted. She became so depressed that she considered taking her life. By the end of the summer, deeply ashamed, she told Condit she was ending the relationship. Janet packed up her belongings on Biltmore Street and moved to San Francisco.

Back on the West Coast, Janet tried to set out on her own. She rented an apartment in the city, found a roommate, and began a career in advertising. She told the FBI agents that Condit was relentless. Despite the distance, he continued to pursue her, and Janet found it hard to say no. Every couple of weeks, Condit flew to San Francisco on his way home. He didn't like to drive and had hired a Harley-Davidson-riding bodybuilder from Ceres, Vince Flammini, to chauffeur him around. Flammini would pick up Condit at the airport and drive him to Janet's apartment, and the couple would spend time together in the city. The relationship stretched into the spring of 1996 before Janet ended it for good. Two months later, she met the man she would marry.

As the interview drew to a close, the FBI agents asked Janet if she had heard from Condit again. She told them that she saw him once more, in 1999. Condit had come to San Francisco and Janet agreed to meet him at a Starbucks at Polk and Green streets. Condit told her that cutting him off and not returning his phone calls was wrong. He criticized her decision to pursue an advertising career, telling her that her job was unimportant. Before leaving, the congressman made a final prediction: He told Janet that her husband would bore her one day, and she would ask Condit to return.

Janet told the agents she never spoke to the congressman again.

8
THE WASHINGTON LAWYERS

Abbe David Lowell

Joseph Cotchett was not doing his client any favors. Gary Condit had retained the California lawyer to represent him as the Chandra Levy story exploded in the press. Cotchett launched a vigorous defense and lashed out at the media, but instead of defusing the situation, he created more negative press.

On June 11, Cotchett took on the *Washington Post,* accusing the newspaper of making statements it "knew to be false." Inside the newspaper, Cotchett's claim was a serious allegation and not taken lightly. Cotchett rebutted a report that Condit told D.C. police that Chandra Levy had spent the night at his client's apartment, but the paper had solid sources and stood by the story. Cotchett then accused the *Washington Post* of a "frightening violation of the ethics and standards of American journalism" after the paper reported that Chandra told a relative she was romantically involved with Condit. Steve Coll, the newspaper's managing editor, pushed back: "We believe that our original story accurately characterized the police investigation, as well as what Levy told a relative." Whatever credibility Cotchett might have had at the *Post* was gone.

Cotchett then took a different tack to defend his client. He went on CBS's *The Early Show.* Cotchett declined to confirm or deny a relationship between Condit and Chandra, but he noted that Chandra had called his client. "Let's assume she was calling him to say good-bye, which we suspect was the case," Cotchett said. "The congressman has come forward and said they were good friends, as he is with many interns."

Several members of the California congressional delegation pulled Condit aside on Capitol Hill to tell him that the situation was spiraling out of control. He needed a new attorney, someone who knew how to navigate the treacherous waters of Washington, where politics, the law, and the media intersect and often conspire with one another. They had the perfect lawyer in mind: Abbe David Lowell. Reluctantly, Condit agreed to meet him, but he insisted it be kept secret.

Near dusk on an early June night in 2001,

Lowell opened the passenger door of a white Ford Explorer parked outside the National Democratic Club, set in the shadow of the U.S. Capitol. He stepped inside and reached over to shake the driver's hand. Lowell had never met a prospective client in a car before, but he understood why Condit wanted it this way.

Condit could not go anywhere without television cameras trailing him and reporters calling out his name and barking questions. "Where's Chandra?" they shouted. Camera crews camped outside his Capitol Hill office. Reporters lined the crowded sidewalk outside his apartment building; pedestrians could barely squeeze by. Curious motorists slowed to gawk at the media circus that had come to the neighborhood. The last thing Condit wanted was to be spotted in the presence of a well-known attorney, or to have cameras snap a photo of a lawyer of Lowell's reputation entering his congressional office or his apartment building. Condit believed his best bet for privacy was at night, inside a nondescript car belonging to one of his closest aides, Mike Dayton.

The son of a decorated World War II flyboy, Lowell was a fast-talking, forty-nine-year-old New Yorker who held a Columbia

Law School degree. With a healthy ego and seasoned in the ways of Washington, he was fierce in the courtroom. Around town, he was known for representing powerful people who had highly publicized falls from grace. His client list read like a Who's Who of prominent politicians who found themselves mired in trouble. House Speaker Jim Wright of Texas, charged with sixty-nine violations of House campaign finance rules. House Ways and Means Committee chairman Dan Rostenkowski of Illinois, charged with fraud, conspiracy, and obstruction of justice. New Jersey senator Robert G. Torricelli, under investigation for accepting illegal gifts and cash from a businessman and campaign contributor.

Three years earlier, in the midst of the Monica Lewinsky scandal, Lowell served as the chief Democratic investigative counsel for the House of Representatives, during impeachment proceedings against President Bill Clinton. The president was impeached by the Republican-controlled House, but acquitted of perjury and obstruction of justice by the Senate two months later.

Lowell also served as special counsel to the House Ethics Committee, and he represented Charlie Wilson, a notorious Democratic congressman from Texas who engineered the financing of one of the largest covert operations in U.S. history, which led to the downfall of the Soviet Union in Afghanistan. The CIA trained and funded Afghan rebels in a successful campaign to force the Soviets from the country. Wilson retained Lowell when the Justice Department opened a probe into possible contracting irregularities in the covert operation, but never brought charges. An inside-the-Beltway man about town, Lowell seemed to know everyone. He was involved in charity and cultural organizations and served on the Board of Trustees for the Shakespeare Theatre Company, indulging a longtime passion for the Bard, especially the tragedies of King Lear and Hamlet. But he loved nothing more than standing on the stage of Washington's real-life political dramas.

Condit drove through the streets of Capitol Hill as Lowell tried to break the ice with small talk. *We have to stop meeting this way,* he jokingly said, noting the crazed media frenzy, the gaggle of reporters growing by the day. Lowell did not press for details or ask Condit too many questions. He knew better. Since it was their first meeting, he probably wouldn't be in the car for long. He wanted to make Condit feel comfortable; trust would come later. As they drove around Capitol Hill that night, they passed the neoclassical Capitol dome illuminated in the darkness, the marble columns of the U.S. Supreme Court, the grand Library of Congress.

Condit had resisted the idea of hiring Lowell. He had already talked to the police, and he had offered ten thousand dollars from his campaign toward a reward fund to help find his constituent, shortly after Chandra's disappearance. For weeks Condit had been trying to ignore the media spectacle around him. He flashed his trademark smile at colleagues and joked that he wasn't paying attention to the news; he couldn't watch the train wreck that had become his life. When he turned on the television, he flipped to the Weather Channel. When colleagues on Capitol Hill asked him how he was doing, Condit tried to stay upbeat and jokingly said he could give them the five-day forecasts for their cities. But his calm demeanor was masking a growing dread.

Television correspondents from every network and cable news station were demanding to know the details of his relationship with Chandra. Steve Friedman, the senior executive producer of CBS's *The Early Show*, attributed the growing media frenzy to the fact that Chandra's disappearance was every parent's nightmare. "You want your son or daughter to do an internship, get a leg up on a job. And then, out of nowhere, comes a fear for the worst — a child's death." Friedman echoed the sentiments of Susan and Robert Levy, who thought Chandra would be safe working in Washington, surrounded by some of the nation's preeminent public servants who were sworn to uphold the law.

The D.C. police helped to fuel the media frenzy. The police department's number-two man, Terrance W. Gainer, a gregarious and media-savvy Chicago cop who once headed the Illinois State Police, was front and center, responding to a barrage of questions from the press by consenting to interviews almost every day. He felt that his department was under enormous pressure to talk to the press and keep the public informed about the course of the investigation. He wanted to shield the front-line detectives from the press. He told reporters the congressman was not a suspect. Chandra's disappearance was a missing persons case, and there was no evidence that a crime had been committed. No crime, no suspect, he said. But the cynical Washington press corps wasn't buying it; if Condit wasn't a suspect, why were police officers walking the hallways of his apartment building, carrying photographs of Chandra and asking his neighbors if they had ever seen her? Why were the police searching the woods of Rock Creek Park near his building with cadaver dogs?

Another police official, Assistant Police Chief Ronald Monroe, gave them an answer. Condit's top aide in Washington, Dayton, denied the congressman had a romantic relationship with Chandra and said she had only come by his office about a half-dozen times to ask for typical constituent favors, White House tour tickets, or schedules of Capitol Hill events. But Monroe said the police had discovered that Chandra had visited Condit's apartment "more than a couple times." Condit was livid. The police had already leaked information to their favorite reporters about his first interview with detectives. Now a top police official had spoken out of turn, disclosing details of what was supposed to be a confidential conversation. Police Chief Charles Ramsey tried to tamp down the story by saying the assistant chief had merely repeated a rumor. But the reporters assigned to cover the story immediately picked up the scent of a summertime scandal, a ritual in Washington when real news is hard to come by. More people seemed to be talking about Chandra's disappearance than tax reform or the landmark McCain-Feingold campaign finance bill.

All of this had led Condit to consent to the car ride. Lowell was good at quickly sizing up people. During the thirty-minute ride, he could see why Condit was popular in his California district. He was charming and good-natured, giving neither the impression of intellectual elitism nor simpleminded naïveté. Still, Lowell thought the congressman was in over his head. The story about the missing intern was potentially more explosive than any case he had ever handled. Not only did it involve sex, it could involve a murder. Lowell had some advice for Condit: If you don't go on the offensive, act strategically, and show that you are concerned about this young woman, this story is going to become even bigger.

Lowell was right. On June 14, not long after his evening meeting in the car, Robert and Susan Levy took a dramatic step: From Modesto, they went on national television, urging Condit to break his public silence. They pleaded with him to come forward and disclose what he might know. The Levys were openly frustrated with Condit and they thought he was concealing knowledge about their daughter and her disappearance. Susan told reporters that she knew of an affair between her daughter and Condit.

On Saturday, June 16, two days after their television appearance, the phone rang at the Levys' home in Modesto. Susan picked it up. "This is Gary Condit," the congressman said. Susan Levy was taken aback. She told him she didn't want to talk to him without her attorney present. She and her husband had hired their own big-time Washington lawyer to turn up the pressure on Condit and the D.C. police. With television trucks parked up and down their street, they had been trying their best to cope. For seven weeks, they had meditated and prayed, hoping their daughter was still alive. Now they were turning to one of Washington's best and brightest, a smooth and seasoned litigator named William Martin, known around town simply as "Billy."

At fifty-one, Martin was equally comfortable on the streets and in the halls of official power, a go-to guy in Washington's legal world. As a former prosecutor with the U.S. attorney's office in Washington, Martin had helped build the famous crack cocaine case against the former mayor of the city, Marion Barry. When Martin left the prosecutor's office, he became a defense lawyer, representing several sports stars. They included Philadelphia 76ers basketball star Allen Iverson, who was facing assault allegations that were eventually dismissed, and former heavyweight boxing champion Riddick Bowe, who had abducted his estranged wife and five children from their Charlotte, North Carolina, home. He was eventually sentenced to eighteen months in federal prison.

Like Lowell, Martin had been a legal player in the Clinton sex scandal story, serving as the attorney for Lewinsky's mother when prosecutors summoned her before a grand jury. Martin and Lowell had something else in common. They once worked together in the D.C. office of the Los Angeles–based Manatt, Phelps & Phillips, a large corporate law firm. For lawyers, Washington was a small town full of revolving doors between the Justice Department, the White House, Congress, federal agencies, and the city's plethora of private practice law firms and lobbying outfits.

After the car ride, Condit reluctantly hired Lowell. He didn't want to admit that he needed him, but the situation was growing worse. The detectives continued to focus on him, and it did not appear that they were interested in pursuing any other suspects.

He decided to defer to his friends and colleagues. One of the first things Lowell did after Condit hired him was to call the police. Lowell wanted to introduce himself to the detectives and their supervisor, Jack Barrett, and let them know he would now be representing Condit. But he also wanted to get a sense of what they were doing. Lawrence Kennedy, a detective who investigated a wide range of crimes during his career, had joined the lead investigator, Ralph Durant. They had gone through the police academy at the same time and worked together for nearly three decades, but had never handled a case this big. In fact, they had never worked in the homicide unit as lead detectives. The detectives wanted another interview with the congressman, and Lowell told them he would try to make that happen, but he had a question for them: What other leads are you following? In his gut, he believed that the congressman had nothing to do with Chandra's disappearance. The police were wasting their time by focusing on his client. They needed to be figuring out what had really happened.

Lowell's job was to protect Condit, but the lawyer was also concerned about the Levy family. He had two daughters himself, one twenty and the other sixteen, and a baby girl on the way. He couldn't imagine the pain of not knowing what had happened to a child. He understood why the Levys were doing everything they could to keep their daughter's disappearance in the news. It would be easy, as the days went by, for the case to get shuffled out of sight and all but forgotten. Or, in the glare of the media attention, for the police to fixate on the photogenic and headline-generating congressman — regardless of the lack of any real evidence tying him to Chandra's disappearance. Lowell wanted to know whether the detectives were seriously chasing other leads. They insisted that they were.

In reality, the police were at a standstill. The detectives had interviewed dozens of people, including Levy's neighbors and members of her health club near Dupont Circle, where she was last seen. They had combed through her phone records but found nothing helpful. They had asked for Condit's financial and phone records. They had drawn up a confidential "suspect list," which included several of Levy's acquaintances and the "CM," which stood for the congressman. The police had three different theories about what happened to Chandra — that she ran away, committed suicide, or fell victim to foul play.

"No theory holds any more weight than any of the others," Barrett told reporters. Barrett was technically in charge of the case, but the former FBI man was new to the department. Gainer and Ramsey both appeared on national television and requested briefings on the progress of the case nearly every day. With nothing much else to go on, Gainer and Ramsey released a new missing poster to the public. It contained four computer-generated images of Chandra with a smile, differentiated by hairstyles that looked as if they came from the 1970s. In one, her hair was cut in a shag; in another, it was short and frizzy like an Afro. Some investigators ridiculed the poster. Not only did it look absurd, they thought it was a waste of time. By now, they thought Chandra was probably dead.

To the Levys and their lawyer, Martin, the poster was more evidence that police had no idea what they were doing. They thought the suicide and runaway theories were off base and that the police were bungling the case by not moving fast enough. To put pressure on the police, Martin hired two former D.C. homicide detectives he knew from his days as a prosecutor. One was Dwayne Stanton, a stocky African-American with a shaved head, neatly trimmed beard, and an infectious charm. His partner was J. T. "Joe" McCann, a thin, white, street-smart New Yorker with a roguish smile and a distinct Long Island accent. After they retired from the D.C. police department, the two had started their own private-eye firm, conducting background investigations for corporations and hiring themselves out to trail spouses suspected of cheating. With Stanton and McCann in tow, Martin pledged to conduct his own investigation of Chandra's disappearance. In a public swipe at the police, he set up his own 800 number to take tips. The parallel investigation created even more tension between the police and the Levys' legal team and became another distraction for the department.

On the evening of June 19, the Levys prepared to fly back to Washington. A friend of the family suggested that they take duffel bags so they could fill them with the belongings that remained in Chandra's apartment. Robert Levy refused; filling duffel bags felt too final. Two days later, the Levys accompanied Martin to police headquarters for a short briefing with Ramsey and other top police officials. The Levys again said they thought Condit was somehow involved in the disappearance of their daughter and he was trying to protect himself. They also thought that Condit was exercising his political power by slowing down the pace of the police department's investigation. They pushed the police to pursue Condit more aggressively. To Barrett, the Levys' insistence was becoming the "albatross" of his investigation. He thought Ramsey and Gainer were responding to the couple by devoting the department's resources to Condit at a time when the chief of detectives was uncertain whether the congressman had anything to do with Chandra's disappearance.

At the same time, Susan Levy wanted to confront Condit and ask him about his relationship with her daughter. Martin and Lowell agreed to set up a private sit-down between the Levys and the congressman, off the record and far away from the television cameras. Lowell briefly considered another scenario. Would it help if Condit went to the hotel where the Levys were staying and made a public showing that he wanted to talk to them? Lowell was torn about how much to play to the media. He wanted reporters to know that his client was cooperating, but if he told them Condit was going to see the Levys, it would create bedlam outside the hotel.

Lowell knew several secluded meeting

spots around the city. To elude the press, he suggested that they meet in a private dining room at the Jefferson, a hotel a block from his office and four blocks from the White House, on Sixteenth Street. The Jefferson is an elegant, old-world hotel, filled with European and American antiques and frequented by well-heeled lawyers, Washington dignitaries, and famous out-of-towners. The hotel, known as "White House North," was where President George H. W. Bush held meetings to select members of his cabinet. The Jefferson also hosted less distinguished guests. President Clinton's chief campaign strategist, Dick Morris, was accused by the *Star,* a tabloid newspaper, of using a room at the Jefferson for his rendezvous with a prostitute. He was forced to resign in 1996 after a photographer for the *Star* caught the prostitute and a man the paper identified as Morris embracing on a hotel balcony.

Lowell met Condit in front of the Jefferson, and they walked in together, past the lobby where original documents signed by the third president hung on the wall, and into the private room Lowell had reserved. Condit wanted to have this meeting, but Lowell knew it wasn't going to be easy for his client or the Levys.

Susan Levy entered the room shortly

afterward with Martin. Robert was not with her — when it came down to it, he could not face meeting Condit. The congressman was disappointed Robert hadn't come. He had wanted to show his concern to both of Chandra's parents. Condit extended his hand toward Susan, but she backed away and refused to shake it. "Let's all sit down," Lowell said. Susan and Martin faced Condit, who was flanked by Lowell at the long dining room table. Susan's face was etched with pain and anger.

Susan began to ask Condit questions, her hands quivering. The two lawyers had agreed on the questions she could ask: When did you first meet Chandra? How often did you see her? When was the last time you saw her? Do you have any information about where she is now? For Susan, it was surreal, like she was outside the scene, watching it from a distance. She didn't see why her daughter had been attracted to the man sitting across from her. He didn't look like the actor Harrison Ford, whom Chandra had told her aunt he resembled. She thought he was slight and not all that handsome. She could barely focus on Condit's answers. His mouth was moving and words were coming out, but they all seemed meaningless because he wasn't saying where

Chandra could be found. When Susan asked Condit if he knew where Chandra was, he said, "Mrs. Levy, I don't know. Really, I don't."

When Susan finished asking her questions, there was nothing more to say. They had been in the room together only fifteen minutes. Condit was surprised. He expected the meeting to last longer. He had prepared himself for a grueling, emotional exchange with both of Chandra's parents, but before he knew it, the meeting was over.

After an awkward silence, Lowell spoke up. "I appreciate the time we've had to talk," he said. "I assure you we are doing all we can. We are so sorry."

Susan and Martin pushed back their chairs and stood up. Condit approached Chandra's mother.

"Can I give you a hug, Mrs. Levy?" he asked.

"Absolutely not," she said, and walked out of the room.

9
DEAR GARY

Anne Marie Smith

As Anne Marie Smith braced for the shame and unwanted attention that was coming her way, she opened the travel journal she had been keeping and began to compose a letter to the man who once stood at the center of her life, Congressman Gary Condit.

He had made so many promises during their whirlwind, coast-to-coast affair, reassured her so many times that everything would work out. Now, in June 2001, the attractive, thirty-nine-year-old redhead with a soft voice and a sweet smile felt manipulated and utterly alone. She didn't want the world to know what she had done. Newspapers and television stations were beginning to report that Condit had been secretly seeing Chandra Levy, and Smith realized that it wouldn't be long before the press corps found out about the affair she had been having with the congressman. She began to write the letter.

Dear Gary:
   You told me you wanted to explain every-thing to me. I am praying that you had no involvement in this situation.
   I know that I should listen to my intuition. Repeatedly, I asked you to be honest w/me to no avail. I know you were seeing someone besides me; I sensed it in my heart. I was a fool to think I was special to you and to listen to your denials & ex-cuses. I knew something was going on because you said there was a situation you wanted to discuss but when I would broach the topic you said you didn't feel like discussing it. You were reluctant to invite me to visit.
   I feel sick and betrayed that I thought you were a man with integrity, but the whole time you were lying to me. You told me my suspicions would ruin everything but in the end, you were the one to ruin the situation. I don't understand how you could be so stupid as to get involved with someone so close to home. It must be an ego thing with you or are you just a sick maniac? I pray that I don't get drawn into any scandal.

It was a difficult letter to write, and in the end, she never sent it. For months, Smith had filled her secret journal with a series of far more sanguine entries. She documented the excitement of a new relationship with Condit, someone she deserved to be with after all the disappointments that came and went before. She wrote about their rendezvous and the possibilities for the future, how she could become a better person as she approached her fortieth birthday.

Smith had been with United Airlines as a flight attendant for a few months before she met Condit in the summer of 2000. After working for a commercial construction company in Seattle, Smith loved her new wanderlust lifestyle; the free trips to Toronto and Australia, El Salvador, London, and France. She dreamed of joining a Paris-based flight crew one day, maybe finding a place to live on a lovely side street lined with flower carts and produce stands. Things that once seemed beyond her reach now seemed possible. Smith mused about something else in her journal, the man with short gray-blond hair and bright blue eyes whom she met in the business class cabin of her San Francisco–to–Dulles flight. He ordered cranberry juice and introduced himself as "Gary." They talked about exercising and he offered her a piece of his power bar. Before leaving, he gave her his phone number and a restaurant recommendation for a place called Pasta Mia in Adams Morgan. On the ground in Washington, one of Smith's flight crew colleagues checked the passenger manifest: "Congressman Gary Condit," it read.

July 10: Met a new friend, Smith wrote in her journal.

Smith called the number Condit gave her, and two days later she met him for dinner in Georgetown, one of the oldest sections of Washington, with its stately mansions and town houses that stand proudly along the Potomac. She was nervous as she gathered the courage to ask the question she had wondered about from the moment they met.

"Are you married?"

"My wife and I don't have a relationship," he answered. He said she had a chronic illness and had been sick since childhood.

At first Smith was hesitant. She didn't date married men, but she found Condit charming, kind, and polite, a perfect gentleman. They began to see each other, clandestine get-togethers at his condominium in Adams Morgan and hotels in Washington and California. Sometimes, Condit's personal driver, Vince Flammini, would chauffeur the congressman to meet Smith in San Francisco. When they were together in public, Condit would wear a baseball hat and dark glasses. In private, Condit showered her with attention, jewelry, a gold bracelet, and a leather bracelet with sterling silver hearts.

Aside from his $145,100 congressional salary, Condit had no other income or assets, other than his home in Ceres and his condominium in Washington. Between 1990 and 2001, Condit used campaign funds to purchase $80,000 worth of gifts and flowers, which he said he gave to his constituents. On December 5, 2000, one of his fund-raisers purchased six fourteen-karat gold bracelets for a total of $690.74 from Bella Gold Imports in downtown San Franscisco. An investigation by his hometown paper, the *Modesto Bee,* found that none of the congressmen whose districts bordered Condit's used campaign funds to buy gifts and flowers for their constituents.

Smith felt the rush of an emotional high. It was a new year, and she had new purpose. She opened her journal and jotted down a few resolutions for 2001: stop smoking, run a marathon.

January 8: I have been learning so much about life and being patient. Gary said there was some reason why we met and I think that is one of them. Just living one day at a time instead of worrying about the future is such a feeling of control over self. We can't control the actions of others — only over our own. Gary means a lot to me — he has taught me to like myself. I don't think he knows that he has helped me so much.

Three days later, Smith penned another passage.

January 11: I drove to Sacramento yesterday to see Gary. We had a nice time, however, he got really sick. I was worried about him. I was really sad when I left him but I need to remember that he does like me and to be secure in that. Our schedules don't always coincide so I need to be patient w/that. Should I write a book? How [to] stay healthy and fit on the road. I have a lot of ideas but I need to initiate them. I think I should start volunteering w/children. Something to keep me busy. What to do about Gary? Need to live my life and be his friend. If and when I get to see him, great. I can't freak out. I need to make him feel secure w/me and that he can trust me. Don't freak out!!

By the spring, Smith started to suspect she was not the only woman waiting on the sidelines of Condit's life. Their meetings became less frequent; her phone messages sat longer without a reply. One morning, when she was staying with Condit in his Adams Morgan apartment, she found a long strand of dark curly hair in the bathroom. Condit told her he didn't know how it got there. Smith chose to believe him, but deep down, she knew better.

On May 9, Smith received an odd call from Condit. He told her that she shouldn't contact him for a while, that he would have to call her.

"Is it your family? Is it your job?" Smith asked.

"No, I can't tell you," she heard him say. "I might have to disappear for a while."

It was an unsettling, confusing conversation, and it didn't start to make sense until May 17, when Smith flew into Washington to visit some of her friends. She asked Condit if they could get together. He told her he was busy and couldn't clear his schedule. The same day, the *Washington Post* published a story that noted Condit's press office had been fielding dozens of calls from reporters asking about an alleged affair between the congressman and Chandra. That evening, an NBC News affiliate in Washington quoted law enforcement sources as saying Condit had told police he was a friend of Chandra's but "refused to elaborate."

The news started to confirm Smith's suspicions that she was not the only one. After she returned home to San Francisco, she received the call that she'd hoped would never come. A reporter from the *Star* magazine heard that she, too, had been involved with the congressman. Smith's mind raced. How did the reporter find out? She had told her roommates and a few friends. Maybe one of them betrayed her, but which one? More important, what should she do now? All she could think about was the shame she was about to bring upon her family.

On June 1, Smith received an unwelcome visit from the FBI. Special Agent Margaret Eason wanted to ask her some questions. Smith was frightened but she told the agent how she met the congressman and provided her with details about the affair — times, dates, and places that she had documented in her travel journal. Smith told Eason that Condit was a decent man, but when she considered whether he might have played a role in Chandra's disappearance, she acknowledged that she didn't know what to think. Smith also said she was concerned for her safety. She thought someone was following her, perhaps a reporter, maybe someone else. She couldn't be sure, but she had spotted a man in a white sedan parked outside her apartment building several days earlier. She thought he had been watching her. Eason forwarded her report to her supervisors in the FBI's San Francisco field office; a copy was transmitted to Jack Barrett and his detectives in Washington.

The day after the interview, Smith decided to call Condit. She thought he needed to know about the interview with the FBI.

"You don't have to talk to them," he said.

"I talked to them."

"I'm going to hang up."

The line went dead. Smith retreated to one of the few remaining sanctuaries in her life — her journal. She began to compose another letter to Condit.

Gary — Our conversation took a wrong turn this a.m. I assure you I don't believe the media or the press. I know what they are trying to do. I believe you & your integrity. The contact I had was a matter of routine. They asked me not to tell you that they contacted me. I know you have a lot of shit to deal w/ right now but you have to trust me that I am on your side. Don't doubt me & don't let this come between us. Maybe I am being foolish in thinking that you even care but I want to see you after this all blows over which it will.

I asked you to call me back to no avail. When I call you now it is not some small trivial pursuit. You need to know that the Star has been calling me incessantly & knocking on my door as well as the neighbors' doors. They said they have been talking to my "friends." I have been offered $$ if I cooperate. I have not and will not respond. I want you to know if something is printed it did not come out of my mouth. These individuals don't really care who they hurt in the process, do they? I know this isn't about me, but there is a leak someplace!!

Smith was reeling. She was an uncomplicated person who found herself in an increasingly complicated situation, and she didn't know quite what to do. The *Star* reporter was following her, hounding her, promising to go with the story regardless of whether she cooperated. At the same time, the mainstream media was pursuing the Chandra Levy story with the same passion. On June 7, the *Washington Post* reported for the first time that Chandra and Condit were romantically involved and that she had spent the night at his apartment. The information was attributed to unnamed police sources and a Levy family relative. The *Post* reporter had tracked the relative down to her home in Chesapeake City, Maryland. It was Chandra's aunt, Linda Zamsky, who had agreed to talk as long as her name wasn't used. Like Susan and Robert Levy, Zamsky thought that Condit might have had something to do with Chandra's disappearance. By coming forward, she hoped to put more pressure on the police to find her niece. The first five paragraphs of the *Post* story resonated in newsrooms around the nation:

U.S. Rep. Gary A. Condit told D.C. police that Chandra Levy has spent the night at his Adams Morgan apartment, according to law enforcement sources, who also said the missing intern told a close relative that she was romantically involved with the congressman.

The California Democrat has said he is simply a good friend of Levy's, and his office has denied a romance between the two. Mike Lynch, chief of staff in Condit's Modesto office, said Condit told him yesterday that he had not made statements to police about Levy spending the night.

"We have nothing to hide" about Condit's relationship with Levy, said Mike Dayton, a spokesman at the congressman's office on Capitol Hill.

But the Levy relative said, "Chandra has told me things that seem to contradict what the spokesmen for Congressman Condit have been saying."

The relative, who spoke to *The Washington Post* on condition of anonymity, said that she spent last Thanksgiving and Passover in April with Levy, 24, and that the intern told her about her romantic life in Washington. The relative declined to provide more detail.

A week later, on June 13, Smith received a call from Condit staffer Michael Lynch. He said he was calling on behalf of the congressman and told Smith to contact someone named Don Thornton, a private investigator for Condit's California lawyer, Joseph Cotchett. Smith turned to a friend of her family who practiced law in Seattle,

James Robinson. On June 15, Robinson called Smith to say he had received an affidavit from Thornton that the private investigator wanted her to sign. Smith was perplexed as she read over the document.

It said: "I do not and have not had a relationship with Congressman Condit other than being acquainted with him. I do not and have not had a romantic relationship with Congressman Condit. I declare under penalty of perjury under the laws of the United States of America that the forgoing is true and correct."

Smith couldn't believe what she was being asked to do. Robinson notified Thornton that his client would not be signing the affidavit. Later that day, Smith received a call from Condit.

"I don't know why your attorney won't let you sign it," she heard Condit say.

"I won't sign it because it's a lie," she said before hanging up.

Smith felt utterly betrayed. She realized that she amounted to nothing in Condit's life. The *Post* story and the affidavit made that point perfectly clear. She didn't want to admit that Condit had deceived her, but at least now she knew where she stood. It was over. She wondered how she could have been so wrong about so many things. She felt consumed by all the unanswered questions as she wrote to Condit in her journal.

I really hope that you learn from this situation the importance of honesty. You have betrayed so many people who deeply care for you. I have never felt so ashamed or saddened in my life.

I am really trying to be objective and not believe the media, but what am I supposed to do?! How did they connect your name? I don't understand why you lied to me or wanted to sleep with 2 people simultaneously. I wish you would have been honest with me and would have let me go. I would have had much more respect for you. I do not want to hear your explanation regarding what occurred. I am not letting you slide by it again. I just ask why? Obviously you were having a relationship with this person. Did it get too close for you? Were you unable to get out of it? Why why why?

I am a good, caring person & understood the parameters of this relationship. You cheapened it by lies and deceit. Why?

Smith's attorney had a plan to shield his client from Condit and the press. He told her that she needed to go public and put the affair on the record. The *Star* published its story on June 26 without her co-operation. Even though the story didn't name her, Smith knew she could no longer keep what happened a secret. She could head off Condit and the media, take control of the story, and prevent the congressman from casting her as a whore angling for fame and money. It was a common ploy used by many men caught having affairs. Crudely referred to as the "Nuts or Sluts Defense," it was often used to portray female accusers as sexually promiscuous or so crazy they made it up, and sometimes both. President Clinton's proxies had used the defense seven years earlier when Paula Jones came forward to allege he had groped her in an Arkansas hotel room. That defense could be used in this case and Smith and her lawyer thought that they needed to be proactive. Time was not on their side. In the *Star* story about her affair with Condit, in which Smith was described as a "bubbly 39-year-old beauty" named "Mary," she saw so many inaccuracies that she felt she needed to set the record straight. Robinson told Smith she should do an on-camera interview with one of the most visible reporters covering the story for a large national audience, Rita Cosby at the Fox News Channel.

With her long blond hair and deep, throaty voice, Cosby was a rising star at Fox, which was fast becoming one of the most popular cable news stations. Cosby was smart and aggressive, determined to get on top of the story and put her relatively new network ahead of the competition. She knew the Chandra Levy story had what it took to be a national sensation: a married politician, a missing intern, anguished parents, political intrigue in the nation's capital, and — adding a final dramatic twist — a possible murder. The story was ideally suited to the 24/7 cable culture, and Cosby found herself in the perfect position to catapult the story into the TV journalism stratosphere.

Cosby started on the story shortly after Chandra disappeared. She followed the *Washington Post*'s piece about the "Levy relative," adding more detail about the affair. She also made contact with Robert and Susan Levy and tracked them as they made their way to Washington to meet with D.C. police and hold a press conference at the Marriott hotel in Virginia. Some of Cosby's reporting was inaccurate. That June, citing sources, she reported that Chandra left numerous messages on Condit's answering machine before she disappeared, pleading with him to see her. There were no such messages. She reported that Condit told the police he had broken off the affair two days before Chandra disappeared and that she refused to take no for an answer. There was no evidence to support either assertion, again attributed to "sources." Her reporting was repeated on other Fox News broadcasts and picked up by other television stations and newspapers around the country, repeated as fact.

On July 2, Cosby separated herself from the pack by landing an exclusive interview with Smith. Fox News anchors put the story at the top of their broadcasts. Cosby introduced Smith, who repeated the story of how she met Condit and discussed the affidavit that his representatives wanted her to sign stating that she never had an affair with the congressman.

Smith tried to stay strong as the story grew exponentially with each passing day. Hurt and angry, she wrote in her journal:

Things will never be the same for us because of this. No more secret rendezvous. No more fun in bed. Oh well, you make your bed & sleep in it — literally. I just pray you had no involvement.

I have told several people about my relationship w/you to protect myself. Per-

haps that could have been me that everyone is reading about. I also understand
now why you were so busy all of the time.
I hope this doesn't ruin your career or your
family.

Annie

10
A Predator in the Park

The Western Ridge Trail

Two months after Chandra disappeared, in the early evening of July 1, Christy Wiegand and her fiancé went for a run in the rain in Rock Creek Park at 7:30 P.M. Wiegand, a twenty-five-year-old former varsity rower at Princeton and recent Cornell Law School graduate, was beginning her legal career at one of the finest firms in town, Arnold & Porter, founded by President Franklin Roosevelt's top advisers. Her wedding date was just seven weeks away. She was tall and blond and strong, wearing a Sony Walkman as she ran along Beach Drive, a scenic byway closed to traffic that Sunday evening.

Her fiancé jogged ahead, as he usually did during their runs, and soon he was out of sight. It happened fast: Alone on the trail, she sensed someone closing in quickly from behind. Then, suddenly, a stranger wrapped his arms tightly around her chest and pulled her off the road, toward the creek. The two tumbled down a ravine. Wiegand saw the knife seconds before the man held it to her neck. Wiegand tried to scream, but the man covered her mouth and ordered her to be quiet.

Wiegand tried to fight back, but she soon began to lose her strength. She couldn't believe how quickly this had happened; one moment she was running in one of the most peaceful places in Washington, and the next she was fighting for her life. She realized that her assailant had selected this spot because it was perfectly isolated — few people hiked along the creek in that section of the park. Wiegand thought that the man wanted to rape her, possibly kill her. He hadn't tried to steal her Walkman or her engagement ring. A rush of adrenaline coursed through her body, and Wiegand began to fight as hard as she could. She stopped struggling for a moment, long enough for the attacker to relax his guard, and with a burst of energy she fought again. She broke the man's hold and clambered up to Beach Drive. Her attacker fled into the forest.

Cut, bruised, and badly shaken, Wiegand flagged down a motorist on a nearby street. She told the driver she had just been attacked and pleaded with him to help her find her fiancé. They spotted him about three-quarters of a mile up the road and the motorist took the couple to a U.S. Park Police station. The Park Police, which has jurisdiction over national parks such as Rock Creek, scrambled "Eagle One," a blue-and-white Bell helicopter, and officers fanned out in search of a Hispanic man wearing a white T-shirt, baggy shorts, and sneakers. At 8:15, two officers in a squad car spotted a man matching the description. His clothes were wet. He was covered with dirt and pieces of leaves.

The officers took the man to a stone stationhouse nicknamed the Rock Creek Hotel for its lodgelike appearance. There they identified him as Ingmar Adalid Guandique, a nineteen-year-old day laborer from El Salvador who lived in a northwest Washington neighborhood not far from the park. He had been arrested two months earlier, on May 7, for burglarizing an apartment on his street, and he had been released on the promise that he return to court. He never did. At one the next morning, three Park Police officers, including a translator, entered Guandique's cell inside the stationhouse. They tried to win his confidence. They left the door open. They gave him some food and water and they allowed him to use the restroom. Guandique agreed to talk without a lawyer. He said he worked as a carpenter, but he was out of a job. Leading the interrogation was Joe Green, a seasoned detective with nearly thirty years on the force. A big, balding man with a laid-back demeanor, the D.C. native prided himself on knowing the city and getting people to talk.

Through the translator, Green asked Guandique if he had attacked a female jogger in the park about six hours earlier. No, Guandique said. Green tried another tactic. He asked Guandique whether it was possible that he bumped into a woman and the encounter was a misunderstanding. Yes, Guandique said. He explained that he was jogging along Beach Drive when he felt a sharp pain in his knee. He bent over to massage it and a female jogger came up from behind and banged into him, causing both of them to fall off the trail and down a ravine. He said he tried to help the jogger, but she began to scream instead. Not sure what to do, Guandique said, he ran away.

Green recalled another unsolved attack in Rock Creek Park that had occurred six weeks earlier, on May 14. On that day, Halle Shilling decided to take a run in the park. She was thirty, a journalist who had just completed her master's thesis for a nonfiction writing program at Johns Hopkins University. At around 6:30 that night, she pulled her blond hair into a ponytail, put on her running clothes, picked up her yellow Walkman, and left her apartment near the Washington National Cathedral. She drove down to the Peirce Mill and started to jog along a path that cuts past the flour mill. North of the mill, she spotted a young Hispanic man sitting on a curb in a parking lot. She noticed the man watching her. He made her feel uncomfortable, but she frequently caught men staring at her. *How annoying,* she thought to herself as she crossed the intersection of Broad Branch Road and Beach Drive and ran up a desolate trail that disappeared into the woods. As she neared a ridge high above the creek, a patch of clouds blocked out the sun, casting a shadow on the ground and turning the air sharply cooler. It felt ominous, being alone in the forest, the temperature falling, the light fading away. She saw a stick on the ground and picked it up for protection, but it was rotted out and she tossed it back. As she ran farther in the woods, she realized a man was jogging behind and closing in fast. She thought he must be in training, pushing his limits by sprinting through the forest. She looked over her shoulder and he had fallen back. Shilling continued to jog, listening to the songs on her mix tape: "Tiny Dancer" by Elton John, "Dancing Queen" by ABBA.

After hitting a crest in the trail, winded from the climb, Shilling began to slow her pace on a flat section of the hill when she felt a pair of hands on her shoulders. She turned and realized it was the same man she had seen in the parking lot.

"No! No! No!" she shouted.

"Shhh," he ordered.

She saw the blade of a knife. He grabbed her around the throat and they crashed to the ground.

Shilling realized that she was in the worst possible place for an attack — high above the creek, the sound of water cascading over the boulders, and farther off, the traffic noise from Beach Drive echoing through the river valley and drowning out her screams. Shilling knew she was in serious trouble. The man didn't try to steal her Walkman; he didn't demand her 1.5-carat diamond engagement ring. He didn't say a word. Shilling had taken a self-defense class and she knew she had to ready herself for a sustained fight. She kept saying to herself: *There is no way this is going to happen. No way. No way. No way.*

She went for his eyes with her fingers, but she missed. His mouth was open, so she thrust her nails into the soft palate beneath his tongue. The man cried out and bit down on her fingers, hard, leaving teeth marks, but the defense-class maneuver had worked. The man released her, and Shilling scrambled to her feet and ran as fast as she could. She made her way to the U.S. Park Police station and reported the crime, telling the officers that she didn't believe her assailant was trying to rob her — she thought he was trying to rape her. Park Police officers searched the park, but the man was nowhere to be found.

At the Rock Creek Hotel, Detective Green was feeling lucky. He had already tricked Guandique into confessing to the Wiegand attack. He tried the same ploy with the attack on Shilling. He asked Guandique if there were any other times he had accidentally bumped into someone in the park. No, Guandique said at first, but then he changed his story. Yes, he said, there was an incident a month or two earlier. He had seen a tall woman with long blond hair running with a yellow radio; he jogged behind her, and she looked over her shoulder and she stumbled to the forest floor. Guandique

181

said he tried to help her up, but she started to scream. He was frightened, he said, and he ran away.

Green had a hunch. He posed one more question to Guandique. He showed him a D.C. police "missing person" flier with a photograph of Chandra Levy. Have you ever seen this woman in Rock Creek Park? Green asked. He decided to show Guandique the flier because D.C. police had been searching for Chandra across the city and in some sections of Rock Creek Park, near the headquarters at Klingle Mansion. Guandique said he had seen her. He spotted her when he was hanging around a parking lot near the Peirce Mill one day. Green then asked Guandique if he thought she was attractive. Yes, he answered, but he never saw her again. Green ended the questioning and he did not include the comment Guandique made about Chandra in his report, nor did he tell the D.C. police, a separate department that had jurisdiction over the rest of the city. The two departments were supposed to coordinate their efforts, but sometimes they failed to communicate. Green didn't think the remark was important enough to pass along to the D.C. police; Guandique hadn't admitted to anything more than supposedly seeing Chandra.

Green kept his focus on the two assault cases. Chandra's disappearance was not his case or the responsibility of the U.S. Park Police.

11
AN INDELICATE REQUEST

Detective Ralph Durant

Abbe Lowell was desperate. Despite his best efforts, the Chandra Levy investigation remained squarely focused on his client, Gary Condit. In another effort to move the spotlight away from the congressman, Lowell arranged a face-to-face meeting with Jack Barrett, the chief of detectives.

On the afternoon of July 6, Lowell sat down with Barrett inside a two-story Starbucks across the street from a colorful, seven-roofed wooden arch decorated with painted dragons that served as the gateway to Washington's Chinatown, a collection of about twenty Chinese and other Asian restaurants not far from police headquarters. Lowell liked Barrett. He thought he was a reasonable man, unlike some of the other police officials on the case. Earlier that day, the department's second in command, Terrance Gainer, had told reporters that police were not satisfied with Condit's answers and they were losing their patience with him. "He probably is trying, but hopefully he'll be trying harder," Gainer said.

Lowell thought his client was trying pretty hard. Condit had already given two interviews to the police, speaking to detectives at his apartment in May when Chandra first disappeared, and then agreeing to a second interview in June after Lowell became his lawyer. Lowell would have preferred to make a public show of the June interview and have Condit march up the steps of police headquarters to demonstrate that he was voluntarily consenting to talk to detectives. But that wasn't Condit's style; his biggest concern was keeping his personal life private. Lowell had suggested that they meet at a friend's town house in Georgetown, a place where the press would not find them.

Lowell had accompanied Condit to that second interview on June 23 with Barrett and his two detectives, Ralph Durant and Lawrence Kennedy. Inside the town house, Lowell offered sodas and coffee; he wanted to make everyone comfortable. He hoped that he had identified a strategy that would protect his client and satisfy the police.

At about 3 P.M., as the interview began, Lowell told the detectives: *I want you to assume that Congressman Condit had a roman-*

188

tic relationship with Chandra Levy. Assume it, and ask your questions. Lowell was trying to shield Condit from embarrassing and detailed questions about his relationship with Chandra. Instead of allowing the detectives to get those details in a written statement on the record, Lowell wanted them to assume the two were romantically involved and ask germane questions that might help them find Chandra.

The strategy backfired. The detectives thought they were in charge of the investigation and they had the right to ask whatever questions they wanted; they didn't want to assume anything. They wanted answers.

During the nearly hour-long interview, Condit repeated what he had told Durant during their first talk. He had no idea what had happened to Chandra. He described her as "a constituent who became a friend." He restated what he had told them before, that he had met Chandra in the fall of 2000 when she and her friend Jennifer Baker stopped by his Capitol Hill office. He last saw her at his apartment on April 24 or April 25, nearly a week before she disappeared on May 1. He couldn't remember everything about their conversation; they had talked about the end of her Bureau of Prisons internship, her plans to return to

California, and her future job prospects with the CIA or FBI. He didn't notice anything unusual about her mood; they had not argued. She didn't seem angry with anyone.

Barrett asked Condit to account for his whereabouts between April 28 and May 3. Condit said he had not seen Chandra during that time. He listed his day-by-day activities: On Saturday, April 28, he rode his bicycle to a Capitol gym and returned to his apartment that night. The next day, he spent the day and night with his wife, who had come to Washington for the luncheon hosted by First Lady Laura Bush. Around noon that day, he had called Chandra on his cell phone and had spoken to her for less than two minutes. On April 30, he attended the luncheon to mark the first hundred days of President Bush's administration and worked in his congressional office. On May 1, the day Chandra disappeared, Condit said he left his apartment at eleven in the morning, had lunch with Vice President Cheney to discuss energy problems in California, and worked until 6:30, when he went to dinner in Adams Morgan. On May 2, Condit said he worked on Capitol Hill and then went shopping and to dinner with his wife. On May 3, his wife returned to California. That same day, he called Chandra twice and left messages on her voice mail, asking where she was. Chandra never returned his calls, he said.

Durant pressed Condit for more details about the extent of his relationship with Chandra, but Lowell interrupted, directing his client not to answer. Lowell was frustrated; he had asked the detectives to assume Condit had a romantic relationship with Chandra. Why did they need the details? To Lowell, it seemed as though they had a prurient desire to force Condit to say the two had a sexual relationship. *Assume the relationship,* he repeated to them. What would be your next question? The detectives were just as frustrated by what they thought were unworkable guidelines. They wanted details about the relationship, and they wondered what the congressman might be hiding.

Before the investigators left, Condit told them he was upset by all the police leaks. Why were his confidential comments to police about Chandra spending the night at his apartment ending up in the newspaper and on the cable newscasts? Barrett and his detectives assured him they were not leaking to the press. The interview ended cordially, and Lowell left with the impression

191

that the detectives had obtained all the information they needed from Condit.

Now, sitting with Barrett in the Starbucks two weeks later, Lowell was being asked to make his client available for a third interview. Condit's alibi seemed solid, but the detectives still had a lot of questions. It had been more than eight weeks since Chandra vanished; the high-profile case had expanded to two coasts, drawn in the FBI, and resulted in about two hundred interviews. Detectives interviewed friends, neighbors, gym members, colleagues from the Bureau of Prisons, and current and former Condit staffers in Washington and California. The detectives didn't want to rule out the possibility that someone close to Condit might be connected to Chandra's disappearance.

At Starbucks, Lowell told Barrett: Condit is not your man. What more does he need to do to convince you of that?

Barrett answered directly: He needed Condit to give him more information about his relationship with Chandra. Lowell understood then that the police would never be satisfied until they knew everything about the relationship between the congressman and the missing intern.

Barrett had an additional request: He

needed the congressman's DNA. Barrett had an indelicate issue on his hands, which he explained, in blunt terms, to Lowell: The police department had a pair of Chandra's underwear with semen stains on them.

When his detectives had searched Chandra's apartment, they found several items of clothing. One was a pair of black underwear among the other dirty laundry that Chandra had stuffed in a Williams-Sonoma bag and left on her breakfast countertop. It was stained with semen. The police needed to know if it belonged to Condit, or if Chandra was seeing another man they didn't know about. The only way to find out was to test Condit's DNA against the DNA found on the underwear. Barrett told Lowell he had a choice: The department could obtain his client's DNA by subpoena, a court order, or Condit could voluntarily provide a sample.

Lowell hadn't expected the request. Just before meeting Barrett at the coffee shop, he had driven across the Potomac River to Alexandria, Virginia, to huddle with Condit at the home of one of his most trusted aides, Mike Dayton. In Dayton's backyard, far from the clamor of the media and the police, Lowell paced with his client while they smoked cigars. They were in a tight spot, Lowell explained to Condit. The only way to get the police to focus their investigation elsewhere was to give them more details about his relationship with Chandra. Condit reluctantly agreed to a third interview.

It had been a terrible week for the congressman, and the pressure was rapidly intensifying. First, Anne Marie Smith had appeared on the Fox News Channel and created a sensation when she revealed her yearlong affair with Condit and the affidavit that she said his representative had asked her to sign. Cable news stations couldn't get enough of the story, and it was picked up by newspapers around the world: the *Mercury* in Australia, the *Daily Mail* in London, the Xinhua News Agency in China. NASCAR driver Stacy Compton put Chandra's photo on the bumper of his car before he ran the Pepsi 400 at the Daytona International Speedway in Florida. Tabloids were offering cash payments for details about Chandra and Condit and the investigation. Reporters and television satellite trucks were staking out players in the story on both coasts. Lowell had to hire a well-connected public relations specialist, Marina Ein, to handle the onslaught of press calls. The stories were withering. "Gary, Gary, Gary! What have you been thinking?" widely read Style writer Sally Quinn wrote in the *Washington Post.* "Dance around the truth — about sex or anything else — and people wonder whether you have something else to hide. Wouldn't it be better to be known as an adulterer — if that's all that happened — than to get mired in what could turn out to be a murder investigation?"

Two days after Smith came forward, Condit took heat back home for missing Modesto's Fourth of July parade. For nearly twenty years, the parade, festooned with red, white, and blue balloons and banners, had been a celebration of sorts for one of Modesto's favorite sons. Condit customarily rode in a convertible driven by one of his interns, flashing his famous smile as he rolled down the city's main thoroughfare lined by war veterans and children waving American flags. But this year, parade-goers held placards with pictures of Chandra. Friends of Chandra's family had organized a silent march along the route and were followed by about a dozen others who carried signs with Chandra's face and long yellow ribbons that fluttered behind. "We want answers from Congressman Condit," one shouted out. Condit's chief of staff in California, Michael Lynch, told the press that the congressman had "another circumstance" that prevented him from attending. He didn't disclose that Condit was in Washington with his wife, Carolyn. She was preparing to be questioned by police and prosecutors the next day about her husband and Chandra. It was difficult for Condit to watch as his wife was pulled into the investigation, but Lowell wanted everyone connected to his client to cooperate. He believed that none of them had anything to hide.

On July 5, in an FBI office near the sprawling Tysons Corner Center in Virginia, two prosecutors began to press Carolyn about her husband's relationship with Chandra. They worked for the U.S. attorney's office in Washington. Because Washington is not a state, it does not have a district attorney who prosecutes criminal cases. Instead a lawyer appointed by the president serves as the U.S. attorney and oversees local and federal prosecutions in the city. Assistant U.S. Attorneys Barbara Kittay and Heidi Pasichow had been assigned to work with the detectives to investigate Chandra's disappearance and ensure that they were putting together a court-ready case in the event of an arrest. Kittay had worked as a prosecutor in Philadelphia

and at the Justice Department before joining the U.S. attorney's office in Washington.
A tough-talking Long Islander, she had
been a television reporter in Wilkes-Barre,
Pennsylvania, before attending law school at
Syracuse University. Pasichow was a veteran
of the D.C. office, serving as a deputy of its
homicide division at one point. Both women
had won convictions in a number of high-
profile cases, and they had their sights
trained on Condit.

Carolyn Condit told the prosecutors that
she had a close relationship with her husband of thirty-four years and they talked
twice a day on the phone when he was in
Washington. She went through the chronol-
ogy of her trip to Washington around the
time Chandra disappeared. She said that
she flew to Washington on April 28 for the
Congressional Club's annual First Lady's
Luncheon at the Washington Hilton, a tradi-
tion dating back to 1912. While in town,
she stayed with her husband at his Adams
Morgan apartment and met him for brunch
and dinner. One day, they shopped together
in the neighborhood. After the May 3
luncheon, she flew home to Ceres. The
prosecutors asked her when she first heard
about Chandra. She described the phone
call she received in Ceres on May 6 from

Robert Levy, who wanted to talk to her husband about his missing daughter. She told the prosecutors that the missing intern and her husband were just friends. Kittay then asked her if she was aware that Chandra had visited her husband's apartment as "just friends."

Kittay thought she was doing her job by asking tough questions to elicit information from a potentially important witness. But Lowell was offended that Kittay had rubbed the "just friends" comment in Carolyn's face. Worse, he was angry that Kittay violated his only ground rule: Lowell had specifically told prosecutors beforehand that private conversations between Carolyn and her husband were off-limits because they were protected by spousal privilege. Despite Lowell's instruction, Kittay kept trying to ask Carolyn what she and her husband had discussed. Lowell halted the interview, advising Carolyn not to answer.

Barrett was also displeased with the way the prosecutors had treated Carolyn Condit. To Barrett, Carolyn seemed like "Harriet," the happy homemaker from the 1950s sitcom *Ozzie and Harriet.* He thought the prosecutors had treated her with unnecessary roughness. Barrett was starting to think that Condit probably had nothing to do with Chandra's disappearance, that he was simply an adulterer who wanted to keep his affairs secret. But Barrett thought the prosecutors believed otherwise, and they were putting too many demands on his detectives, ordering them to follow all leads relating to Condit and his aides and leaving little time to follow other investigative paths. He thought that Kittay and Pasichow were wasting his time by insisting that Condit should be the focus of the investigation.

The next day, at the Starbucks, on July 6, Lowell told Barrett that his client would consent to one more police interview. Condit had nothing new to tell them, but if another interview would end the police department's interest in his client, they would consent. The DNA request, however, was a surprise. Lowell hadn't discussed it with Condit, and he didn't know how the congressman would respond. Lowell told Barrett that he and his client would proceed with the interview, but for the moment, he wanted to put the DNA request on hold. Barrett didn't object, and they set the third interview for that night. Barrett explained that the meeting would not only include Detective Durant, but also Kittay, the federal prosecutor.

The interview began at 8:30 and the tension from Carolyn Condit's questioning spilled over into Lowell's law firm conference room. A pack of reporters were waiting for Condit to arrive outside the firm at Fifteenth and M streets in downtown Washington, but the congressman managed to slip past them and pull into the underground garage. Lowell was not thrilled that Kittay was going to be part of the interview. He thought she was clearly after his client, and that she had crossed the line in her questioning of Carolyn.

Kittay asked the congressman to be precise about the nature of his relationship with Chandra. Up until that night, Condit had given the police few details about his affair. But Chandra's forty-year-old aunt, Linda Zamsky, had just gone public, providing an explicit account of the affair in interviews with newspaper and television reporters. Zamsky was tired of hearing the denials from Condit's aides. She knew things about Condit and her niece that no one else could know and she recounted them in exacting detail: Zamsky said she and Chandra took long walks and had numerous conversations when Chandra visited her for Thanksgiving in 2000 and Passover in 2001. Chandra referred to Condit as "my guy." She said he kept cactus plants in his apartment, his favorite ice cream was Ben & Jerry's low-fat chocolate chip cookie dough, and he loved to ride his Harley-Davidson motorcycle. He had given Chandra a couple of plane tickets to California, along with Godiva chocolates and a card for Valentine's Day. He also gave her a gold bracelet that she had showed her aunt in April.

Chandra had confided in Zamsky that she and Condit spent a lot of time in his apartment; sometimes he would cook, other times they ordered in. They were fond of body-oil massages. If they went out, Chandra would go downstairs first, hail a cab, and get inside. Condit would then come running down, wearing a baseball cap and jeans. Sometimes they would go to the suburbs for Thai or Chinese food. Condit enjoyed working out, as did Chandra. Condit suggested that she date other men, but Chandra wanted to be monogamous and was willing to do what Condit wanted in order to make it work. Chandra told her aunt that they talked about moving in together so she could save money on rent, keep up his apartment, and be there for him. Chandra organized her evenings so she could remain available; she avoided making plans because she wanted to wait to hear from him, and she never knew what he was doing. She understood that she was in a complicated situation, but she hoped for the best because she was in love.

Condit set rules to keep their liaisons secret, and he warned Chandra that he would stop seeing her if she told anyone. To get in touch with him, Chandra would dial a number, soft background music would play on the answering machine, and then she would leave a message. If she was in the elevator of his building and someone pressed his floor, she was to press a different floor. If anyone asked if she was new in the building, Condit told her to say she was visiting a sick friend. "He was emphatic," Zamsky told reporters. "It had to remain secret. If anybody found out about this relationship, it was done, over, kaput."

On April 29, the day Chandra last spoke to Condit and the day before she was last seen at the Washington Sports Club, she left a message on Zamsky's voice mail: "Hi, Linda. This is Chandra. My internship is over. I'm planning on packing my bags in the next week or ten days. Heading home for a while. Don't know what I'm going to do this summer." And then Chandra said that she had some "big news" to tell her aunt. "Call me," she said. Zamsky did not get a chance to call Chandra back before she disappeared.

The details of Zamsky's account were already familiar to everyone in Lowell's conference room. Kittay asked Condit to fully describe in his own words his relationship with Chandra. Kittay thought he was a viable suspect and fair game. She didn't think he was being forthcoming and she wasn't going to treat him any differently just because he was a congressman. Condit appeared to be closer to Chandra than anyone in Washington and it was critical for investigators to know her behavior, her habits, and her mood in the days and weeks before she disappeared. Condit said his relationship with Chandra started in November 2000, and she came over to his Adams Morgan apartment a couple of times a week, usually showing up in her gym outfit and carrying a backpack with a change of clothes.

Condit said he had once given her a gold bracelet. He had not ended the relationship before she vanished and did not know of anything that could explain her disappearance. Condit acknowledged to the police and prosecutors that he and the young intern had had a sexual relationship. Kittay then brought up the other women featured in the press, such as flight attendant Anne Marie Smith.

Lowell was outraged; the media reports about other women professing to be Condit's girlfriends had nothing to do with Chandra's case. This wasn't what he had agreed to in his Starbucks meeting with Barrett. He objected: The questions were irrelevant. Barrett looked uneasy and tried to get the interview back on track by returning to some of the previous questions about Chandra. But Kittay pressed on. She asked Condit to submit to a DNA test. Lowell was stunned. He turned to Barrett. He said he thought they had an agreement to table the DNA test.

Kittay erupted in fury. She thought Barrett had made a side deal with Lowell without talking to her and she was "tired of being fucking gone around." Then she and Lowell were in each other's faces. Kittay told Lowell, "Don't be such an asshole." To Barrett, it was like a bomb going off, sudden and devastating. Here they were, an assistant U.S. attorney and a prominent defense lawyer swearing at each other, calling each other "motherfuckers." Barrett looked over at Condit, and the congressman rolled his eyes. Barrett rolled his eyes, too. He thought it was one of the most unprofessional scenes he had ever witnessed. Lowell stood up abruptly and declared, "We're done." At

10:10 P.M., Lowell walked Barrett, Durant, and Kittay to the elevator. He turned to Barrett: "I'm sorry it ended this way." "Me, too," Barrett replied.

In the car on the way back to their offices, Barrett dressed down Kittay. No matter how much Lowell might have provoked her, he thought her outburst was unprofessional. Kittay thought that Barrett should "man up" and that he was overreacting to what she believed was a heated but fair interrogation in a potential murder case. Barrett had been working so hard to keep his relationship with Lowell on an even keel. Kittay had caused a scene — and for what? She had accomplished nothing to advance the case. The next morning, Barrett went to see Police Chief Charles Ramsey. "We have to replace these prosecutors," he told him. After the Carolyn Condit interview and the session at Lowell's office, Barrett no longer had confidence in them.

The bad blood between the police and the prosecutors was mutual. Kittay was furious about all the police leaks in the case. Every day it seemed as though police officials were holding press conferences or confidential information from the case file was being leaked to the media, compromising the integrity of the investigation. The day after

205

the interview in Lowell's office, Gainer went before the cameras to confirm that a third interview had taken place. In a front-page *Washington Post* story, a source was quoted as saying Condit had acknowledged that he had had an affair with Chandra. From Kittay's vantage point, the situation was impossible to manage, and she wanted off the case.

Barrett called Lowell. He said the police were going to obtain a DNA test one way or the other, and it would be better to voluntarily submit a sample. Lowell realized that Condit would have to take the test and he thought that perhaps it could be the final step toward ending the nightmarish predicament.

About 10 P.M., on July 9, Condit and Lowell met Detective Durant in a dimly lit parking lot behind the Giant supermarket near the Washington National Cathedral on Wisconsin Avenue, one of the main thoroughfares in the city. It was a convenient location for Durant, across the street from 2D, the police department's Second District.

The D.C. detectives were amazed at how much publicity this case was generating in Washington and around the world. Chandra Levy had become a household name. Yet there were dozens of missing people in Washington every year, and the hundreds of people who were slain on the city's streets — most of them African-Americans — never received this kind of attention. The officers in the mostly black police force whispered about the case, saying it had received so many resources because it involved a white girl and a congressman. Why was the media paying so much attention to one missing white girl in a city where more than two hundred people had been murdered in the year before Chandra's disappearance? For many blacks in the city, the discrepancy seemed racist.

Condit stepped out of a car in the Giant parking lot and Durant walked over to him. With a cotton swab, the detective swiped the inside of the congressman's cheek and walked away. It took only seconds. Lowell had been trying for weeks to protect Condit, to shield him from more embarrassment — and now it had come to this: his client, a United States congressman, standing in the darkness of a supermarket parking lot, opening his mouth so a detective could stick a long Q-Tip inside and take a sample of his saliva.

12
THE INAUGURAL BALL

Inauguration Day, 2001

D.C. police and FBI agents worked feverishly to fill in the blanks of Chandra's life in Washington — her habits, her hangouts, her acquaintances. They found that she spent much of her time alone and followed a simple routine: working out at the Washington Sports Club, taking the Metro to her internship at the Bureau of Prisons, and spending as much time as she could with Gary Condit. The investigators kept their focus on the congressman, but they wondered whether there might be another man in Chandra's life, someone they missed during their frantic search for clues to her disappearance.

They were intrigued that Chandra had placed her final cell phone call to a man named Sven Jones just three days before she vanished. Jones was a colleague of Chandra's at the Bureau of Prisons who worked out at the same gym. Chandra was just a friend, Jones explained; she had told him that she was dating someone powerful in government. Jones described her as a loner who was friendly and flirty, with a memorable, sarcastic sense of humor. She also could be serious and conservative, and she was a whiz with computers. Jones said that he was in Canada the day Chandra called and left a message, asking if he was free for lunch. Investigators corroborated his account. After Jones passed a polygraph exam, the detectives excluded him from their case.

Investigators were also fascinated by another man on the fringe of Chandra's life; though he was quickly eliminated as a suspect, he provided important insight into Chandra's state of mind in the months and days before she disappeared.

Robert Kurkjian was a USC graduate who arrived in Washington around the same time as Chandra. He was twenty-eight, a newly hired accountant for Pricewaterhouse-Coopers with a quick smile and a charismatic charm. He met Chandra at the Washington Sports Club and he invited her to a party and USC events in Washington. Each time, Chandra politely declined. Kurkjian got the message; she was busy, serious about her work, and she probably had a boyfriend.

On January 20, 2001, Kurkjian received an unexpected call. He and a friend had tickets to the inauguration of George W. Bush that morning, and he was walking home from the swearing-in ceremony that afternoon when his cell phone rang.

"Hey, it's Chandra. I have tickets to the Inaugural Ball. Are you free?"

Kurkjian was surprised to hear from her, but he had no plans that night. He thought that going to one of the balls would be a quintessential Washington experience, something he couldn't pass up.

"Hey, why not?" he said. "Where do I need to be and how do I get there?"

Kurkjian put on a tuxedo — he kept one on hand for unexpected formal events — hopped into his blue Acura coupe, and drove over to Chandra's apartment from the row house he shared with two friends on the other side of Dupont Circle. It had been a cold, miserable day, and as he drove, it began to snow. Dressed in a long evening gown, Chandra slipped into the Acura and Kurkjian pulled away from her building, squinting to see through the swirling flakes of the January storm.

"We have to pick up the tickets," Chandra said.

"Okay, where are they?"

Chandra told Kurkjian she needed to go to her boyfriend's apartment in Adams Morgan. When they reached the neighborhood, Chandra directed Kurkjian to pull into a gas station parking lot and told him to wait. She opened the car door and ran into the wintry night. Kurkjian was confused, but he was also intrigued by her mysterious behavior. *Who was her boyfriend? Why wasn't he taking her? Why did she tell me to stay in the car?*

About ten minutes later, Chandra reappeared. In her hand was an envelope containing a pair of tickets to the Ball After the Ball featuring R&B singer Macy Gray.

Once inside the National Museum of Women in the Arts, a splendid hall that once served as a Masonic temple, near the White House, Chandra wasn't interested in dancing. She didn't want a drink or anything to eat. She and her date climbed a grand staircase to the balcony, rested against the railing, and looked out over the crowded dance floor.

"So, who's your boyfriend?" Kurkjian asked.

"He's a member of Congress," Chandra said.

"You're kidding me!"

"No."

"Who is he?"

"I can't say."

"Is he a Democrat or a Republican?"

"I can't say."

"What state is he from?"

"I can't say."

"How long has he been in Congress?"

"I can't say."

"Is this guy married?"

"I really can't talk about him."

Chandra was resolute. Kurkjian began to believe that she had been schooled to be highly secretive when questioned about her boyfriend. He also came to understand that Chandra's Washington experience revolved around this man, whoever he was. As far as he could tell, she had no significant circle of friends, just a loose network of casual acquaintances. As the night came to a close, and Kurkjian drove Chandra home, he began to feel sorry for her. She was obviously in love, but she couldn't share a single detail about her boyfriend or their relationship. Kurkjian was relieved to find the strange night finally over.

Nearly three months later, on April 27, Kurkjian heard from Chandra again. He had invited her to alumni happy hours twice since the ball — she had declined each time — and he was surprised to receive her call.

"It's my last weekend in D.C.," Chandra said. "I wanted to know if you want to go out to a bar."

Kurkjian told her that it had been a long week at work. "I'm pretty much done for the night." But he said he and one of his roommates planned to order pizza and watch a movie, and she was welcome to come over.

"Okay," she said.

Kurkjian was expecting her to turn down the invitation; in truth, he had hoped to hang out with his roommate that Friday night and go to sleep early. It all seemed so odd to Kurkjian. *What about her boyfriend? Why couldn't he take her out? Where was he?*

Chandra told Kurkjian that the Bureau of Prisons had ended her internship because she had completed her graduate coursework the previous December. She said that she was technically no longer a student and therefore no longer eligible for the internship. This wasn't completely true. The bureau had extended her internship beyond December, but a female supervisor terminated Chandra's position after she violated the strict chain of command within the agency by going around a supervisor and asking for a raise from the personnel department. Chandra also didn't mention the reason she wasn't with her boyfriend on her last weekend in Washington: His wife was in town to attend Laura Bush's luncheon for congressional spouses.

In the living room of Kurkjian's row house, Chandra poured her heart out. She was disappointed to be leaving Washington, especially her boyfriend. She insisted that he planned to give up his seat in Congress, become a lobbyist, divorce his wife, marry Chandra, and start a second family.

Kurkjian realized it would be a long night. He and his roommate ordered pizza and began to watch *The 6th Day,* an Arnold Schwarzenegger action movie. As Chandra continued to talk about her boyfriend, Kurkjian was stunned by her naïveté. He tried to change the subject.

"Are you moving home?" he asked.

She wasn't sure.

"What are your plans?"

She didn't know.

"Was your boyfriend able to help you find a job?"

Surely, Kurkjian thought, this unnamed member of Congress could find her a job if he really wanted her to stay in Washington. Kurkjian was incredulous. He couldn't believe that someone who seemed to be so smart and ambitious could be so hood-winked.

Kurkjian asked her: "So, you're telling me that a sitting, married member of Congress, with two children, is going to resign his seat, divorce his wife, and marry you?"

Chandra seemed certain.

Kurkjian tried one last time to be direct, to try to get through to her.

"Chandra, this guy is totally playing you. This is not a healthy relationship."

To Kurkjian, it seemed as though Chandra had been brainwashed. Nothing he said resonated. She was in love, her boyfriend promised it would all work out, and there was nothing more to say. Chandra said she wanted to watch another movie and continue talking, but it was after one in the morning. The conversation faded; Kurkjian began to nod off. He decided it was time to call it a night. He walked Chandra to Sixteenth and R streets. The White House was barely visible twelve blocks away as they stood near the curb and flagged down a cab. He felt badly for her as the taxi pulled up and she climbed in for the short ride across Connecticut Avenue to her home.

"Good luck with the move," Kurkjian told her.

"Okay, thanks."

He would never see her again.

13
THE FISH BOWL

The Pack

At *CBS Evening News* headquarters in New York, the images of the Chandra Levy story flashed across the newsroom's many TV screens. The same scenes played again and again: a congressman ducking reporters, family photos of an attractive young intern missing for more than two months, her grieving parents pleading for information to help them find their only daughter. As executive producer of the *Evening News* and a veteran journalist for nearly twenty years, Jim Murphy had seen his share of Washington scandals, but none quite like this.

Some of the more memorable episodes involved members of Congress, many of them at the height of their careers, all of them accused of behaving badly. Representative Melvin Reynolds of Illinois: sex with a sixteen-year-old girl. Representative Barney Frank of Massachusetts: sex with a male prostitute. Senator Brock Adams of Washington: drugging and molesting his staff members and associates. Senator Robert Packwood of Oregon: sexually harassing and groping his staff members and lobbyists.

The list stretched back to the earliest days of Washington with its exhilarating mix of power, politics, and money. In a city that idolized power, politicians were treated like rock stars. Entourages of staffers escorted them nearly everywhere they went. Television camera crews and reporters trailed them on the Hill. They took expense-paid trips around the world. They met with heads of state, high-powered lobbyists, the president of the United States. They were away from their families for much of the year, and when they weren't working on the Hill, they were often ensconced in fashionable Washington town houses and condominiums. Wherever they went, groupies seemed to tag along, women who were attracted to their star power and craved inclusion in Washington's inner circle, no matter how fleeting their social standing might be. For some women, the prospect of having an affair with a powerful politician was full of risk, passion, and promise.

One woman who had an affair with a member of Congress around the time of the Clinton sex scandal told the *Washington*

Post that she felt validated and empowered by the romantic relationship. She relished her proximity to other members of Congress and the president of the United States and felt that she was at the center of the action. At night, after everyone left the congressional building, she said she and the lawmaker "had some pretty steamy times" in his office, the lighted dome of the Capitol visible from the window. She said she had fallen in love and the affair was like a drug; it made her feel invincible. "You're totally wrapped up in the glamour of the place, the power, the access and the people you're hanging around with. You're meeting the president, congressmen, senators and other important people. I sat on the Capitol steps with him after a vote. I thought: This is so cool. It just feels great."

She and the lawmaker were never caught, but other members of Congress were not as fortunate. While President Clinton's dalliances with Monica Lewinsky received the most attention in recent history, Washington's record is replete with sex scandals that ruined the careers of many members of Congress. In 1974, Wilbur Mills, chairman of one of the most powerful legislative panels in Congress, the House Ways and Means Committee, created a sensation when a stripper named Fanne Foxe bolted from his car during a police traffic stop and leaped into the Tidal Basin near the Jefferson Memorial. Two years later, California congressman Robert Leggett acknowledged that he had fathered two children with a Capitol Hill secretary and then had an affair with an aide to House Speaker Carl Albert. News about Congressman Wayne Hays of Ohio overshadowed the scandal that same year. Hays had hired an attractive young blonde to work as a fourteen-thousand-dollar-a-year clerk in his Capitol Hill office. Her name was Elizabeth Ray. When he married his longtime office assistant in 1976, Ray went public, famously telling the *Washington Post* that the congressman had placed her on his payroll for pleasure, not business. "I can't type, I can't file, I can't even answer the phone," she told the paper. In 1980, the *Washington Post* magazine published the "Diary of a Mad Congresswife" by Rita Jenrette, who described in detail the infidelities of her husband, Congressman John Jenrette of South Carolina. She noted that women in Washington gained status by proximity to powerful men, and she revealed that members of Congress had frequent liaisons — referred to as "nooners" — in meeting rooms in the basement of the U.S. Capitol and in rented rooms near the Hill. She also disclosed that she and her husband had had sex near the steps of the Capitol behind a marble column on the portico. She revealed more in a *Playboy* pictorial and in a tell-all book she authored, titled *My Capitol Secrets.*

While some of the men who crashed because of their promiscuous behavior during the 1970s and '80s were influential members of Congress, none was more powerful than Gary Hart. The senator from Colorado was the front-runner for the Democratic nomination for president in 1988, and many thought he might win the White House. But rumors swirled around the senator that he had been carrying on extramarital affairs, and in an interview with the *New York Times* in 1987, Hart issued an invitation to the press corps: "Follow me around. I don't care. I'm serious. If anybody wants to put a tail on me, go ahead. They'll be very bored." Reporters for the *Miami Herald* followed the senator to a Washington town house, where he spent the night with a twenty-nine-year-old model from South Florida named Donna Rice. Hart eventually dropped out of the race, but the public was more outraged by the behavior of the press than the conduct of the senator. A

Gallup poll found that nearly two-thirds of the nation thought the news media's treatment of Hart had been "unfair," and more than half of those surveyed believed that infidelity would play little or no role in a president's ability to lead.

While Gary Condit was surprised by the intensity of the news coverage of his relationship with Chandra, he shouldn't have been. The covenants guiding politicians and the press and the public had been permanently altered by the Gary Hart affair, and Condit's case added a new, irresistible angle to the timeless Washington sex scandal: a possible murder. It was a classic Washington thriller with the potential to define the careers of those assigned to cover it, particularly if they returned to their newsrooms with scoops to put on their front pages or at the top of their broadcasts. The story also had one other critical element — timing. It broke in the spring of 2001 but blossomed in the summer as Congress wound down the legislative session, when the city was largely devoid of headline-generating news. Hundreds of reporters and producers and camera crews based in Washington had plenty of time on their hands. Aside from the stories about shark attacks that terrified swimmers along the East Coast, the Chandra Levy story became the perfect antidote for the dog days of summer. Anne Marie Smith's July 2 appearance on the Fox News Channel had ramped up the story, and now it was ready for prime time — which meant *all* the time in the 24/7 cable news world.

The cable stations were consumed by the unfolding story that some had dubbed "The Chandra Drama." CNN, MSNBC, and Fox News repeated the story five times every hour, often without any new information to report. It was the number-one topic of conversation on *Crossfire, Hannity & Colmes,* and *Hardball.* Cable anchors Wolf Blitzer, Greta Van Susteren, Geraldo Rivera, Larry King, and Bill O'Reilly put it at the top of their broadcasts. Most of the nation's leading newspapers showed some restraint; two months into the story, the *Washington Post* had played it on the front page three times, *USA Today* once, and the *New York Times* not at all. There were important stories to cover that July: escalating tension between India and Pakistan; violence in Israel's West Bank; the push to rewrite the Medicare prescription drug plan; and key developments in the story of double agent Robert Hanssen, who sold American secrets to Soviet and Russian intelligence services in the biggest security breach in FBI history.

But the TV screens in the CBS newsroom in New York bayed with the breathless reports from competing networks about Condit's affair with Chandra, his past sex life, and speculation from a parade of "experts" and "analysts" and "news consultants." Each of the retired homicide cops and criminal profilers and criminal defense lawyers and prosecutors theorized about the fate of the intern and how the congressman might be involved. None of them had any direct, firsthand knowledge of the case.

Amid the crazed media coverage, being first became more important than being right, and the facts began to suffer. The *National Enquirer* was wrong when it reported that Carolyn Condit had a "heated screamfest" with Chandra just before she disappeared. The *New York Post* incorrectly reported that Chandra made a series of frantic phone calls to Condit before she vanished. One of the nation's leading reporters stumbled as she stepped into the story. NBC's Andrea Mitchell reported that a 7-Eleven store security camera in suburban Virginia had videotaped Chandra shortly after she disappeared. NBC dropped the report two hours later when Mitchell's sources said they had been mistaken.

At the *Evening News,* inside a glass-covered meeting room in New York called the "Fish Bowl," where Jim Murphy, anchor Dan Rather, and several senior CBS producers spent much of their days, Murphy didn't like what he was seeing. He had a reputation as a hard-driving newsman, a raconteur who liked a good story just as much as anyone else in the news business. But Murphy thought the reporting on the Chandra story was crossing and often obliterating the lines of journalistic principle. Ever since the story broke in May, the *Evening News* had stayed away; not once had Rather mentioned the name "Chandra Levy." Murphy went public with his criticisms of the overheated coverage in a July 10 article by Howard Kurtz, the media writer for the *Washington Post.* Murphy said he was sickened by the press's relentless focus on Condit. "It looks to me like this feeding frenzy of people who are excited that maybe he was involved in her murder. It feels like people are hoping, dreaming that it'll be a sensational story that will see them through the summer. I just find it beyond tasteless. It's nauseating."

Murphy's remarks became the talk of the nation's newsrooms. Some praised Murphy for taking a principled stand; there was no evidence that Condit had anything to do with Chandra's disappearance, and the *Evening News* was right to pass on the story. Others derided Murphy, saying the newscast and its anchor were being sanctimonious at best, and politically biased at worst. They accused Rather, a favorite target of Republicans, of ignoring the story because Condit was a Democrat.

Inside the *Evening News* offices, many were beginning to believe that Murphy and Rather had taken their stand too far. ABC's *World News Tonight* had aired a story about the case. So had the *NBC Nightly News*, ten times in the first week of July alone. ABC's *Nightline* was the only other major network news program to pass on the story. The story raised a journalistic dilemma: Was it news, or was it gossip masquerading as news? Many *Evening News* staffers insisted that the story was news, and they received some potent ammunition to support their argument on July 10.

At 11:15 that night, D.C. police officers and FBI agents pulled up to the curb of Condit's apartment in unmarked cars and walked past the pack of reporters assembled on the sidewalk. Condit stepped from the building and climbed into a waiting car as reporters called his name and shouted out questions. Once inside, crime-scene technicians began to search the apartment. They collected hair from a shoe in a closet. They extracted fibers and hair from a clothes dryer lint trap. Cameramen on the street shot footage of the technicians as they moved behind the windows of the apartment. Toward the end of the search, the technicians turned on ultraviolet lights to illuminate possible traces of forensic evidence — blood, fingerprints, saliva — anything that might provide a clue to the case. The lights bathed the congressman's apartment in an eerie purple glow as the pack of reporters and cameramen watched the extraordinary scene playing out four flights above them.

At 2:45 the following morning, the investigators and technicians emerged from the condominium. They quietly loaded file folders and large paper evidence bags into one of the unmarked cars and drove off without saying a word. Condit had consented to the search in an attempt to clear his name, but to the pack of journalists assembled on the sidewalk, it looked like he was the prime suspect.

Cable news had a field day with the story, running it hard and repeating it throughout the day on July 11. Still, the *Evening News* stayed away, and inside the CBS newsroom, reporters and producers were starting to revolt. Some were embarrassed that their newscast was still holding out. The network was being ridiculed. The FBI had searched a congressman's home for evidence of a possible murder, and that was not news? Media personalities publicly criticized the mainstream media for punting on the story. Said Fox News commentator Bill O'Reilly in the "Talking Points" segment of his show:

As we reported yesterday, *Nightline* and the *CBS Evening News* have ignored the story entirely, and ABC's *World News Tonight* has only done one report. So if the cable news networks did not exist, the pressure on Congressman Condit and the D.C. police would be at a minimum. "Talking Points" believes the elite media is out of touch with the American people. The Condit story is about abuse of power and shoddy behavior by an elected official. Most Americans understand the validity of the situation and see the bigger picture here. Apparently, some in the elite media don't see that picture.

After the search, Murphy started to second-guess himself, wondering if perhaps it was time for the *Evening News* to get in the game — but Rather refused to budge. He thought it was a tabloid story, void of facts, full of conjecture, and beneath the dignity of the network. The reporting he saw was slipshod, and it appeared that the reputation of a congressman was being shredded without verifiable, on-the-record information.

Early in his career, Rather covered the police beat in Houston, Texas, and he had a gut feeling: The D.C. police didn't have much to go on. Rather had been in the news business for nearly fifty years, and he established his reputation as a crusading journalist who didn't like to run with other reporters. He made his mark at CBS as the first to report that President Kennedy had been assassinated and then as a longtime correspondent for *60 Minutes*. In 1981, he ascended to the anchor chair, taking over from legendary broadcaster Walter Cronkite. During the course of his career, he came to despise the dynamics of pack journalism. The packs were often ugly — reporters shouting questions, pushing and shoving each other, and surrounding their subjects with cameras and microphone booms, blindly following each other and creating an echo chamber of information that rarely served the public. He compared the pack to a flock of turkeys: If two of the turkeys leaped over a cliff, the rest of the flock would follow. As the managing editor of the *Evening News,* Rather had made a judgment not to follow the pack. He wasn't about to change his position.

One of Rather's bosses was Andrew Heyward. The president of CBS News, Heyward was a gregarious, Harvard-educated newsman who made a habit of knowing the names of everyone in the news division, from the pages to the producers. He oversaw the *Evening News,* the *Early Show, Face the Nation,* and every other network news program. He gave his anchors and producers wide latitude over how they ran their shows, making suggestions but almost always deferring to their judgments. That July, Heyward was on vacation in the medieval city of Brugge, Belgium, when the calls started to arrive from New York. His colleagues at CBS told him about the search of Condit's apartment and the decision not to air the story. They pleaded with him to intervene; the most venerable program in CBS News history was becoming the laughingstock of the industry.

Heyward considered the arguments. He, too, viewed the story as pack journalism at its worst and not worthy of the *Evening News*. But he was also aware that the cable news stations were devoting unprecedented airtime to the story, and he wondered whether viewers of the *Evening News* deserved a piece by CBS about the missing intern and the congressman. The case had become a cultural phenomenon; 63 percent of Americans were following it closely. Still, the story gave him pause. The cable stations were running the same flimsy facts over and over, day after day, without anything new to report. Frequently, the broadcasts were filled with speculation and rumor, and he thought that the coverage was failing to advance the public's understanding of the case. It seemed prurient and pointless. But the search of Condit's apartment was a significant development and Heyward thought it deserved to be carefully and responsibly reported by the *Evening News*. He spoke to Murphy from his hotel room in Brugge and told him so.

Murphy had also come to believe that the development was legitimate news and the *Evening News* should run a story. Murphy told Heyward that Rather was the only person standing in the way and he asked Heyward to talk to the anchor and convince him to air a piece. Heyward considered the request but stuck to his management style; the decision would be left to Rather.

In the Fish Bowl in New York, Murphy and his senior producers huddled around the conference table. They were in agreement: It was time to report the story. Murphy met with Rather and asked the anchor if he would acquiesce to the consensus of the team. Rather repeated his arguments. Finally, Rather told Murphy: "If you really want to put this on the air, I won't anchor the show."

Replied Murphy: "I don't think that would be right. Let's do the show that you prefer."

The next day, on July 12, a story would play out in a way that would support the legitimacy of Rather's reluctance. The *Washington Post* broke the story about the Pentecostal minister who moonlighted as a gardener for the Levys. He had since told the FBI the same story he told Susan Levy in April, that his daughter also had an affair with Condit. The article, played on page one, began:

FBI agents looking into the disappearance of Chandra Levy have approached and interviewed a Pentecostal minister who described an affair between his then-18-year-old daughter and Rep. Gary A. Condit, telling investigators that the congressman had warned her never to speak of the relationship.

Four law enforcement sources confirmed that the father, Otis Thomas, has been questioned by the FBI and that investigators are interested in talking to his daughter. Thomas, in an interview in which he described what his daughter told him of the affair, said that he has encouraged her to talk to the FBI but that she is afraid to do so and has gone into hiding.

Thomas said the relationship took place about seven years ago and that it ended in a tense breakup initiated by his daughter. . . . Thomas's daughter, who is now in her mid-twenties, declined to discuss any aspect of the case. "I don't want to talk about any of that," she said in a brief telephone conversation this week.

Marina Ein, a spokeswoman for the Democratic congressman from California, yesterday accused The Washington Post of joining "the ranks of tabloids who have come to us with specious questions about a supposed affair."

"These questions are destructive,

unfair and irrelevant," Ein said. "In fact, we are constantly placed in the impossible position of having to prove a negative. This is something we will not do."

Condit's attorney, Abbe D. Lowell, said, "This is beneath the dignity of The Washington Post."

The report was picked up around the nation. It triggered a fresh round of newspaper stories and topped the cable news broadcasts. Not only was the young woman eighteen at the time of the alleged affair, but she was black, a political death sentence for a white conservative congressman from the Central Valley of California. Some news organizations went beyond the allegations contained in the *Post* article, reporting that the girl became pregnant and gave birth to Condit's child. But there was a problem. Days later, Thomas recanted the tale he told to the *Post.* He confessed to FBI agents that he had fabricated the story. Susan Levy told her friends that she thought Thomas had been truthful but someone had persuaded him to change his story. Why would he have made up a story about his daughter and the congressman and told not only her but also the *Washington Post* and the FBI? On July 21, the *Post* ran an article, retracting the

Thomas story. It began:

.MODESTO, Calif. — A Pentecostal minister who told the FBI of an affair between his then-18-year-old daughter and Rep. Gary A. Condit informed investigators this week that he had fabricated the story, a law enforcement source said today.

The account provided by Otis Thomas, published by The Washington Post on July 12, was widely circulated in the media and increased the pressure on the California Democrat. A note signed "Jennifer Thomas" that appeared on the front door of the Thomas residence that same day dismissed the minister's story and said: "I never met the congressman who's involved in all of this."

It is unclear whether the minister disavowed all or parts of his account, which he provided to the FBI in May. But one law enforcement official said that the FBI had been trying to interview Thomas's daughter and that Thomas "backed off" the story in the last few days.

Condit's representatives, who called *The Post*'s July 12 story "reckless and deplorable," did not return telephone calls seeking comment today.

That same story noted another important development in the case — an undeniable one that spelled trouble for Condit. About three hours before the police and FBI agents started to search his apartment, the congressman and his top aide, Mike Dayton, drove across the Potomac River to Alexandria in Dayton's black Volkswagen Jetta. At about eight that night, the Jetta pulled to the curb near a McDonald's. Daniel Olson, a law firm temp who lived in the neighborhood, was driving home when he saw a man he recognized as Condit step out of the passenger side of the car. Olson pulled over and watched as Condit strolled over to a trash can, pushed something deep inside, and returned to the Jetta. Olson was intrigued. When the Jetta pulled away, he walked over to the trash can and looked in. He spotted a small black square, the size of a CD, and pulled it out. It was a cardboard box for a TAG Heuer watch. The box was torn and flattened. Inside, Olson found a manual and a warranty, but no watch. He brought the box back to his apartment and showed it to his roommates. The next day, Olson tossed it back into the same trash can and went to work, where he told the story to his colleagues. One of them, who once worked for the Baltimore Police Department, urged Olson to call the D.C. police.

D.C. detective Lawrence Kennedy drove to Alexandria and retrieved the box, the manual, and the warranty. Police traced the serial number and determined that the box had contained a watch that "Janet," Condit's former girlfriend who worked on his staff, had given to him years earlier. Detectives were puzzled. Why did he keep a watch box for nearly seven years? And why did he throw it out hours before their search of his apartment? The story, first reported by a Washington television station, was picked up around the nation.

At the *Evening News* in New York, Rather began to relent. He and Murphy decided to put one of their best reporters on the story: Jim Stewart. A wiry man with a distinct southern accent, Stewart covered the Justice Department for CBS News and his sources in the law enforcement world were deep and dependable. It wasn't long before Stewart called Murphy back with a scoop that would propel the *Evening News* ahead of its competitors and cast the Chandra Levy case in an entirely new light.

14
A SEARCH IN THE PARK

Police in Rock Creek Park

With Chandra missing for eighty-five days, the police stepped up their search. To the public, it seemed as though the police had been looking for her everywhere: Using searchlights and crowbars, they had pried open boarded-up and abandoned buildings across the city; they scoured the Potomac River around Ronald Reagan Washington National Airport and the Anacostia River near the South Capitol Street Bridge; detectives returned to Chandra's apartment building in Dupont Circle to interview residents and conduct criminal background checks; they canvassed the Washington Sports Club for leads.

The police were also forced to follow a flood of bizarre tips that poured in from all over the world, each one stranger than the last. Dozens of psychics and oddballs were calling with their hunches, their visions, and their sightings. Some of the tips were plausible; others were not. All took time away from the case.

Police were frustrated. They were spending an unprecedented amount of time on the case and not getting a meaningful break — a witness, a piece of physical evidence, a solid tip from an informant. Instead they were hearing about ghostly visions.

One psychic said that Chandra's throat had been slashed and that she was put in a body bag and stowed in the basement of a Smithsonian storage building. Police checked the building but found nothing. Another said Chandra was murdered and dumped in the Potomac near the Memorial Bridge. A dive team found nothing. Another caller said Chandra was a victim of a suicide bombing in Israel. Police called their counterparts there; it wasn't true. Another psychic said Chandra was buried in Maryland. State troopers checked the site, but it was one more false lead. One tipster said that Chandra died in Nevada during a botched abortion by a veterinarian and that she was buried in the desert, a tip that fed a persistent rumor that Chandra was pregnant. The two private investigators for the Levy family went out West, but they came back empty-handed.

One of the strangest tips of all came from

Monty Roberts, a seventy-six-year-old horse trainer who was known around the world as the "Horse Whisperer." Roberts was on a flight from Seattle to Phoenix when he struck up a conversation with a well-dressed Middle Eastern man seated next to him. The man told Roberts that he organized events for embassies and was arranging one in Phoenix. The man then told Roberts that he knew what had happened to Chandra Levy. He said Gary Condit was a frequent guest at Middle Eastern embassies and the congressman had told his embassy friends that he was having a problem with the intern: She was threatening to go public with their affair. The man said he saw a group of five men on the tarmac of an airport in late April taking a woman out of a limousine and putting her onto a private jet. The woman was in a zombielike state, as if she had been drugged. He said the woman was Condit's girlfriend, that she had been kidnapped and taken to a Middle Eastern country, where she would be sold into a sex slave ring.

Roberts called Dominick Dunne, a writer for *Vanity Fair*. The FBI heard about the tip and began to pursue it along with the U.S. attorney's office in Washington. Prosecutors obtained flight records for private planes taking off from Dulles International Airport. They reviewed flight information from the Federal Aviation Administration and a D.C. detective interviewed employees of a charter plane company that flew to the Middle East from Dulles. They also examined a company that owned the jets used by the ruler of Dubai. After spending weeks chasing the tip, FBI agents and prosecutors determined that it was false.

On June 7, a month after Chandra went missing, the FBI received the report from the analysis of her computer. For detectives working on a case that might involve a murder, the delay seemed like an eternity. The investigators noted what they thought was an intriguing clue: Among the Web pages that Chandra visited on the day she disappeared was one showing the address for the Klingle Mansion. On June 9, the D.C. police searched the grounds of the mansion. The news media didn't find out until July 15, when executive assistant D.C. police chief Terrance Gainer told reporters that on May 1, before Chandra logged off her computer, she looked up the mansion that served as the park's administrative headquarters.

Built in 1823, the Klingle Mansion sits on

a hill north of the National Zoo, overlooking a block of large homes near a wooded area that is a popular destination for dog walkers, bikers, hikers, and joggers. Police department commanders sent recruits to search the underbrush and the woods near the mansion. Police officers also contacted the city's taxi commission to check whether anyone took Chandra to the mansion or anywhere else. They requested that all 1,600 registered taxi drivers in the city turn over their logs for the period between April 30 and May 2.

But investigators misinterpreted Chandra's computer search when they briefed Gainer. She had actually been looking up Rock Creek Park that morning. She clicked on a washingtonpost.com "Entertainment Guide" to the park at 11:33 A.M. When that site popped up on her computer, the URL at the top of the page listed the address of the park headquarters: 3545 Williamsburg Lane, Klingle Mansion. The investigators focused on that URL and the mansion, but they failed to focus on the searches Chandra conducted minutes later, when she went deeper into the site and clicked on links for a map of the park and its hiking trails.

Gainer's comment to the press about the Klingle Mansion was repeated on television and in newspaper reports for weeks and it set off a flurry of theories that were repeated at dinner parties, around office cubicles, and in supermarket aisles. Why did Chandra look up the mansion? Did Chandra meet Condit there for a rendezvous? Did someone else lure Chandra to the Klingle Mansion and then kill her?

Reporters continued to besiege the department with an unprecedented number of interview requests, and Gainer thought that he needed to respond. The prosecutors assigned to the case, including Barbara Kittay, however, were furious about Gainer's repeated press conferences and media interviews. The new chief of detectives was also angered by the constant press briefings. As a former FBI official, Jack Barrett had been trained to stay away from the media. He thought that talking to the press rarely helped a criminal investigation and it often resulted in trouble. In this case — his first as a D.C. police official — it seemed as though every time the police discovered something new, Gainer or one of his colleagues alerted the media. Barrett took an unusual step, warning his detectives not to tell him about sensitive information that they didn't want to read about in the newspaper; if they did tell him, he would have to report it up the chain of command and he thought it would likely be leaked to the media or become the topic of a press conference.

Behind the scenes, Gainer was clashing with Condit's lawyer, Abbe Lowell. The battles began when the Levy family publicly called on Condit to take a polygraph exam. After the police took Condit's DNA, Lowell had hoped that the detectives would back down, leave his client alone, and refocus their investigation. By the second week of July, Condit had voluntarily provided a saliva sample, submitted to three interviews, and consented to the search of his apartment.

But Condit was under increasing pressure. A poll of likely voters in his California district found that 44 percent believed he had not been as helpful to the investigation as he could have been. When law enforcement sources leaked to the news media that, during his third interview with the police, Condit had acknowledged a romantic relationship with Chandra, Robert and Susan Levy again went before the reporters and television cameras lining their street in Modesto. They thought that Condit had been untruthful for two months and hadn't told the police all he knew about the disappearance of their daughter. The Levys urged the police to force Condit to take a lie-detector test.

The Washington press corps followed their lead. One afternoon as Lowell walked out of his law office building, reporters besieged him and demanded to know whether Condit would submit to a polygraph. Lowell soon received a call from Barrett, asking if Condit would take the test.

Lowell didn't believe in polygraphs; they were inadmissible in court and infamously unreliable. They were so unreliable that Aldrich Ames, a former CIA counterintelligence officer, committed one of the biggest breaches in agency history by spying for the Soviet Union while passing polygraph exams designed to catch double agents. In 1994, he and his wife pleaded guilty to passing top-secret documents to the Soviets using drop boxes in and around Washington in exchange for more than $2.5 million.

Lowell also worried about false positives — Condit was under tremendous stress and scrutiny and he could become nervous during the test. What if he appeared deceptive when responding to a question about Chandra's disappearance? Lowell told Barrett he saw no benefit to his client taking the test.

If Condit passed, people would say he was a good liar; if he failed or the test was inconclusive, the police could come under pressure to charge him. Besides, Condit didn't want to take a polygraph administered by the police. He had cooperated in the beginning, but he had lost faith in the department long ago.

Everywhere Lowell went, reporters pressed him about the polygraph. Lowell crafted another strategy to shift the media spotlight and end the investigation of his client. He made some calls and found a former FBI agent, Barry Colvert, who was considered one of the most respected polygraph examiners in the country. Colvert had been an interrogator assigned to the FBI Washington field office for seventeen years. Retired from the bureau, he taught FBI agents how to administer the test. Lowell considered hiring Colvert to administer the exam at a private location, and suggested the possibility to Condit: If he passed, they could decide what to do with the results. If he failed, no one would ever know. Condit agreed.

On the afternoon of July 12, Lowell and Condit eluded the pack of reporters by meeting at the town house of one of Lowell's colleagues in Washington's Cleveland

Park neighborhood. In an upstairs bedroom, Colvert set up the polygraph equipment. Downstairs, Lowell paced the floors while he waited for the results. Twenty minutes passed. Lowell nervously looked at his watch; it seemed like the exam was taking forever. He began to second-guess his strategy. What if his client failed and that somehow leaked out? After nearly an hour, Lowell heard the upstairs door open. Condit walked down the stairs, Colvert behind him. Lowell braced himself for the verdict, which would be one of three possible outcomes: deceptive, not deceptive, or inconclusive. "Not deceptive in any way," Colvert told Lowell. The former FBI agent concluded that Condit "had a probability of deception of less than one-hundredth of one percent to the only questions that mattered." He had asked Condit three key questions: Did he have anything to do with the disappearance of Chandra? Did he harm her or cause anyone else to harm her? And did he know where she could be found?

The next day, Lowell called Barrett. Lowell wondered if he could reach a compromise with the police department. He asked Barrett if the department would accept a privately administered polygraph exam. Barrett checked with his superiors. The answer came back in no uncertain terms: unacceptable. It would have to be performed by an examiner chosen by the police and conducted according to department protocol.

On July 13, Lowell called a press conference at the Madison Hotel, across from his office in downtown Washington. Standing before the gaggle of reporters and television cameras, he announced that Condit had passed a privately administered polygraph. He then held up a poster that described the extent of Condit's cooperation with investigators: the interviews, the search of his apartment, and the voluntary submission of DNA. Lowell noted that his client had taken the exam during the most stressful week of his life, and he had some harsh words for the reporters, castigating them for spreading misinformation to the point that "the truth has become invisible." Lowell told them: "I think he has done what a person could do. Should you not be asking if others have done as much?"

The privately administered polygraph angered the D.C. police more than anything Lowell or Condit had done in the two and a half months since Chandra disappeared. Police Chief Charles Ramsey dismissed the test as a farce with "no investigative value."

He told reporters: "He may have tried to sell it to us, but we're not buying it." Ramsey also dismissed Lowell's claims on the poster as a "very upbeat and very bright portrayal of the openness and honesty of the congressman." Ramsey added: "I would not paint quite as rosy a picture as that." Gainer was more critical. He told reporters that the police wouldn't have needed to interview Condit a third time if he had been more forthcoming in the first two interviews. Then Gainer went a step further: In a fury, he picked up the phone and called Lowell.

"You guys are bordering on obstruction of justice," he told him.

"Chief, I know that you have a lot more law enforcement experience than I, but I don't recognize why you're angry," Lowell replied. "When you calm down and recognize that we have had three interviews, a DNA test, had Mrs. Condit come to be interviewed, allowed the congressman's place to be searched, and have subjected him to the world's best polygrapher, it is the strangest definition of obstruction of justice."

Gainer lost his composure. "Goddamn it," Lowell heard him say before he hung up.

Gainer wasn't through. He told reporters

that the police had been negotiating with Lowell about conducting a polygraph of Condit when Lowell went behind their back and hired his own examiner. Gainer thought Lowell had lied to him. "My impression was that we were going to continue that dialogue. I took him at his word," Gainer said.

Gainer then did what Lowell predicted the police would do if the congressman passed the test: He said polygraphs were not foolproof, based on his past experience as a homicide detective in Chicago. "I can tell you, in my homicide days, I had people who passed who were the murderers, and I had people who failed the polygraph and in fact were not the murderers."

The Levys' lawyer also lashed out at Lowell. "It seems the congressman and his attorneys snuck off to a private polygraph examiner," Billy Martin told reporters. On the Sunday morning television show *Meet the Press,* Martin got personal: "The way this thing was set up by his attorney is slippery, it's slick."

Lowell offered to turn over the raw polygraph data and results to the police, but that made matters worse. On July 18, Ramsey told the press that the FBI had reviewed Condit's polygraph but was unable to match specific questions to the graphs that showed the congressman's reaction. The FBI "had no way of telling with certainty the results of each question," he said. Within days, a series of damaging stories about Condit were leaked. It was payback from the police department, Lowell thought.

First came the story about the congressman throwing away the wristwatch box in Alexandria. An article in the *Washington Post* attributed to "law enforcement sources" said prosecutors were trying to determine whether the incident was part of an "attempted cover-up" of his previous affair with "Janet." Then came stories, again attributed to law enforcement sources, that said prosecutors were exploring allegations that Condit's staffers may have obstructed justice by telling "Janet" that she would be ruined if she went public and by asking Anne Marie Smith to sign the affidavit denying the affair.

There was one embarrassing detail the police didn't leak: Condit's DNA test had come back from the laboratory at FBI headquarters in Quantico, Virginia, about an hour south of Washington. His saliva sample was compared with the semen found on Chandra's underwear. It was a match. The test result was a closely kept secret; only a few people involved in the investigation were told. To Barrett, it seemed that the match was an "aha" moment for the prosecutors, strengthening their suspicions of Condit. But Barrett thought the match added little to the case. It simply confirmed what he already knew — that the congressman had been having an affair with Chandra and had been covering it up to save his marriage and his political career.

Barrett had come to believe that the congressman was probably not involved in Chandra's disappearance, but in many ways, it was too late to stop the momentum of the investigation. Prosecutors, as well as the news media and the public, were fixated on the congressman. Reporters were drilling into his past and writing about his family, including his two brothers, Darrell and Burl Condit. They reported that his younger brother, Darrell, had an arrest record for drug possession, vehicle theft, and attempting to cash a forged check. They reported that his older brother, Burl, a Modesto police officer, had been reprimanded for shooting his service revolver for fun in a park. Reporters also tracked down Condit's driver, Vince Flammini, who had since been let go by the congressman. Flammini said he constantly covered for Condit. "I lied for him a million times," he told Fox News. "If his wife said — she'd say, 'What time did his plane came [*sic*] in?' And I would say, 'Ten.' It probably came in the day before."

It seemed as though everyone wanted Condit to be involved, and the congressman didn't help himself by suspiciously discarding the wristwatch box. Even though Barrett thought it was another "silly" attempt by Condit to hide an affair, the incident forced his detectives to open a new line of inquiry into the congressman.

With tensions between police and Condit at an all-time high, the detectives asked the congressman to submit to a fourth interview. Condit was reluctant to sit down with the police again. He tried to maintain his work routine on Capitol Hill, but he was being publicly bludgeoned regardless of what he or his lawyer did. His real-life soap opera unfolded hour after hour on cable television. In typical Washington fashion, a long lineup of talking heads, political observers, and media pundits jumped into the fray. Even Lanny Davis took a shot. The former special counsel for President Bill Clinton and the author of the book *Truth to Tell: Tell It Early, Tell It All, Tell It Yourself* urged the Democratic Party to demand full public disclosure from Condit.

The congressman couldn't believe that his

name was being linked to a possible murder, and the commentators didn't have to prove a thing. The stories were based on false-hoods reported as fact: He was engaged in bisexual and gay relationships. His wife didn't have any thumbs. He rode his Harley with the Hells Angels.

At 8:58 on the morning of July 25, 2001, three D.C. police sergeants gathered twenty-eight recruits along Glover Road, one of several roads that crisscrossed Rock Creek Park. Since early July, they had been search-ing for any trace of Chandra in the park, one of the last sites she visited on her computer before signing off more than two and a half months earlier. It was above 80 degrees, the start of another steamy day in Washington, when the recruits formed a line near a picnic area known as Grove 17 and executed an order issued by Barrett: Search one hundred yards from the roads that run through the park.

But someone had made a mistake. Ramsey thought that he had ordered Barrett to direct the recruits to search one hundred yards off the park's roads *and paths.* By limiting the search to the areas off the roads, the police would canvass a much smaller portion of the park and exclude deeply wooded areas. Either Ramsey miscommunicated his order, or Barrett misunderstood it.

After one that afternoon, the sergeants called off the search and the weary recruits boarded a bus and headed for another area of the park. Not far from where the recruits had canvassed was the Western Ridge Trail, a leafy path that winds its way through stands of poplar and oak trees perched above a steep ravine that runs down to Rock Creek. Off the Western Ridge Trail, beneath the dark green canopy of the forest, a pair of sunglasses rested on the ground. A few feet away was a white Reebok sneaker trimmed in blue. A little farther, on the edge of a ravine, was a pair of black ProSpirit stretch pants turned inside out, each leg tied in a knot. And nearby lay the body of Chandra Levy. It was seventy-nine yards below the trail.

15
THE WRONG MAN

Brad Garrett

Three years before Chandra Levy came to Washington and seven thousand miles from the place she disappeared, FBI Agent Brad Garrett approached a dilapidated hotel on a dusty street in Pakistan. It was four in the morning. He and the three other agents who accompanied him wore traditional Pakistani clothes over their jeans and weapons. Garrett had long anticipated this moment. Inside the hotel was the man he believed had opened fire outside CIA headquarters in Langley, Virginia, in 1993, killing two agency employees and injuring three others.

The agents burst through a door of a three-dollar-a-night room at the Salimar Hotel in Dera Ghazi Khan, their guns drawn, but the man on the bed did not fit the description of the killer. The man was bearded and heavier.

"Turn him over!" Garrett yelled to the other agents. He straddled the man, took his left thumb, and pressed it onto an ink pad. Garrett pulled out a copy of Mir Aimal Kasi's fingerprints and examined them through a magnifying glass. The four-and-a-half-year international manhunt was over. "It's a match!" Garrett said. On the plane from Pakistan back to the United States, Garrett persuaded Kasi to confess to shooting the CIA employees with an AK-47 as they waited in traffic to turn into the agency's headquarters.

Garrett's 1997 arrest of Kasi made him a legend within the FBI and the world of counterterrorism. It added to a reputation that had been growing since he obtained a confession from Ramzi Yousef, the mastermind of the 1993 World Trade Center bombing, and after he worked with a D.C. police detective to solve the execution-style slaying of the three employees at the Georgetown Starbucks. The former Marine from Anderson, Indiana, with a Ph.D. in criminology was so successful at closing murder cases that he was nicknamed "Dr. Death." Garrett dressed the part — black turtlenecks, black jeans, black jackets. He was tall and thin, handsome enough to briefly work as a model during college.

When the Chandra Levy case hit a standstill toward the middle of July, it was natural for the FBI to assign one of its top agents to the case. The D.C. police department was technically in charge of the investigation, but the FBI had been called in because of Chandra's connection to a member of Congress. The FBI turned to Garrett, along with his partner, Melissa Thomas. Together they worked cold cases, the hard-to-crack investigations that dragged on for months, sometimes years.

When investigators contacted Abbe Lowell and told him that Garrett would like to interview Condit, Lowell's first impulse was to laugh; what could Garrett possibly ask Condit in a fourth interview that hadn't been asked in the previous three? The investigators explained that this interview would be different. Garrett was less interested in Condit; he wanted to build a profile of Chandra. What was her lifestyle? Her habits? What did she like to do when they weren't together? Who were her friends? Were there any people she expressed concerns about? Lowell was intrigued. Finally, he thought, someone from law enforcement who wasn't interested in his client's sexual past.

At the *CBS Evening News* in New York, executive producer Jim Murphy received a proposed script from one of his top reporters in Washington, Jim Stewart. After the *Evening News* passed on covering the search of Condit's apartment, Murphy had assigned the veteran journalist to work his law enforcement sources to see what he could develop on the Chandra story. As he read Stewart's script, a smile came across his face. At first he thought Stewart was pulling a prank, but it soon became clear that his reporter had a solid scoop: The FBI believed that the focus of the investigation on Condit was misplaced and the bureau had assigned one of its top agents to examine the case from scratch.

It was a good "get" for the *Evening News*, which had stayed away from the story for nearly eleven weeks. With a piece of original reporting that advanced the public's knowledge of the case, it was time for CBS to enter the media fray. On the night of July 18, anchor Dan Rather introduced the story: "There is news tonight worthy of national note in the case of missing person twenty-four-year-old Chandra Levy. The young woman disappeared in Washington more than eleven weeks ago and became one of tens of thousands of missing persons across the country. CBS News correspondent Jim Stewart reports that now both the status and the nature of this widely publicized investigation have changed."

Stewart began his report by saying the case had been transferred to the FBI's cold-case squad, an elite unit within the bureau that focused on the toughest cases with the fewest clues. Quoting unnamed law enforcement sources, he said the shift coincided with the belief that the D.C. police department had placed an "inappropriate emphasis" on Condit. He noted that the Metropolitan Police Department would continue to serve as the lead agency, but FBI agents would "start at ground zero" and "focus on areas other than Representative Condit."

Stewart added that prosecutors were increasingly uneasy over the public spectacle the case had become, and they were "particularly unhappy over the multiple press appearances local police make each day with essentially nothing to report." Stewart said the FBI had named Garrett as its lead agent and noted he had spent four years tracking down Kasi in Pakistan. Stewart briefly mentioned the search of Condit's apartment by saying that laboratory tests on a hat, a jacket, and other items taken from his home "have thus far disclosed no traces of blood or other useful evidence."

Stewart concluded his report: "The real significance of the FBI reassignment is in the very name of the unit handling it. 'Cold case' means cold leads, few tips, and little to go on. The media spotlight may stay hot, but the investigation now appears to be in the hands of people prepared to take years to do their work."

Lowell and Condit felt emboldened. Perhaps the focus of the investigation had finally shifted. Lowell agreed to meet Garrett at the U.S. attorney's office on the morning of July 24 to explore the possibility of a fourth interview. At the table were the two D.C. police detectives assigned to the case — Ralph Durant and Lawrence Kennedy. When Garrett walked in with Thomas, his partner, Lowell thought they looked like they had come straight from central casting: Garrett strode into the room confidently, wearing his trademark outfit: black jeans, black shirt, black jacket. Thomas was attractive, self-assured, the quintessential special agent. She had helped actress Julianne Moore prepare for her role as FBI agent Clarice Starling in the movie *Hannibal* by taking her around to Quantico and FBI offices. She and Garrett resembled stars in their own television crime show — not unlike the one Garrett used to watch as a kid, the 1960s police drama *Adam-12*.

As Garrett explained the reasons for the

interview, Lowell realized that the tone of the questioning had changed. Garrett told Lowell that he didn't see his client as a suspect, but rather as a source of information. Lowell left the U.S. attorney's office feeling for the first time that professional investigators were on the case. Lowell told Condit about his meeting with Garrett and the agent's reputation within the bureau: his arrest of Kasi, how he helped to solve the Starbucks triple homicide. Condit was impressed. He agreed to sit for one more interview.

On the evening of July 26, Garrett and Thomas arrived at Lowell's downtown Washington office, where they met up with the D.C. detectives assigned to the case. Garrett had already examined the police files in the investigation — the interviews, the searches of Rock Creek Park, the reviews of Chandra's home and cell phone records, and the results from the search of Condit's apartment. After nearly three months of investigating, the D.C. police department had few leads, and the police chief now thought the chances of solving the case were less than fifty-fifty. It became clear to Garrett that Chandra's world in Washington revolved around her internship, the Washington Sports Club, and Gary Condit. He hoped that the congressman would disclose something new that would give him a clue about where she could be.

When the interview began at 7:50 that night, Garrett took the lead. He immediately set out to establish a personal connection between himself and Condit, noting that they were both the same age, fifty-three. Condit smiled at the tall, tan agent with the model good looks and asked, "Why do you look so much better?" Garrett returned the smile and replied, "I haven't been through what you've been through."

The approach was classic Garrett: Show compassion and find common ground. Garrett had a calm, Zen-like way of interviewing witnesses and suspects, and Lowell wasn't surprised by the chemistry between his client and the special agent. In his mind, they were two cowboylike characters whom Lowell could imagine hanging out together in California's Central Valley, talking about guns and the outdoors.

Garrett told Condit that this interview would be about Chandra. He needed to know everything the congressman could recall. Any information that could round her out as a person might provide a lead. Condit described Chandra and provided details about their relationship, some of them new. He said she was a vegetarian. She was always upbeat. She took vitamins and shunned drugs and alcohol. Garrett asked about her spending habits, and Condit said she was frugal. Her wardrobe looked like it came from Macy's, not Nordstrom. Condit said that he and Chandra didn't spend a lot of time together; when they did, they mostly stayed at his apartment. He said he was surprised to learn that Chandra had ended the lease on her apartment. He expected her to return to Washington after her May 11 graduation from the University of Southern California. There were no plans to stop seeing each other.

As the interview progressed, Garrett began to see a more complete portrait of Chandra. Garrett pictured Chandra as smart and driven, but also naïve. Garrett was familiar with the Chandra Levy case file, and he noted that her relationship with Condit was reminiscent of another relationship that she once had with a police officer in Modesto. Chandra was twenty when she dated the officer, Mark Steele, who was in his late twenties at the time. Garrett knew from interviews that investigators had conducted with her friends that Chandra found men her own age to be immature, and she was drawn to older, largely unattainable men in positions of power.

As Lowell listened to the questions, he felt a sense of relief. For the past two months, as he dealt with the D.C. police, Lowell felt as though he had been operating in a foreign country, a chaotic world he didn't understand and didn't know how to navigate. Now he had returned to familiar ground. Gone was the tension, the fighting, the swearing, the accusatory words.

During the interview, Condit raised the issue of police leaks. He wanted to know if he was going to read about this meeting in the newspaper. Garrett and Thomas assured him that he would not. They, too, were troubled by the leaks. As the interview came to an end an hour and a half later, Condit told Garrett that he wished he could help him more, and he hoped that the FBI and the police could solve the case. Garrett realized that Condit didn't know a lot about Chandra's personal life outside of their sexual relationship.

Garrett left the interview with a prevailing sense that Condit simply didn't care enough about Chandra to harm her or kill her. The congressman was not their guy.

Jack Barrett, the chief of detectives, and his superior officer, Terrance Gainer, dispute what happened next. After the interview, Barrett said he received a call on his cell phone. Gainer was on the line. He asked Barrett how the interview went and he wanted to know what Condit had to say. Barrett said the call pushed him to a breaking point. He refused to tell his commanding officer what had taken place. He told Gainer that he no longer trusted him, that every time he provided him with details of the investigation, they would wind up in the press. He told Gainer that he would be fired if he worked for the FBI.

He said Gainer asked again.

"That's an order," Barrett heard him say.

Barrett, who had spent his career following the chain of command, complied.

Gainer is adamant: He says the phone call never happened.

To help the investigators, Garrett and Jim Trainum, the D.C. detective who had worked with him to solve the Starbucks triple homicide, went outside the department for help. In early August, two weeks after Garrett interviewed Condit, they decided to contact one of the world's leading criminal profilers, who worked in Washington, and ask him to examine the case. They told him the investigation had gone "a little sideways" because of the focus on Condit, and they wanted to take a fresh approach.

Kim Rossmo, director of research for the Police Foundation, had created a widely respected computer program that analyzed geographic patterns in murders, rapes, and other crimes. He used the program to assist police departments in Canada, England, and the United States. In Lafayette, Louisiana, he used it to aid police in their search for a serial rapist who had been assaulting women for nearly a decade in the 1980s and '90s. Ernest "Randy" Comeaux, thirty-seven, a top investigator in the juvenile division of the Lafayette Parish Sheriff's Department, pleaded guilty to the rapes in 1999. Rossmo had also used the program to help D.C. police track down a serial murderer who was strangling women in the city between 1996 and 1997. Darryl Donnell Turner, a liquor store clerk, was convicted of raping and strangling two of those women.

Rossmo based his computer program on the premise that detailed examinations of crime-scene locations can help investigators narrow down suspect lists. He theorized that criminals rarely travel far from "anchor points" to commit their crimes; they stay

278

near neighborhoods, shopping centers, parks, and other places they know well. To construct a geographic profile, Rossmo put crime-scene locations into his computer program and cross-referenced them with a list of possible suspects and the places they had lived, spent time, and committed other crimes.

Before he could get started, Rossmo gave Garrett and Trainum a long list of questions to help him fully understand Chandra and how she lived her life in Washington. He wanted to know where she ate, where she went for coffee, and whether she spent time with anyone else besides Condit. Did she take bike rides, Rollerblade, or jog, and where? Did she use her credit card or debit card shortly before she disappeared? Had she hailed any cabs? Did she have a Smar-Trip fare card for the city's subway system that might have recorded her train travel? Rossmo waited for weeks. Garrett was having a hard time filling in the blanks. Trainum told Rossmo he was having difficulty obtaining the answers from the Metropolitan Police Department. The detectives working the case declined to disclose any information about their open investigation.

16
PRIME TIME

Gary Condit and Connie Chung

After the FBI's top cold-case agent dismissed Gary Condit as a credible suspect in the Chandra Levy case, Abbe Lowell decided that the time had come to salvage what remained of his client's political career. Condit's son and daughter, Chad and Cadee, two of his closest advisers, believed that their father needed to launch a public relations campaign to put the past behind him. His colleagues on Capitol Hill agreed, and so did Lowell. Without an act of contrition and an explanation of why he had stayed silent in the face of the ferocious media pack all these months, there was no way he could ever retain his congressional seat.

Condit stood on the precipice of political ruin. Voters in California were losing their faith, and his hometown newspaper, the *Modesto Bee,* was calling for his resignation. The *Bee* had endorsed Condit in every political contest dating back to his days as the mayor of Ceres, but on August 12 the paper's editorial board declared that the congressman had "violated the public trust" and "knowingly hindered" the police investigation into Chandra's disappearance. "His self-absorption has been a lapse not only of judgment, but of human decency," the editorial board concluded. In what Condit perceived to be an act of betrayal, a former staff member considered running against him in the Democratic primary eight months away. At forty-two, Dennis Cardoza had once served as Condit's chief of staff in Sacramento and won a seat in the California State Assembly after Condit was elected to Congress. Cardoza had said he would not run for Condit's congressional seat unless his mentor retired, but the political landscape had suddenly changed.

Deep down, Condit didn't want to conduct a public relations campaign, but as distasteful as it was, he thought that his children, his political advisers, his party's leaders, and his lawyer might be right. Only one question remained: Which national newscast should he choose to carry his plea for political salvation? The nation's top anchors and media personalities clamored to provide Condit with a platform: Diane

Sawyer, Katie Couric, Ed Bradley, Connie Chung, Barbara Walters, Stone Phillips, Rita Cosby, Larry King. The anchors and their producers and bookers behaved like lobbyists, pleading with Lowell, cajoling him, penning personal notes, making their pitches for why they should be the one to get the exclusive interview. They made many of the same claims: Their own network was the best, the most watched; their program was fair, the others were not. Condit was sickened by the spectacle. He had come to despise the news media, first for eviscerating him and now for their groveling. It was unseemly, but he knew he needed at least one member of the pack to be on his side if he were to have any chance of remaining in Washington.

Of all the anchors and the media personalities vying for the interview, Connie Chung made her way to the front of the line. Since her days as a local television reporter in Washington, Chung had built a reputation for beating her competitors and bringing in the big interviews. Smart and dogged, she rose through the ranks of the broadcast news world, ascending to the *CBS Evening News* in 1993 as co-anchor with Dan Rather. Although the arrangement ended in acrimony two years later, Chung landed at ABC, where she was seen as the go-to correspondent for interview "gets." She thought there was nothing wrong with aggressively pursuing interviews with celebrities and newsmakers, as long as reporters didn't compromise their integrity. It was a cutthroat business, the increasingly crowded landscape populated by tabloid television shows, cable news programs, and mainstream TV magazines like hers, and interview gets meant big ratings, more advertising dollars, and guaranteed time slots. To succeed, Chung believed in walking a fine line between appearing sympathetic to the interview subject and not coming across as a shill.

Condit and his advisers considered their options. They thought a woman might ask softer questions, and Chung was not known for roughing up her interview subjects. She sounded earnest and came across as fair and forthright in her pitches. ABC's *Primetime Thursday* had millions of viewers, and Charles Gibson, a highly respected newsman, anchored the program from New York. Condit made his pick: The get would go to Chung. It was the biggest scoop since Barbara Walters convinced Monica Lewinsky to discuss her dalliances with President Bill Clinton in 1999, when 48.5 million people tuned in. On August 22, the day before his *Primetime* appearance, Condit wrote to his constituents. He wanted to explain why he had decided to take his case before a national television audience.

Dear Friends and Neighbors,

Chandra Levy has been missing for nearly four months.

I'm sorry that the pain the Levy family and Chandra's friends are feeling has grown worse with each passing day.

When Chandra's dad called me to tell me she was missing, he asked for my help. I contacted the police to see if a reward fund would help find her. They said it would, so I helped start one.

Since that day, and every day since, I have cooperated and worked with law enforcement to find Chandra. I invited the police to my apartment. I asked the FBI to help.

Despite my best attempts to help the police find Chandra, some in the media have criticized me for remaining "silent."

I have not been silent with those in charge of finding Chandra.

I have answered every single question asked by the police and FBI.

When tabloids turned the tragedy of

Chandra's disappearance into a spectacle and rumors were reported as facts, I decided that I would not discuss my private life in the media.

Some suggest that not talking with the media could mean I had something to do with Chandra's disappearance. I did not. I will be interviewed on television and hopefully I will be able to answer questions that help people understand.

It is not something I look forward to. But things have gone on long enough.

Before speaking to the media, I wanted to write to you. I have known so many of you for a long time. You know me to be hard working, committed to our issues and dedicated to my community and my family. I hope you also will understand that I am not perfect and have made my share of mistakes.

For 30 years as local Mayor, County Supervisor, State Assemblyman and Congressman, thousands of people have come to me with their personal problems.

A son in trouble, a mother in a nursing home, a job that was lost, a farm going broke, a mortgage that couldn't be paid.

And each time, people trusted that I would treat their problems with care.

I hope our relationship is strong enough

to endure all of this.

For now, I want my work in Congress to improve our communities. Please know that you can still bring me your concerns and your problems.

Thank you for the kindness you have shown Carolyn and my family.

Sincerely,
Gary Condit

The *Primetime* team packed its equipment and headed to the West Coast. Chung began to prepare her questions. Her producers and technicians set up for the interview, to be held in the house of a friend of the congressman on a ranch near his home in Ceres. They cleared furniture from the living room, rearranged the remaining pieces, put up stands of lights and filters, and snaked cables through the house, connecting the television cameras to monitors in a bedroom and to Gibson's anchor desk in New York.

The day of the interview, Lowell sat in the house and wondered whether he and his client had done the right thing. How would the congressman handle embarrassing questions about Chandra and the other women who had been romantically linked to him? Would he appear defensive and elusive? Would he be able to keep his composure, show empathy for Chandra and her family, and convince the public that he had done everything he could to help find her? Lowell had prepared Condit like a defendant before a jury trial. He rehearsed his client's testimony and put the congressman through a mock cross-examination. If his client was going to make a blunder, better that he do it in private than before millions of viewers.

Condit was nervous when he met Chung at his friend's home an hour before taping time. He told her that he was second-guessing his decision, and Chung took him for a walk along a tree-lined road on the ranch. She assured him everything would be all right, and he calmed down. By the time they returned to the house, he was ready for the interview. They sat down in the living room, facing each other in high-back chairs. Lowell was too nervous to stay in the same room; he retreated to a bedroom and sat in silence before a television monitor as the questioning began. Nearly 24 million people were tuned in.

"Congressman Condit, do you know what happened to Chandra Levy?"

"No, I do not."

"Did you have anything to do with her disappearance?"

"No, I didn't."

"Did you say anything or do anything that could have caused her to drop out of sight?"

"You know, Chandra and I never had a cross word."

"Do you have any idea if there was anyone who wanted to harm her?"

"No."

"Did you cause anyone to harm her?"

"No."

"Did you kill Chandra Levy?"

"I did not."

Condit started to reel, feeling as though he had been betrayed. Chung had assured him she wouldn't do a "gotcha" interview. He suddenly saw Chung as a hated foe, someone not to be trusted. He considered ending the interview, standing up, and walking off the makeshift set, but he knew he was trapped; he had to stay. He thought to himself: *I'm not going to cooperate. She could torture me, and I'm still not going to give her the interview she wants.* Chung continued.

"Can you describe your relationship? What exactly was your relationship with Chandra Levy?"

"Well, I met Chandra . . . last, uh, October. And, um, we became very close. I met her in Washington, D.C."

"Very close, meaning . . . ?"

"We had a close relationship. I liked her

291

very much."

"May I ask you, was it a sexual relation-ship?"

"Well, Connie, I've been married for thirty-four years, and uh, I've not been a . . . a perfect man, and I've made my share of mistakes. But um, out of respect for my family, and out of a specific request from the Levy family, I think it's best that I not get into those details uh, about Chandra Levy."

The interview quickly spiraled out of control. Chung hammered Condit, repeat-edly asking him about the nature of his relationship with Chandra and whether it was sexual. She wondered to herself, *Why won't he be more forthcoming, why is he stonewalling me, how much longer can I pursue this line of questioning?* Condit stuck to his talking points: He had nothing to do with Chandra's disappearance; he had co-operated fully with the police and the FBI; and his thoughts and prayers were with Chandra and her family. Chung continued to press.

"I'm simply asking you if it was more than just a friendship."

"Well, let me say, the details included they didn't know, didn't want to know what, how I felt about her, or how she felt about me.

So I'm trying to honor that. I'm try—"

"Forgive me, I —"

"And I think the . . . I think the American people understand that people are entitled to some privacy. I'm entitled to try to retain as much privacy as I can. The Levys are entitled to retain as much privacy on behalf of their daughter as they can. I'm going to honor that."

"But, but you are protecting your privacy, your family's privacy at the expense of a, of a woman who is missing."

"Well, that's not correct. That's not correct at all. Because I have cooperated with law enforcement. The people who are responsible for finding Chandra. No, I haven't held a news conference, and no, I don't do talk shows. But I have cooperated . . ."

"Forgive me, but we have gone over this area already."

"Well, I have cooperated."

"The police even said that you impeded the investigation. They do not believe that you have fully cooperated. In fact, the word from the police is that your lack of candor impeded the investigation."

"Well, I'm, I'm confused if you're making reference to Chief Ramsey's latest comments. Let me tell you, Connie, I have interviewed four times. I interviewed with the Metropolitan Police Department. I've interviewed a second time with the Metropolitan Police Department and the commander. I interviewed with the Department of Justice, the federal prosecutor, also with the MPD. I interviewed with the FBI. I allowed them to search my home, where they ripped up my carpet, they took the paint off the walls, they put the drains down the, the pipes."

"I understand."

"Now let me finish. I have, I . . . because this is a very important point. I have done everything, to the point where I've let them interview my staff, they've searched the cars . . ."

"Did you at any time ask the staff to lie?"

"I flew my wife . . . I flew my wife to Washington."

"Did you at any time ever ask your staff to lie?"

"Well, let me, let me finish this. Let me finish this. Because you're making the accusation, I think it's a very important one. That I have not been cooperative. And I'm puzzled by why the police chief would say that. I don't think there's anyone in Washington, D.C., who's been more cooperative in this investigation than myself. And I'm confused by why the police chief would say that. Several weeks before that, the chief and —"

"Because you didn't reveal the true nature of your relationship with Chandra Levy until the third interview."

"Well, that, that's just not correct. In every interview, I answered every question, gave every detail."

"So you're suggesting that the police didn't quite ask you the right questions?"

"No, I'm not suggesting that at all. I'm, I'm suggesting that, that you're, you're going on unnamed sources of the third interview of people who were not even in the room."

"But you can clear the air."

"And a lot . . . well, I'm clearing the air."

"You can clear the air now by, by revealing exactly what kind of relationship you had. Because it, isn't it obvious to you that it, when you're dealing with a missing persons case, that any relationship with the missing person is important for police, authorities to know?"

"Well, but you and I work under two different assumptions here, I think. I think it's my job to work for the people who . . . have the responsibility to find Chandra. Not to go out and do news conferences and do talk shows to talk about that."

"But are you . . . aren't you?"

"I worked with the law enforcement people in every step, provided them information in every interview, and gave up a lot of my civil liberties to make sure that they had all the information that they needed."

"But aren't you here to set the record straight?"

"I think I am setting the record straight."

"Would you like to tell the truth about the relationship with her?"

"I've told you and responded to, uh, the relationship question. And I think the American people, and people watching out there understand. I think they understand that . . . that I'm entitled to some of my privacy. My family's entitled to some of their privacy. And certainly the Levys are, as well."

The cause was lost. Condit could feel it all slip away — his seat, his career, the life he had before the frantic phone call he'd received from Robert Levy nearly four months earlier. Lowell could barely watch; it was too painful. He felt horrible that he had encouraged Condit to go on national television. Lowell felt an urge to pull the power cord connecting the cameras, to put a stop to the seemingly endless interview. Chung was handling the congressman like a prosecutor. What did Chandra say before she disappeared? Was she pregnant? Why did he dump the wristwatch box in a garbage can on the eve of the search of his apartment? Who gave him the watch? What was his relationship with her? What was his relationship with Anne Marie Smith? Did he ask her to obstruct justice? Condit appeared evasive as he tried to stick to his script.

Chung opened a new line of questioning.

"Um, why won't you take a polygraph test administered by the police? And why won't you cooperate with Chandra Levy's parents' investigators?"

"Well, let me say that, that uh . . . you know, this is sort of new to me. But when the polygraph issue came up —"

"What is sort of new to you?" Chung asked.

"This polygraph issue, in that uh . . . I'm not familiar with the polygraph people. But we went out to find the best."

"I understand."

"The best in the country."

"But why won't you take one . . . from the police?"

"We found the best in the country that . . . He trains the FBI agents who give the polygraph tests. And so we took the test. We passed the test. And his credibility is unchallenged by people in the industry. And I'm, I'm confused by the police chief's comment immediately after we take the polygraph test. He did not read the polygraph test. Uh, I think you'll find that people in the FBI now have seen the polygraph test, they can read the polygraph test, and it makes total sense to them. So we basically thought we were being helpful, just found the best guy we could find. And that's what we did. And I don't know if —"

"Why, why won't you cooperate with uh, the Levy family investigators? And why won't you take . . . if you, if you are guilty of no criminal wrongdoing, if you're not guilty of any criminal wrongdoing, why don't you take a polygraph test given by the police, and cooperate with Chandra Levy's —"

"But we've taken a polygraph test. And it, and it proves that I'm innocent. And it's by, it's by a . . . a guy who's one of the highest-regarded gentlemen in that field in the country."

"I understand. All right."

"And let me . . . on the investigate, the investigators with the Levys, um, we have offered information that we have on all the issues to the investigators. We have sent letters to them. They have not responded. Now I'm a little bit concerned about the sincerity of their requests, the investigators' requests, if they're not willing to take some of the information that we have, go through it, and see what it is they need. Once they go through it, if there's something that we can be helpful with, we . . . we're open to do that. But they need to be uh . . . they, they need to at least show that they're really interested in . . . finding out what we've already done, what's been said, what the investigation that we've been through says. And once they do that . . . I, we, we're open to . . . talk to them."

"All right."

"But, but we just don't want it to be a TV show, or, or sort of . . . sort of publicity stunt."

"We have just a few minutes left. Uh, what has all of this done to you and your family?"

"Well, it's been tough. I mean, it's been tough on my family. Uh, we, we've gone through tough times. I mean, as I mentioned, uh . . . they dragged my wife across the country for an interview, because they refused to do it here, and they were going to subpoena her. They tried to uh, go through her medical records, uh, they reported she didn't have thumbs, and they chased my children around. The tabloids have. But the fact of the matter is, is this is not about the Condits. This is about the Levys. And that's minor . . . minor pain, and that's minor . . . uh, interference with our life, compared to what . . . Dr. and Mrs. Levy are going through. Sympathy and our hearts go to Dr. and Mrs. Levy. Not the stuff that we've gone through."

"Uh . . . do you . . . I, I . . . at the end of this interview, we're, we're . . . we only have a few minutes left. Uh . . . do you fear that uh, the public out there um, may be very disappointed that you didn't come forward and reveal details today, as we sit here to-night?"

"Well, I think I have revealed details. The details that I've been fully cooperative uh, with law enforcement. I've answered every question on every occasion. I've given up my civil liberties . . ."

"You don't think you're stonewalling?"

"No, I don't think I'm stonewalling at all. I think that people expect that you can maintain some of your privacy. I think the Levys expect to maintain some of their daughter's privacy. And I'm trying to honor that. I'm trying to do that with dignity. I, I'm trying to retain some privacy for my family and for their family. And I think your jurors out there will understand that."

"I'm, I, I would think that many people would want you to maintain your privacy. However, you have constituents out there, something like six hundred . . . six hundred and eighty thousand. Do they deserve the truth?"

"They deserve the truth. And the truth is that I have done everything asked of me by the people who are responsible to find Chandra Levy. I have done everything. I've given you the list. I mean, I have not been part of the media circus if, if that's your point. But it's not the news media's responsibility to find Chandra Levy. It's law enforcement. And I made a decision that I would work with law enforcement to do just that."

"What do you think happened to Chandra Levy?"

"I don't know."

"You have virtually no idea?"

"No idea."

"Can you survive, can your career, your marriage, survive this?"

"Well, my, my family's intact. It's going to take more than the news media . . . with, with innuendos, half-truths, unnamed sources, to, to split my family up."

301

"But . . . isn't much of what has happened partly your doing?"

"In what respect, Connie?"

"You said to. . . . yourself, to your constituents, in a letter, that you've made mistakes, and you said that to me earlier."

"Right."

"What mistakes are you talking about?"

"Well, I haven't been a perfect man. And I think people, your viewers will understand that. I have not been a perfect man. I've made mistakes in my life. I acknowledge that."

"But what mistakes are you talking about? Are you talking about moral mistakes?"

"Well, there's a variety of mistakes. I mean, I, I've made . . . uh, all kinds of mistakes in my life, but I'm not going to go into details on this program about the mistakes that I've made in my life."

"Do you, do you . . ."

"I acknowledge them. And I'm sorry for them."

"Do you think you're a moral man?"

"I think I am a moral man. Yes."

"Okay. Um, I think we are out of time, Gary. Thank you so much, Congressman Condit."

"Thank you."

"Thank you, I appreciate it."

"Thank you."

The interview had lasted thirty-one minutes. It felt like an eternity. Chung and Condit stood from their chairs and Lowell approached his client. He told him he had done the most difficult thing in his career and he should be proud of himself. Privately, Lowell was furious. He thought Chung had behaved like an interrogator, not an interviewer, that she'd treated the congressman as though he was a suspect in the case. Chung thought she had done her job. She asked the tough questions and held the congressman's feet to the fire. Still, she was drained by the intensity of the interview and wondered how it played on television. Off the air, Lowell watched as Gibson appeared on the monitor from New York. "You go, girl!" he told Chung.

For Chung, the interview turned out to be one of the best gets of her career. It was the most watched television show of the summer and the most viewed news program since Walters interviewed Lewinsky. Chung outperformed her previous big interview, when she sat down in 1995 with the mother of Newt Gingrich, who had engineered the Republican takeover of the House. Chung leaned in and asked Kathleen Gingrich what her son thought of First Lady Hillary

Clinton. Gingrich hesitated. With 15 million people watching, Chung urged her: "Why don't you just whisper it to me, just between you and me." Gingrich replied: "She's a bitch."

The ratings of the Condit interview tied another big get in terms of ratings — Chung's exclusive with figure skater Tonya Harding on the eve of the 1994 Winter Olympics, after Harding had been accused of taking part in a plot to maim her Gold Medal rival, Nancy Kerrigan. But for Condit, the interview was an absolute disaster. Media pundits and public relations specialists said that he appeared evasive and behaved like a guilty man. Robert and Susan Levy were appalled. They said they had made no "specific request" that Condit be discreet about their daughter. Condit knew he should have gone with his gut; he never really wanted to go on national television. He believed he hadn't done anything wrong. He had told the police and the FBI everything he knew, and no good would ever come from talking to the news media. The *Primetime* gamble, he realized, had probably cost him his career.

Nineteen days after the interview, the satellite TV trucks parked along Robert and

Susan Levy's street suddenly pulled away. It was early on a Tuesday morning, near dawn on the West Coast. The trucks had been camped outside most of the summer. Susan Levy had been planning to fly to Chicago that day for an appearance on the *Oprah* show, then to New York for an interview on the *Today* show. She never made it to the airport. A friend from the East Coast called. Susan turned on the television and watched the historic news unfolding in words and images that would become tragically iconic: A pair of passenger planes had hit the World Trade Center; another had slammed into the Pentagon, and a fourth had crashed into a field in Pennsylvania. Instantly, on that bright September morning, the story about the intern and the congressman was simply no longer a story.

17
A SATELLITE ISSUE

Ingmar Guandique

Five months after the attacks of September 11, downtown Washington looked as though it had been transformed into the set of an apocalyptic action film. Soldiers clad in full battle gear guarded the U.S. Capitol. Military vehicles surrounded government buildings and installations. Police officers halted taxicabs and trucks at security checkpoints; bomb-sniffing dogs checked for explosives. Heavily armored Humvees took up positions near the entrances to the Pentagon, their machine gun turrets trained on the traffic lanes of the George Washington Parkway that skirted the banks of the Potomac River.

Far from the chaos of a city still on high alert, in a quiet third-floor courtroom near Pennsylvania Avenue, on the afternoon of February 8, 2002, Ingmar Guandique sat behind a wooden defense table and waited to learn the punishment he would face for attacking two women in Rock Creek Park. Guandique listened to a translator as Assistant U.S. Attorney Kristina Ament told the judge about the twists and turns of what she called one of the strangest cases of her career.

Ament explained that there was a confidential matter she needed to discuss before Guandique could be sentenced for his crimes. With no newspaper or television reporters present in the courtroom, Ament proceeded to tell D.C. Superior Court judge Noël Anketell Kramer what police and prosecutors had kept secret from the public: Guandique's name had come up in connection with the disappearance of Chandra Levy.

In mid-September 2001, a lawyer for a man being held in the D.C. Jail called the U.S. attorney's office in Washington. He said an inmate at the jail, Ingmar Guandique, told his client that he had murdered Chandra in Rock Creek Park. On September 21, U.S. marshals removed Guandique from his cell and brought him to the U.S. attorney's office for questioning by prosecutors and D.C. detectives. Guandique, accompanied by a public defender, was shown a picture of Chandra. He denied knowing anything about her and said that the only place he had ever seen the missing intern was on television.

He had told a different story to the man he met in the D.C. Jail that summer, Ramón Alvarez. Like Guandique, Alvarez was from El Salvador. He had befriended Guandique during language classes. Both men were waiting to be sentenced: Alvarez for armed sexual assault, Guandique for his attacks on Halle Shilling and Christy Wiegand in Rock Creek Park. Alvarez told his lawyer that he ran into Guandique on August 26 in the gym of the jail while their cell block was being fumigated. Guandique seemed depressed. After some small talk about their criminal pasts, Guandique confided that he had murdered the woman whose picture was being splashed repeatedly on television news reports.

Guandique said more: A congressman named Gary Condit had paid him to do it. He said he didn't realize who Condit was until later, when he saw the congressman's picture on TV. According to his story, Guandique was walking in the Adams Morgan neighborhood when a car pulled to the curb. Condit offered him money — twenty-five thousand dollars — to murder a woman. The congressman provided him with a picture of Chandra and a location where he

311

could find her. Alvarez said that Guandique had told him that he took drugs and drank alcohol to steel himself for the attack. He then went to the location that Condit had provided and saw Chandra running on a path. Guandique hid in the bushes. When Chandra circled back, he jumped out and attacked her, stabbing her in the neck and the stomach. She fell to the ground, and Guandique carried her body deep into the woods. He scooped out a hole in the forest floor with his hands and covered Chandra with dirt and leaves and sticks. He said he left the knife in her body and later considered retrieving it, but he never did. Guandique sent the twenty-five thousand dollars to his family in El Salvador.

Alvarez told his lawyer he wanted to come forward because he felt badly for Chandra's parents after seeing them on TV. The prosecutors and detectives weren't sure what to make of Alvarez's story. They thought the claim that Condit had hired Guandique was farfetched, but they wondered whether Guandique still might have been involved in her disappearance. Could he have embellished his account, adding the part about Condit to make himself seem particularly tough in the violent confines of the D.C. Jail?

On September 24, three days after the meeting with Guandique in the U.S. attorney's office, D.C. detectives Ralph Durant and Lawrence Kennedy wrote a report detailing information they had in their files on Guandique.

The detectives said they had received a tip about Guandique two months earlier. They wrote in the September report that they received information on July 20 from the U.S. Park Police that a Hispanic man had accosted a woman named Karen Mosley in Rock Creek Park. The twenty-nine-year-old massage therapist was walking her dog along a path not far from the Peirce Mill, on a day near the end of May, several weeks after Chandra vanished. Mosley heard some rustling in the brush on the hillside above. At first she thought it was another dog, but she looked up to see a man exposing himself. Mosley's dog began to bark, and the man took off into the woods. She ran back to the mill and called the police from a pay phone. Mosley provided a Park Police officer with a description of the man — young, Hispanic, no shirt, denim shorts. Police searched the park, but the man had fled.

On July 24, four days after learning of Mosley's encounter, the D.C. detectives wrote in their report that they contacted the

Park Police for more information. They were told that a man matching the description in the Mosley case had been arrested after attacking two women in the park. The assailant's name was Ingmar Adalid Guandique, and he was being held in the D.C. Jail. The chief of detectives, Jack Barrett, said he contacted the U.S. attorney's office and asked that prosecutors remove Guandique from jail so his detectives could interview him. Barrett thought the prosecutors were too fixated on Condit. By the end of the summer, they still hadn't arranged the interview. Barrett's detectives weren't able to talk to Guandique until the September meeting in the U.S. attorney's office.

Now, with an explosive but unverifiable allegation on their hands, the prosecutors and detectives were not sure how to proceed. They decided to polygraph Alvarez and Guandique. On November 28, Alvarez, who spoke little English, took his exam at the U.S. attorney's office. He failed. The results of the FBI-administered polygraph test showed that he was "deceptive" when he answered yes to two questions: "Did Guandique tell you he stabbed Chandra Levy?" and "Did Guandique tell you he received twenty-five thousand dollars from a congressman for stabbing Chandra Levy?"

Nearly ten weeks later, on February 4, 2002, Guandique took his polygraph. When asked by the FBI examiner whether he was involved in Chandra's disappearance and if he caused her disappearance, Guandique answered no. The readings were inconclusive, but the official result was listed as "not deceptive." It was a judgment call made by the polygraph examiner, reflecting his interpretation of the results. Because polygraphs are not a precise science, examiners have latitude to draw their own conclusions. It was the examiner's prerogative to score Guandique as "not deceptive."

Polygraphs can be a useful law enforcement tool, but the results are not admissible in court because they are considered too unreliable. There was another problem with the polygraph exams in the Chandra case: Neither Alvarez nor Guandique spoke much English, and the FBI polygraph examiners were not bilingual. A translator was used for both exams, a variable that can compromise test results. Polygraph equipment measures minute changes in breathing, sweating, and other bodily functions. If the polygraph examiner and the translator are not in sync, the test results can be skewed. Barrett wanted a Spanish-speaking polygraph examiner to administer both exams, but he would have been forced to wait; the FBI was focused on terrorism, and Guandique was not a priority within the bureau. With Guandique's sentencing hearing coming up, Barrett and the prosecutors didn't have the time to wait.

Four days after taking his polygraph, Guandique appeared in Judge Kramer's courtroom and sat next to his court-appointed lawyer, D.C. public defender Gladys Joseph. A presentence report noted that Guandique had a wide range of behavioral, alcohol, and drug problems. In a twelve-page report to Judge Kramer, the court officer who wrote the report issued a warning:

His arrest history shows that the defendant has transitioned from the role of victim to that of predator, and it is quite clear that he is becoming more psychopathic in his behavior. The defendant appears to be targeting victims that can be overpowered, as well as carefully selecting the location of his crime to minimize the possibility of witnesses and his chances of getting caught. His employment history dissuades from believing that the value of the stolen objects is the motivating factor, but rather, the defendant appears to be drawing some kind of satisfaction in attacking helpless victims. . . . Although he admitted that he feels bad about his behavior after the crime is committed, it is alarming how he can block out any concern for the victim, much less control urges to take their property.

Guandique's explanation of his behavior was disturbing. He told the court officer during his interview for the presentence report:

I feel bad about what I did. I am repentant for what I did. When I'm about to commit an offense, I tell myself to go ahead and do it, but afterwards, I feel bad about it. I feel good when I see someone alone and carrying something of value on their person because it makes it easy for me to take it from them. Then it crosses my mind, that after doing it so many times, I will eventually get caught. Sometimes, I cannot control myself when I see someone alone in a secluded area with something of value.

Equally troubling was Guandique's performance on a battery of tests administered by a court-appointed psychologist. On a Beta III exam, a standard intelligence assessment in use for nearly a century, Guandique scored in the second percentile for men in his age group. In nearly every testing category — verbal, nonverbal, neurocognitive — he scored at the extreme low end of the scale. Guandique also exhibited deep psychological problems. The psychologist who evaluated him said he appeared to be experiencing symptoms of depression: feelings of hopelessness, worthlessness, failure, and profound sadness. Other times he exhibited signs of an overly elevated mood, accelerated thoughts, and a disorganized approach to routine tasks and activities. His performance on the exams also showed that he was experiencing anxiety-like symptoms, including fear and tension. Guandique complained of uncontrollable sweating, trembling, and shortness of breath. The psychologist concluded that the symptoms were indicative of a major mental disorder marked by hallucinations, flashbacks, magical thinking, and delusional beliefs.

As the sentencing hearing continued, the prosecutor told Judge Kramer that Guandique had been a cooperative defendant. Ament said that Guandique had voluntarily spoken to prosecutors and police about the

Chandra Levy case as part of his agreement to plead guilty to two reduced counts of assault with intent to commit robbery, and that he had passed a polygraph exam when asked if he knew anything about her disappearance.

"In other words, there's no suggestion that he is involved in the Chandra Levy case?" Kramer asked.

"There is no suggestion at this point now that he is involved. And his polygraph went a long way in defusing the suggestion," Ament said. "I do believe, as does Ms. Joseph, that he should receive credit for the fact he voluntarily did come in and submit to a polygraph examination in that case, which he was not required to do under the plea agreement."

Ament also told Judge Kramer that no one from the U.S. attorney's office had demanded that Guandique take the polygraph as a precondition to his sentencing, an accusation that Guandique's lawyer, Joseph, had included in a memorandum to the judge.

"I want to tell you something both candidly, on the record," Judge Kramer said. "This is such a satellite issue. This is a serious case. I never for a moment thought that he had anything, after reading your memo, that he had anything to do with Chandra Levy. Just to me it doesn't have anything to do with this case."

Joseph tried to persuade the judge to give her client a light sentence. She asserted that Guandique's only motive was robbery, that he never intended to harm Shilling or Wiegand, and she disputed their accounts that her client had a knife during the attacks.

"Mr. Guandique was trying to get a Walkman and go. And really just did something incredibly stupid, and incredibly dangerous, even to himself," Joseph said.

Ament challenged the public defender's explanation.

Your honor, this defendant claims that all he intended to do was to take a Walkman. But in neither case did he take a Walkman that was readily available to him. So while he might have wanted to take property from these women, it would be the view of the government that the evidence shows that there was more going on than that, not that that wasn't part of it, but that he wanted to terrorize them and made a plan that allowed him to do that. The government does not believe that the complainants were mistaken when they claim that he held a knife. And although Mr. Guandique argues through counsel that they had no injuries consistent with having a knife brandished at them, they never said that they were cut. They said it was held to them, to threaten them, to get them to do what Mr. Guandique wanted. The government does not believe that either victim was mistaken about that. But the fact there are two of them who describe the same thing only serves to reinforce it.

I don't know if Mr. Guandique intended to hurt them, to rape them, to simply scare them, but he intended and he did act as a predator. In both cases, as the court will note, he watched, he followed, and he picked the location at which he was going to accost the women. He picked places that were isolated, and if you remember from Ms. Shilling's statement, she talks about screaming even knowing the cars in that location would drown out the noise of her screams. Those things were planned, Your Honor. At least he took an opportunity and made it so these women would be, the isolation would be maximized in these cases. And as I said before, we can only be glad that they were able to fight him off and that no one had to discover what it was that he really intended to do had he had his way with them.

Judge Kramer then asked Shilling and Wiegand if they had anything to say before she sentenced Guandique. Shilling was eight months pregnant, fighting off a cold, feeling exhausted. She wasn't really up to talking, but she wanted the judge to know that she didn't believe Guandique was interested in robbing her. She thought he wanted to rape her and she wanted him to receive as much time behind bars as possible. Shilling walked past a low, curved wooden wall that divided the well of the courtroom from the benches set aside for spectators, stood several feet away from Guandique, and began to read her statement:

Good afternoon, your Honor. Thank you for giving me an opportunity to speak. I would just like to say that, though I understand my attacker pled guilty to assault and attempted robbery, I reject the notion that he intended to simply rob me. This attack was a physical one, pure and simple. He stalked me for a mile. He attacked me with a knife. We struggled on the ground. He left my valuables on the path when he fled. I do not doubt for a second that, given the chance, he would repeat this crime against another woman. I would request that this person be given the harshest possible sentence for his crime and that he lose the privilege of living in this country. Thank you for your time.

Wiegand spoke next:

I'm very grateful to be here today and to be able to stand before you without ongoing physical injuries. But I also want to say that being attacked by Mr. Guandique was a terrifying experience, and it changed me, and it changed how I will view the world. I completely agree with the other victim, that given the opportunity, Mr. Guandique will attack another woman. I don't think that he should be given the opportunity to do this to someone else or to do it to me again or do it to the other victim. So I, too, would ask that you award him the maximum sentence.

Judge Kramer asked Guandique if he had anything to say. Through an interpreter, he said: "Well, I would like to ask the judge for forgiveness. And also of the two people I assaulted. I am sincerely repentant for the two offenses I committed. And please give me another chance in order so that I would be able to work and help my family. Thank you for listening to these words."

Judge Kramer was perplexed by the circumstances of the case. As the deputy presiding judge of the criminal division of the D.C. Superior Court, where nearly half of her cases involved robbery, she told Ament and Joseph that she had seen nothing quite like it.

It fits no pattern. Other than robberies that may have occurred because of a grudge, most robberies take place, particularly those on the street outside, relatively quickly. The purpose is to get the property and run, and escape, and not be caught. Now, I am not here to say that Mr. Guandique had no intention of robbing either victim of property, but that is only a beginning. It is not usual if one wants to grab a Walkman to pick someone and trail them and then drag them off and fight with them in this way. And, Ms. Joseph, you make a good point. There appears to be absolutely none of the indicia of a sexual assault. There was no fondling of the breasts as far as I know; there was no effort to pull off clothes. There was no effort to take off his clothes. So, it may be that this had nothing to do with assault of a sexual nature.

But I do agree with Ms. Ament's comment that Mr. Guandique acted as a real predator here. He went out of his way to struggle, to have a physical encounter with each of these women. And another interesting part of this is that now that I have seen each victim, and neither one is one that you would think of as easy prey. So, I'm left to wonder, as we all wonder, what was really going on here.

Guandique faced thirteen years on each assault charge: a total of twenty-six years behind bars in a federal penitentiary. Both the defense attorney and the prosecutor asked the judge to give Guandique credit for cooperating with the police and for taking the polygraph exam. At the conclusion of the thirty-eight-minute hearing, Judge Kramer announced her sentence: ten years in federal prison.

18
A GRISLY FIND

Charles H. Ramsey

Robert and Susan Levy sat side by side on a sofa in their white-brick ranch house in Modesto early on the morning of May 22, 2002. Bright television camera lights bathed the living room as their images were beamed across the country to Chicago, where Oprah Winfrey was taping her nationally syndicated show.

After the terror attacks, it seemed as though the world had forgotten about Chandra, but her parents still anxiously waited for any scrap of information about their daughter. With nothing but silence, they tried to rekindle media interest in the case. It had been a year and three weeks since Chandra disappeared, and Winfrey welcomed the Levys on her program. She asked the couple whether they believed Gary Condit knew what had happened to their daughter.

"Oh yes," Susan said. "I think he does."

For Condit, the inevitable had taken place; two months earlier, the six-term congressman suffered a particularly painful loss to his former chief of staff, Dennis Cardoza, in the Democratic primary, losing by an embarrassing 18-point margin. His once-promising political career was over. Condit downplayed the loss. "Look, it's just an election," he told reporters. "You guys are making this overdramatic. Things happen to you in life that you can't explain. Whatever happens, happens. I'll do something else."

The Levys told Winfrey that it was unlikely their daughter would be found alive, but Robert, who wore a button displaying Chandra's photo, said that as a parent he had to maintain hope. After the interview, Susan crawled into Chandra's bed. It offered some faint comfort, a feeling of being close to her missing daughter as she curled in the sheets and drifted to sleep.

Across the country, *Washington Post* reporter Sari Horwitz was having breakfast with Executive Assistant Police Chief Terrance Gainer at Reeves Restaurant & Bakery, a downtown institution for nearly a hundred years, known for its strawberry pies and blueberry doughnuts.

Post Metropolitan Editor Jo-Ann Armao had just given Horwitz a new assignment:

Find out whatever became of the Chandra Levy investigation. Armao knew that Horwitz was fascinated by the story and wanted to work on it the year before, but was working on a different investigation with her colleague Scott Higham. Armao told her to take a month to see what she could find out. One of her first calls was to Gainer. She had known him for about four years, ever since he came to Washington from Chicago. They decided to meet for breakfast on the morning of May 22. But as Gainer ate his scrambled eggs, he said he was not optimistic. He had no new information and suggested that Horwitz find another story. The investigation was at an impasse; only a lucky break could restart it. Either "somebody dimes somebody out," he said, "or we find the body."

As they talked, Gainer's pager went off. He politely ignored it. A few minutes later, it vibrated again. He continued to talk and it went off yet again. Horwitz jokingly told Gainer that maybe he should check his messages. It sounded like something was going on. Gainer finished his breakfast and stepped outside to his police cruiser. When he returned, he seemed stunned. He said someone might have just found the remains of Chandra Levy in Rock Creek Park.

At about 8:30 that morning, 11:30 on the East Coast, Susan Levy awoke to the sound of the phone ringing and climbed out of bed to answer it in the hallway. The call was from the D.C. police department. The remains of a woman had just been discovered in Washington. Police might have finally found her daughter. Susan slumped to the floor. She sobbed so hard she could barely catch her breath.

U.S. Park Police Sergeant Dennis Bosak was the first to respond to the call from Philip Palmer, the bone collector. At first Bosak thought that the man might have stumbled on the remains of a Santeria ceremony. In recent years, the religion that combines practices from West Africa, Cuba, and Brazil had attracted several thousand people in the Washington area with its belief in spirit possession, divination, and animal sacrifice. Bosak had seen evidence of Santeria gatherings in the park before — candles, bones, and the heads of goats and roosters.

At the tree branch where Palmer had previously hung his sweatshirt, he and Bosak climbed up the steep ravine. It was covered with tall, leafy trees that blocked much of the sunlight. Bosak's eyes followed the line of the forest floor as it sloped up to the Western Ridge Trail. Bosak walked to the spot Palmer had marked with his dog's blue leash. He looked at the top of the skull. At first he couldn't tell whether it was human. Bosak took out an extendable baton and rolled it over. He saw teeth and what appeared to be bone cartilage on the bridge of the nose. He ordered Palmer to step back and sit down on a log ten yards away.

Bosak knew instantly that this was not the scene of a Santeria ceremony. On the ground around him, he saw pieces of clothing: a pair of black thong underwear turned inside out, a red Aero sports bra, a pair of ProSpirit black stretch pants, also turned inside out, each leg knotted at the bottom. Nearby lay a black Aiwa AM/FM radio/cassette player. Bones of all sizes were scattered about the site. He saw a dirty gray T-shirt with red lettering: PROPERTY OF USC ATHLETICS. Could this be Chandra Levy, the missing intern from California? he wondered.

Bosak had another thought: Was Ingmar Guandique responsible? The isolated scene was eerily similar to a site Bosak knew well, near Beach Drive in Rock Creek Park, where Guandique had attacked Christy Wiegand a year earlier. Bosak had worked that case, along with Park Police detective Joe Green. Both scenes involved isolated

333

ravines and Walkman radios. D.C. detective Lawrence Kennedy would later take a statement from Bosak.

"Does this scene remind you of any other crime scene that you have been on?" Kennedy asked.

"Yes. The attempted sexual assault case involving Guandique."

"What about this site is reminiscent?"

"Coming from the top of the hill from where the skull was found going towards the creek, the characteristics of the Beach Drive Guandique assault were similar to the Levy crime scene," Bosak said. "Both involved hillsides, both involved Walkman radios, the sliding down the hills, and the location of the clothes."

Within hours of Bosak's arrival, Broad Branch Road was under siege. Word had spread inside the D.C. police department, the FBI, the U.S. attorney's office, and newsrooms across the nation. Television camera crews, satellite trucks, TV anchors, reporters, and photographers descended on the quiet, well-to-do neighborhood of Forest Hills, which bordered Rock Creek Park. It was a clear, 60-degree spring day, and police cordoned off the busy road with yellow ribbons of crime-scene tape. Police officers and technicians from the Mobile Crime

Unit scrambled up the hillside — not far from Glover Road, the Western Ridge Trail, and the Grove 17 picnic area where the recruits had searched ten months earlier. Toward the top of the hill, they found sunglasses. As they moved farther down from the trail, they spotted a white Reebok jogging shoe, trimmed in blue, more bones and headphones. The largest concentration of items and remains were strewn down the side of the ravine in a ten-yard radius from the base of a tree, seventy-nine yards from the top of the Western Ridge Trail. They began videotaping the scene and marking the locations of the bones they found with tiny flags. D.C. police chief Charles Ramsey and Gainer arrived at the scene. So did the detectives in charge of the case, along with Brad Garrett from the FBI.

Shortly after 2:30 that afternoon, Ramsey addressed the reporters assembled along Broad Branch Road. The media was in a full-blown, live-team-coverage frenzy. "We do not know the identity of the person that we've found," Ramsey told the pack. "It could be someone else."

The chief's cautious words failed to tamp down speculation that Chandra had been found. Stories about terrorist threats against the Brooklyn Bridge, a suicide bomber in the Middle East, and President Bush's trip to Europe were wiped off the television screen at noon by the discovery in Rock Creek Park. As though caught in a flashback, the old, familiar images flooded the airways: home videos of Chandra, Condit being pursued by reporters on Capitol Hill, the Levys' anguished pleas, the "missing" poster and childhood snapshots of Chandra. Maps of Rock Creek Park replaced maps of Afghanistan. Reporters staked out the Rayburn House Office Building, where Condit was finishing out his term. Television trucks reappeared outside Chandra's apartment building in Dupont Circle, about four miles from the crime scene. Tied to a tree in front was a faded yellow ribbon.

D.C. medical examiner Jonathan Arden joined the police officers and crime-scene technicians on the hillside. From the scattered bones that were being photographed and marked by police, Arden took the single most important find: the skull. He brought it back to his office on the grounds of D.C. General Hospital in southeast Washington and retrieved Chandra's dental records, which her parents had provided the year before. Teeth are the hardest mineral in the body and do not decompose. They are as unique as fingerprints and DNA. The root canals, the spacings, the fillings, and the crowns amount to a personal signature. Arden X-rayed the skull and hung the exposed film on a light screen next to the dental records. He stepped back and forth, comparing the two jawlines. He turned to the half-dozen police and federal investigators who had crowded into his small office.

"It's her," he said.

Late that afternoon, Ramsey returned to Broad Branch Road and stood before the pack of reporters. He had grim news to announce: Dental records confirmed that the remains belonged to Chandra.

A reporter called out: Didn't the police search this area of Rock Creek Park last year?

"It's possible to search and not find," Ramsey said.

In the days that followed, D.C. Mobile Crime Unit technicians and police recruits conducted what amounted to an archaeological dig. They sifted through layers of the forest floor in the remote section of the park for evidence of how Chandra died and who might be involved. Aided by an archaeologist from the National Park Service and a forensic anthropologist from the Smithsonian Institution, they combed through the dirt and leaves for clues. Cadaver dogs were brought in to help. The police department borrowed lights from the National Guard to continue their search after night fell. On May 28, Arden called a news conference to announce that he had ruled Chandra's death a homicide. Her cause of death: "undetermined." He said he couldn't tell how Chandra was murdered from the skeletal remains, which had been exposed for more than a year and were void of tissue. There were no bullet holes, slash or stab marks on her bones, no depressions or fractures to her skull. Arden also said he couldn't determine whether Chandra was strangled, because his examination of the hyoid bone, a small, fragile U-shaped bone in the upper neck that usually fractures under pressure, was inconclusive. "It is possible we will never know the specific injury that caused her death," he said.

That same day, back in California, nearly a thousand friends, relatives, and residents of Modesto had gathered for a memorial service for Chandra in a downtown auditorium. At the entrance to the service were silver tureens filled with Reese's Peanut Butter Cups. Flowers came from as far away as Finland. The Modesto police chief attended, along with the county sheriff. Flight attendant Anne Marie Smith came to pay her respects. Chandra's twenty-year-old brother, Adam, addressed the crowd. "I feel Chandra's presence every day. She will never be lost; she will always remain in our hearts and in our minds."

Inside Chandra's Washington apartment building, the fading poster of the missing intern taped up near the mailboxes had been taken down. Two weeks after Chandra's remains were found, the two private investigators hired by the Levy family — retired D.C. homicide detectives Dwayne Stanton and J. T. "Joe" McCann — drove to Rock Creek Park. On the morning of June 6, after the D.C. police had concluded their search of the crime scene and reopened that section of the park, Stanton and McCann went to have a look on their own. After all the police missteps the summer before, they didn't trust that the department had conducted a thorough search. Wearing jeans and T-shirts, they came equipped with a shovel, an ax, and two rakes, and they allowed *Post* reporter Horwitz to accompany them. Horwitz had met the pair in the late 1980s while she was covering the police department and they were working as homicide detectives. After Chandra's remains were found, she contacted Stanton and Mc-

Cann, and when they decided to examine the crime scene for themselves, she asked if she could come along.

Horwitz met them in a pull-off along Glover Road near the Grove 17 picnic area and they walked down the Western Ridge Trail. The path was silent, except for the occasional snap of a twig. About three minutes down the path, they turned left and headed down the steep wooded hillside toward the creek and Broad Branch Road. They spotted a tiny police flag that said "shoe" and came across a long metal spike, spray-painted orange, that had been driven into the ground near the location of Chandra's skull. An hour and a half into their search, McCann began to examine an area about twenty-five yards from the spike. McCann's rake scraped against a twelve-to-fourteen-inch bone embedded in the dirt beneath the leaves. Yellow-brown in color, it appeared damaged, as though an animal had chewed it on both ends. McCann and Stanton contacted their former employer, the D.C. police department. Instead of sending the Mobile Crime Unit, the police department dispatched Detective Ralph Durant. The encounter was awkward. Durant was not happy that two former D.C. homicide detectives hired by the Levy family were searching his crime scene. Durant reached down and picked up the bone. He said it looked like it came from an animal, slipped it into a bag, and walked away.

Later that night, after examining the bone, Arden confirmed that it was Chandra's left tibia, the second-largest bone in the body. Somehow the police department had missed it. The department's public affairs office issued a press release that said there was a "strong possibility" that forest animals had moved the bone. "It appears that department technicians did not pass over the bone during the original search," the release said. "There appears to be a greater likelihood that the bone was reintroduced into the area by wildlife."

Ramsey was furious. The chief demanded to know how his crime-scene technicians had missed it. He launched an internal review and lit into a police commander who pleaded with Ramsey to go to the isolated spot in the woods where the bone was found so he could see for himself the difficult terrain — the fallen trees, the slippery carpet of dead leaves, the low branches and tangled underbrush that made footing difficult on the incline, sometimes as steep as 45 degrees. The chief was uninterested in excuses or explanations. He was familiar with the area. He said he didn't need to see the exact spot where the bone was found. Ramsey and his deputies couldn't believe that Mc-Cann and Stanton had found something their search teams had missed. The detectives on the case summoned McCann to police headquarters, where they questioned the veracity of his story. Unconvinced, they asked McCann to take a polygraph exam. McCann refused, insulted by the insinuation that he had tampered with a crime scene. The detectives then turned their attention to the man who found Chandra's skull. They questioned Palmer, asking him whether he might have taken the bone and returned it when he realized it was part of a crime scene. In a statement videotaped by police, Palmer denied ever seeing the bone.

The discovery of Chandra's tibia was deeply embarrassing for Ramsey. The idea that a large bone belonging to Chandra had been somehow overlooked raised troubling questions about how thoroughly and systematically the scene had been searched. *Washington Post* columnist Marc Fisher wrote a scathing piece the next day, ridiculing the police department and urging Ramsey to invest in an "efficient, heavy duty, fully warrantied, American-made garden rake." During the initial searches of the park the year before, the police had missed finding Chandra. Now scores of crime-scene technicians and police officers had missed her tibia. What else did they miss? Ramsey sent the search teams back into the woods, along with a zoologist, to explore animal burrows and other locations that might have been overlooked.

Once again police cordoned off the hillside. Technicians and police recruits spent the next nineteen days digging and raking. They found more bones scattered around the site: small bones from Chandra's hands, feet, and back. They found her heel bone — and they found her femur, the largest bone in the body. It was discovered 170 feet west of the crime scene. Once again, Ramsey blamed woodland creatures. "Animals got hold of the bones," he said. "They're scattered all over. They're pulling them out of burrows."

After Chandra's remains were found, Amy Keller, a writer for the Capitol Hill newspaper *Roll Call,* had a story idea. Maybe the focus on Condit was misplaced after all, and Chandra had been the victim of a random attack in the park. Keller went online and began to search databases about crimes committed in Rock Creek Park. She came across the name of Ingmar Guandique, and discovered that the Salvadoran immigrant was serving a ten-year sentence for attacking two young women in the park around the time of Chandra's May 1 disappearance. The first attack had taken place that same month, the second two months later. Keller wrote a story about her findings and other members of the press corps picked up her piece. Condit's new Los Angeles–based attorney, celebrity lawyer Mark Geragos, said: "I certainly would like to know, as a lot of people would, where was this man on April 30 and May 1?" But both Ramsey and Gainer downplayed Guandique as a suspect. "The press is making too big a deal of it," Ramsey said. Gainer went further. He said he never believed Guandique had anything to do with Chandra's disappearance. If Guandique were a prime suspect, he told reporters, the police would have been on him "like flies on honey."

At police headquarters, investigators were scrambling. The location of Chandra's remains, the details of the crime scene, and the appearance of a violent struggle all seemed to point toward Guandique. The detectives and prosecutors who had been focused on Condit all these months had to retrace their steps. They wanted to reinterview Guandique, but his lawyer from the

U.S. Public Defender Service was ahead of them. Gladys Joseph had already contacted Guandique, who was serving his sentence at the federal Rivers Correctional Institution in Winton, North Carolina. She told him not to talk to anyone — detectives, FBI agents, or private investigators — without contacting her first. She also left strict instructions with the officials running the prison: no interviews with Ingmar Guandique.

19
A VIABLE SUSPECT

Geographic profiler Kim Rossmo

When Halle Shilling heard that Chandra's remains had been found in Rock Creek Park, she felt a chill. She followed the news reports closely and was struck by the similarities between the setting where Ingmar Guandique assaulted her and the scene where Chandra had been attacked just half a mile away. Both were off isolated trails, along steep inclines, and near the old Peirce Mill, where Shilling first spotted Guandique sitting on a curb before he followed her deep into the forest. The timeline of the crimes was equally disturbing: Shilling was attacked two weeks after Chandra disappeared. About seven weeks after the assault on Shilling, Guandique pulled Christy Wiegand down an embankment along Beach Drive. Shilling read the stories about the site where Chandra was found and realized that it could have been her.

Within days of the news about Chandra,

Shilling found herself fending off the media. Reporters who were covering the story had followed up on the *Roll Call* article that first disclosed Guandique's name; a review of the court file revealed the names of the women he had attacked. A few enterprising reporters sifted through computer databases and came across a freelance story Shilling had written for the Style section of the *Washington Post* six weeks before the discovery of Chandra's remains. Published on April 15, 2002, Shilling wrote a first-person account of how a self-defense class she had taken may have saved her life. She described her attack in Rock Creek Park, but she did not name Guandique.

"Despite my success at fending off an attacker, I confess that these days I often prefer the treadmill at my gym to the open trails. But I think that will change soon," Shilling wrote. "Most important, I also have the benefit of knowing that the man who jumped me is off the streets. After attacking another woman in nearly the same spot in Rock Creek Park a month and a half later, my assailant was caught by quick-thinking Park Police officers who made the connection between the two attacks."

It was a scoop for the reporters who put Shilling and Guandique together. They had found a possible suspect in the murder, and they had the name and the firsthand account of one of his victims. They located Shilling and her family, who still lived in Washington. Shilling was besieged. Reporters hounded her for interviews, calling her at home and at work, confronting her on her doorstep. Shilling, a former newspaper reporter for the *Daily Camera* in Boulder, Colorado, wanted no part of the media feeding frenzy. She declined to talk. As she fended off the calls from the reporters, she wondered when she might receive a call from the police department in Washington. Surely one of the investigators on the Chandra case would want to talk to her about what had happened a year before. As the days passed without a call, Shilling couldn't understand why the D.C. police seemed to be so uninterested in her violent encounter with Guandique. She thought to herself, *If I were in charge, I would talk to me.* Maybe, she thought, they already had all the information they needed.

Beyond the glare of the media pack, the investigators began to collect information about Guandique. The similarity of crime-scene locations — coupled with the appearance that Chandra had been attacked as she walked along the trail — was a humiliating

351

development for investigators who for so long had focused on Condit. New prosecutors on the case directed the D.C. detectives to find Guandique's associates, his friends, his co-workers, his family members, anyone who could tell them where he was on May 1, 2001, what his state of mind was in the days before and after Chandra disappeared, and whether he left behind any physical evidence. The detectives decided they didn't need to interview Guandique's other victims because the two women had already provided statements to the Park Police. The D.C. detectives, Ralph Durant and Lawrence Kennedy, couldn't re-interview Guandique. The detectives also faced another problem. They did not speak Spanish, and nearly everyone they needed to interview spoke little or no English. The language barrier bogged down the investigation. "Interviewing slow," they wrote in an investigative report.

Seven weeks after the discovery of Chandra's remains, the detectives finally visited the spot where Guandique had attacked Shilling. On July 12, 2002 — a year after Guandique's arrest — the detectives and a prosecutor met Park Police detective Joe Green in the parking lot near the Peirce Mill, and Green showed them where Guandique had been sitting when he first spotted Shilling. Green then took them into the woods to the section of the trail where Guandique jumped Shilling. The detectives noted that they were about half a mile away from the location of Chandra's attack. "This site is easy walking distance from the Levy crime scene," they wrote in an investigative report.

Four weeks later, on August 11, Durant and Kennedy went to Guandique's old neighborhood on the edge of Rock Creek Park. With the help of a translator, they questioned Maria Portillo, the mother of his former girlfriend. She told them about Guandique's drinking and violent behavior toward her daughter, and said that he punched and bit her. She added that he appeared to be distraught and unstable; for no apparent reason, he sometimes left the apartment and sobbed uncontrollably outside. Durant and Kennedy then talked to Portillo's daughter, Iris, who confirmed her mother's account and said her mother had kicked Guandique out of the apartment in late April 2001 — soon before Chandra vanished.

The detectives searched for physical evidence — clothing and other items that might contain hair, or traces of semen or blood. They were on the hunt for a particular item that had not been found in Chandra's apartment or at the crime scene — a fourteen-karat gold signet ring inscribed with the initials CL that her parents had given to her as a college graduation gift. The detectives checked pawnshops across the city and circulated a bulletin with a sketch of the ring, hoping that whoever had it might also have information about Chandra's murder.

On August 12 — thirteen months after Guandique's arrest — Durant and Kennedy met with one of Guandique's friends, Jaime Flores. He and Guandique had come from the same small town in El Salvador. The detectives learned from Flores that Guandique's half brother, Huber, had picked up Guandique's belongings after his arrest. Twelve days later, the detectives interviewed Huber, who told them he thought a man known as "Juan the Pig" had the belongings and he had no idea where he could be.

To assist the investigation, FBI agent Brad Garrett and his former partner, D.C. detective Jim Trainum, asked geographic profiler Kim Rossmo to return to the case and examine the attacks in Rock Creek Park.

Rossmo visited all three crime scenes: Chandra's, Shilling's, and Wiegand's. He noted the locations and the similarities. Each was isolated, near a ravine or an embankment, and each was shielded from sight by heavy vegetation and dense forest. He also noted that in each attack, the victim had been carrying a Walkman, but Shilling and Wiegand both said that Guandique did not demand anything of value, nor did he take anything when he fled. Rossmo thought that the attacks on Shilling and Wiegand were attempted sexual assaults, and he theorized that the same thing might have happened to Chandra. Rossmo also studied incidents of criminal behavior in the park. He learned that murderers and rapists were rare; more prevalent were car burglars, drunks, and flashers. No similar attacks on women had occurred in this section of the park before Chandra disappeared on May 1, and the attacks ended on July 1, when Guandique was arrested. Rossmo found it noteworthy that Guandique lived in a neighborhood that bordered Rock Creek Park, and the apartment he stayed in with his girlfriend was not far from where Chandra's remains had been found.

Rossmo prepared a report for the investigators. He said it appeared that Chandra went to Rock Creek Park to visit the Planetarium or the Nature Center and was attacked while walking along the Western Ridge Trail, either on her way to or from one of those two places. He concluded that the focus on Gary Condit was misplaced, that it appeared Chandra was the victim of a random attack, and investigators had committed a cardinal sin by having "tunnel vision" and focusing on one suspect to the exclusion of others. Rossmo wrote in his report: "The proximity in time and place between Chandra Levy's murder and the attacks committed by Ingmar Guandique make him a viable suspect in Levy's homicide. The rarity of violent or sexual offenses against women in Rock Creek Park increases the chance that these events are related, therefore increasing the likelihood of Guandique's involvement."

For the investigators working the case, it was a difficult conclusion to accept. Although he respected Rossmo, Garrett was unconvinced. In the mind of the FBI agent, Guandique could not be excluded as a suspect. But perhaps another predator in the park had attacked Chandra, a "stranger crime," as Garrett called them. Maybe she died at the hands of an unknown boyfriend, or someone she met at the Washington Sports Club or the Bureau of Prisons. Garrett hadn't ruled out the possibility that someone connected to Condit might have been involved, someone who acted alone without the congressman's blessing or knowledge. The FBI agent didn't think there was enough evidence to connect Guandique to Chandra's murder, and there was not enough proof to build a case that could withstand the rigors of a criminal trial.

By the time Rossmo prepared his report, a new prosecutor had taken over the case, and she did not share the FBI agent's point of view. Elisa Poteat was a young, promising assistant U.S. attorney who spoke fluent Spanish and specialized in prosecuting sex crimes. The daughter of a CIA science and technology officer who spent thirty years with the agency, the petite blonde was known for her toughness and aggressive approach to her cases. Poteat took a different view of the investigation than her predecessors at the U.S. attorney's office, Barbara Kittay and Heidi Pasichow, who had left the case. Pasichow had moved on to other investigations, and Kittay, frustrated by the persistent police leaks and press conferences, had requested that she be removed from the case. Their chief adversaries, Abbe Lowell and Jack Barrett, cheered their departures. Lowell thought the prosecutors' focus on Condit had ruined his client's career; Barrett thought it had ruined the investigation.

Poteat viewed Guandique as the prime suspect, and she sided with Rossmo's theory of what might have happened in Rock Creek Park. The prosecutor was also frustrated by Durant and Kennedy's slow pace, and on September 22 — more than fourteen months after Guandique's arrest — she stepped up the tempo. While Durant and Kennedy were temporarily detailed to help monitor the protests at the International Monetary Fund in downtown Washington, Poteat moved to have two bilingual D.C. officers assigned to the case. Sergeant Raul Figueras and Detective Emilio Martinez started off by tracking down Guandique's associates, even though Durant and Kennedy had already interviewed several of them. Poteat wanted to question them herself. During those interrogations, Poteat made an intriguing discovery. It appeared that Guandique had not been at work on May 1, the day Chandra disappeared, a fact confirmed by Park Police detective Joe Green.

Brad Garrett joined Poteat in the interrogations. They had different opinions about the case and their personalities didn't seem to match. Poteat was constantly in motion;

Garrett was cool and deliberate. But within months, the two would begin a romantic relationship.

As Poteat ramped up her investigation, Sari Horwitz and two other *Washington Post* reporters, Allan Lengel and Sylvia Moreno, drove to Guandique's old neighborhood and began knocking on doors. They raced to beat their competitors on the story, and in the process, they moved ahead of the police investigation. On October 2, 2002, they knocked on the door of Guandique's landlady, Sheila Phillips Cruz, who recalled that Guandique had a fat lip, a bloody blemish in his eye, and scratches on his throat around the time of Chandra's disappearance. Cruz said Guandique told her that he had gotten into a fight with his girlfriend, and she recalled that Guandique started drinking heavily during that period. "Ingmar just got really strange," she said. "Half the time he didn't know where he was."

Cruz also said Guandique left behind two bags of belongings in a stairwell when he moved out of the apartment on Somerset Place in the spring of 2001. She said the bags contained the T-shirts, baggy pants, and baseball cap Guandique liked to wear. That summer, she had a maintenance man throw away the bags, which could have contained forensic evidence. If the police had contacted her the year before, she would have gladly handed over the bags, but she said she never heard from anyone at the police department.

After learning that the *Post* had interviewed Cruz, the police rushed to talk to her. She repeated what she had told the reporters, and Poteat redoubled her efforts to find whatever remained of Guandique's belongings. Poteat had already built a fairly compelling circumstantial case, but she needed more evidence to take it into a courtroom.

Poteat subpoenaed phone records for one of Guandique's friends, and the new officers learned that Juan the Pig's real name was Juan José Arevalo Escobar. He was locked up on a drunk-driving charge in Newport News, Virginia, but was about to be released. On October 10, 2002, Poteat urged the D.C. police department to send Figueras and Martinez to Newport News. She wrote to the department's central intelligence branch that day: "The witness is believed to have access to a possible suspect's belongings. Should this matter be delayed, I have no doubt we may permanently lose access to this witness. Please keep this matter secret as it is apparent that there are press leaks in this case. Any leak of information whatsoever would seriously harm the investigation."

Figueras and Martinez made it to Newport News before Escobar's release. He told them he had some of Guandique's belongings; they were back in Maryland with a friend whom they had already interviewed. When Figueras and Martinez found the friend, he told them he had thrown the items out — soon after they had left the first time. The officers considered filing obstruction of justice charges, but in the end they knew there was no point. Whatever evidence they might have found was gone, and they didn't want to pursue what had become a moot point.

In early October, an unfolding rampage overtook the Chandra investigation. A sniper was on the loose. By the time Poteat wrote her memo on October 10, there had been nine shootings, including a man mowing a lawn, a woman pumping gas, and another woman sitting outside a post office. The FBI pulled Brad Garrett and Melissa Thomas off the Chandra Levy case and sent them to work on a task force established to stop the shootings that were terrorizing

Washington and its suburbs. The press also abandoned the Chandra story. In all, John Muhammad and Lee Boyd Malvo were tied to the shooting deaths of fifteen people in Washington, Maryland, Virginia, Alabama, Georgia, Washington State, Louisiana, and Arizona — ten of them in the Washington region between October 2 and October 22, 2002.

Poteat pressed on with the Chandra investigation. Durant and Kennedy rejoined the case and they began to examine other possible suspects. They interviewed a man who had been convicted of raping and strangling a jogger in the northernmost reaches of the park in Maryland about eleven miles from where Chandra was attacked and three months before she disappeared. Albert W. Cook Jr. freely admitted to torturing and killing the jogger, Sue Wen Stottmeister, but he denied having anything to do with Chandra's murder. Durant and Kennedy also focused on a D.C. substitute teacher who had been exposing himself in a neighborhood near Chandra's apartment. But with little information to go on, the line of inquiry languished.

In November, Durant and Kennedy returned to Rock Creek Park to interview Park Service employees about what they might have witnessed around the time of Chandra's disappearance. They wanted to know if the park workers had seen any suspicious people or cars. Did they find any clothing or jewelry? On November 7 — sixteen months after Guandique's arrest — Durant and Kennedy visited the Park Service maintenance yard on Glover Road, not far from where Chandra was found. They interviewed Michael Buchanan, who operated mowers in that section of the park. Buchanan couldn't recall seeing anything out of the ordinary, but he had a question for the detectives: Why had they waited so long — nearly six months after the discovery of Chandra's remains — to interview him and his colleagues? The detectives explained that the FBI was in charge of interviewing Park Service employees, but those agents had been reassigned, working on antiterrorism cases.

As the year wound down, Poteat had a hunch. Police searches of Chandra's condominium and the crime scene had never turned up an important piece of evidence: Chandra's apartment keys. The prosecutor reviewed the case files and evidence inventories and wondered if Durant or Kennedy had ever examined a set of keys that was found on Guandique at the time of his arrest and kept by the police. They hadn't. Poteat thought she might have finally found a break. On December 13, she summoned Kennedy to her office and asked him to retrieve a set of duplicate keys from Chandra's building, along with Guandique's keys. A crime-scene technician compared the two sets. They didn't match; it was just one more disappointment.

In May 2003, nearly a year after they were found in Rock Creek Park, Chandra's remains were returned to Robert and Susan Levy in Modesto, California. They were taken to the Lakewood Memorial Park Cemetery in Hughson, a tiny town of low-slung ranch houses spread out beneath a slender white water tower not far from where Chandra grew up. On May 27, the Levys held a private graveside service for their daughter. A rabbi recited prayers. A choir from the family's temple sang. Susan Levy read a poem and twelve white doves were released into the sky. Chandra's parents didn't mark the grave site. They don't plan to until their daughter's killer is convicted. Only then will they put up a stone. Robert Levy knows what it will say: "My God, my God, why have you forsaken me?"

20
AN ARREST

The Levys

On Sunday, July 13, 2008, the *Washington Post* published the first installment of its yearlong investigation into the Chandra Levy case. "Who Killed Chandra Levy?" ran as a serial narrative, in nearly nineteen thousand words over thirteen days on the *Post*'s front page and its website. The series exonerated Gary Condit and identified Ingmar Guandique as the most likely culprit in the murder. Video and audio interviews with Robert and Susan Levy, Condit, Ingmar Guandique, and investigators in the case accompanied the online stories. So did maps, timelines, and documents from police and court files.

The series highlighted the many missteps that plagued the investigation and helped blind investigators to the possibility that someone other than Condit was responsible for Chandra's disappearance. Among the lapses the series documented: the failure to immediately secure surveillance videotapes; the mismanagement of the examination of Chandra's computer; the missed connection between Chandra's disappearance and other attacks in Rock Creek Park; the failure by Park Police to report Guandique's statement two months after her disappearance that he had seen Chandra in the park; the failure by D.C. detectives to interview the two women he attacked; the failure to properly search the park; the omission of a bilingual polygrapher in the examinations of Guandique and Ramón Alvarez; the finding by the FBI polygraph examiner that Guandique was "not deceptive," when the polygraph readings were "inconclusive"; the thirteen months after Guandique's arrest that passed before police discovered that Guandique's girlfriend and mother said Guandique had violent tendencies; the fourteen months that passed before investigators interviewed his landlady, who said Guandique looked like he'd been in a fight around the time of Chandra's disappearance; the fourteen months it took investigators to realize Guandique hadn't shown up for work at his construction job on the day Chandra disappeared.

Each day of the series, the *Post* published a Reporter's Notebook, and Horwitz and

Higham, along with staff writer Sylvia Moreno — who had interviewed Guandique and his associates — engaged in an online conversation with more than five hundred readers, many of them espousing their own theories of the case. Bloggers followed every turn of the series and thousands of readers around the world e-mailed their comments to the *Post.* While many praised the project, others harshly criticized the news organization for devoting so much valuable front-page space to a largely forgotten case.

On the final day of the series, July 27, 2008, the *Post's* reader representative wrote a column titled "A 13-Part Series to Love or Hate." Ombudsman Deborah Howell noted that "the series was phenomenally popular online, outpacing other recent investigative series," but she pointed out that in her two and a half years at the paper, no other investigation had provoked such sharply opposing remarks from readers. Comments ranged from "Fascinating! Totally hooked! Riveting!" to "Lurid! Appalling! A waste of time!" Howell focused much of her column on the readers who complained that the *Post* had turned tabloid, and perhaps racist. Howell quoted *Post* reporter Robert Pierre as saying the emphasis on the murder of a white woman in a city where nearly two hundred people are killed each year, most of them African-American, was "absolutely absurd and dare I say, racist, at its core." Pierre called the series "unconscionable" and questioned whether the *Post* had proclaimed that a "white life is worth more than a black one."

The editors of the project, Jeff Leen and Larry Roberts, pushed back. Leen noted in a response to Howell that the *Post* had previously conducted an investigation into faulty police work on hundreds of D.C. murder cases, most of them involving African-American victims. Howell was undeterred. She concluded that the serial was largely a waste of time. "To me, the project wasn't worth 13 days, all on Page 1," she wrote. "It was simply too much for this impatient, time-starved reader who wanted to know what the reporters found out right away."

Far from the controversy, the Metropolitan Police Department and D.C. detectives quietly stepped up their investigation into the Chandra Levy case. The police boxed up the records containing the Condit leads in the case and began to reexamine the old files that the department had collected on Guandique. They retrieved physical pieces from evidence lockers — clothing belonging to Chandra and Guandique — and prepared to test them for traces of DNA. They began to monitor Guandique's phone calls and mail from a maximum-security prison on the edge of the Mojave Desert in California, where he had been sent because of bad behavior.

By the summer of 2008, Chief Charles Ramsey had left the department to become Philadelphia's police commissioner. At the conclusion of the series, he told Horwitz and Higham that he was troubled by its findings. He didn't know his detectives had not interviewed the two women Guandique had attacked in Rock Creek Park, and he was infuriated by the long list of mistakes his department had made during the course of the investigation. "When I read the series, I said, 'Oh man.' That's ridiculous. That's fundamental and basic. There are a few things that I assumed had been done. People criticized us for micromanaging. In retrospect, we should have micromanaged more."

Ramsey was replaced by Cathy Lanier. In 2007, soon after taking over, Lanier met with Susan Levy at police headquarters. When Levy held out her hand, Lanier hugged her. The chief emerged from the meeting after ninety minutes vowing to solve the case. By then, Detective Lawrence Kennedy had retired, and Lanier removed Ralph Durant. She replaced them with two veterans, Detectives Kenneth "Todd" Williams and Anthony Brigidini. The officers were juggling several other cases and they had not made significant progress on the Levy investigation. A few days before the *Post* series began, Horwitz interviewed Lanier. The chief said she hoped the series would "stir things up. Sometimes people come forward. The possibility of that is still viable."

On September 8, 2008, two months after the series, Detective Williams and two other D.C. police officers arrived at the Victorville Federal Correctional Institution in Adelanto, California, where Guandique was serving out the remainder of his ten-year sentence for attacking Christy Wiegand and Halle Shilling in Rock Creek Park. Ever since Guandique's conviction in 2002, he had been a persistent problem for prison officials, forcing them to move him from facility to facility. While in a federal prison in North Carolina, he mailed pornographic sketches containing written suggestions of explicit sexual acts to a female insurance agent, a stranger whose picture he had seen in a Spanish-language newspaper. In another prison, he pulled down a lighting fixture and frequently masturbated in front of female guards. Along the way, he joined MS-13, the nickname for Mara Salvatrucha, the violent Salvadoran street gang, which was also active inside federal and state prisons systems.

At three that afternoon, detectives Williams, Brigidini, and Emilio Martinez, who worked on the case in 2002, met with Guandique in an interview room inside the prison. They asked if they could talk to him and take a DNA sample. He agreed. Martinez served as the translator during the interview and took a seat next to Guandique at a small table. On the other side sat Williams and Brigidini. Guandique was not handcuffed or restrained, and he could have left the interview room at any time. The detectives said he chose to stay. They asked Guandique about the murder of Chandra Levy and told him they had obtained DNA evidence during the course of their investigation. They expected it would match the DNA sample they had just obtained. It was a carefully crafted bluff. The detectives were familiar with the interrogation of Guandique by Park Police detective Joe Green. They had read the reports and saw how their counterpart had successfully tricked

Guandique into confessing to the two attacks in Rock Creek Park. At first, Guandique was defiant. He told the detectives
that if they had DNA evidence tying him to
the crime they should charge him with
murder. The detectives persisted. They
asked him again to explain why his DNA
would wind up on evidence that had been
recovered in the case. "So what if I touched
her," Guandique told them. It wasn't a
confession, but the detectives solicited an
incriminating statement from Guandique,
one that could prove useful to the prosecu-
tion if admitted during the trial.

The detectives then turned the questioning to the day Chandra disappeared. They
asked Guandique why he was seen with a
fat lip and scratches on his face that first
day of May seven years earlier. He said "two
black guys" had roughed him up during a
robbery attempt. The detectives challenged
his story. They told him that they knew he
had provided a different account to his
landlady, Sheila Cruz — that his girlfriend,
Iris Portillo, struck and scratched him during a heated argument. Guandique altered
his story. He told the detectives that the fat
lip was the result of the encounter with the
"two black guys" and the scratches on his
face came from Portillo.

The detectives also noted that Guandique had a tattoo on his neck that read "Mara Salvatrucha." He had a tattoo of the devil on the top of his shaved head and a tattoo on his back depicting the horror-film character "Chucky" holding a knife. They asked Guandique about the large tattoo of a naked woman with long black hair he had on his chest. They noted the similarities to Chandra and asked him if the tattoo was some sort of "souvenir" that reminded him of the murder. Guandique smirked, then giggled, but he didn't say a word. While the detectives were interviewing Guandique, prison officials were searching his cell. Inside, they found a photograph of Chandra clipped from a magazine.

In the fall of 2008, the detectives interviewed several witnesses who said Guandique had confessed the murder to them. While details of the accounts varied, sometimes wildly, the central claim, that Guandique had murdered Chandra in the woods of a park, remained the same. In November 2008, the detectives interviewed a "confession witness" who told them that Guandique had boasted about being a member of MS-13 and claimed that he had committed numerous rapes and robberies. The witness also said Guandique was known as

"Chucky" because of his fondness for cutting up his victims. The witness told the detectives that Guandique had bragged that he and other gang members would frequently hide on dirt paths and snatch young women as they walked by. Guandique said he would bind their hands and feet behind their backs, and if he didn't have rope, he would use whatever material was available. The witness told the detectives that Guandique said he didn't always know whether the women survived the sexual attacks, but it didn't matter because animals like coyotes and vultures would finish them off.

Guandique was specific about one of these incidents. He claimed he and two other men were in a park one day when they spotted a woman who looked to be Italian. She had thick dark hair and was jogging alone on a path. Guandique said he lassoed her around her neck and dragged her into the woods, where she was knocked unconscious. He and the other man tied her feet together, stuffed something in her mouth, and then raped her. When she began to regain consciousness, Guandique stabbed her and slashed her throat.

Also during the fall of 2008, the detectives interviewed a friend who had corresponded with Guandique five years earlier. Guandique wrote to the friend that he had spent time in a park in Washington and was the person responsible for the murder of a young woman. In a recorded phone conversation with the friend, Guandique talked about the "girl who's dead." The detectives also interviewed Amber Fitzgerald, the young lawyer who had been chased in the woods near the Peirce Mill by a man fitting Guandique's description. Fitzgerald had gone to the police in 2003 after she saw a picture of Guandique on television. D.C. detectives interviewed her but never followed through. The new prosecutor assigned to the case interviewed Fitzgerald and the man she was dating in 2001. They reconstructed their calendars and determined that Guandique had stalked Fitzgerald on May 1, 2001, the day of Chandra's disappearance.

As 2008 drew to a close, the detectives and prosecutors summoned Halle Shilling to Washington. On December 14, they met her, her father, and her sister in Rock Creek Park. Together they walked deep into the woods and up the trail above Beach Drive to the spot where Guandique had attacked her. She reenacted the crime as her father stood silently to the side. As he watched, he was overcome by anger, realizing how close

Guandique had come to taking his daughter's life. One day later, Shilling testified before a grand jury in Washington about what had happened that day more than seven years earlier. The detectives and the prosecutor apologized to Shilling. They told her they were sorry it had taken the police department so long to interview her. They also told her they were upset that Guandique had been permitted to plead guilty to reduced charges in the case, and they were baffled that so much time had been wasted investigating Condit. One of the investigators rolled his eyes and told her: "I can't believe Gary Condit was even a suspect."

After Shilling testified, the detectives continued their investigation. In February 2009, they interviewed an inmate who said Guandique admitted to being involved in Chandra's murder. Guandique told the inmate that he and two teenage men were sitting on a bench in a "big park." They were smoking marijuana laced with cocaine when they spotted a young woman jogging in an area where people normally walk their dogs. He said she had curly hair and he thought she "looked good." He told the other men he was going to get her, and the three started to chase her. When they caught up to the woman, they grabbed her and pulled her into the bushes. Once on the ground, Guandique said the "bitch" started screaming and fighting back, badly scratching his face. He grabbed her by the neck and choked her to death. Guandique said he and the men buried her under some leaves before leaving the park. If anyone ever questioned him about the scratches, Guandique said, he had a cover story. His former girlfriend, Iris Portillo, inflicted them during a fight.

Later that same month, a reporter for WRC-TV in Washington, Pat Collins — who had covered the story since Chandra first disappeared — received a tip that the police department was seeking an affidavit for Guandique's arrest. The story was picked up around the nation. It appeared as though the news media hadn't learned from the mistakes of the summer of 2001. The Associated Press reported that the new evidence against Guandique included a DNA match. While there was no DNA match, the report was picked up and repeated as fact by news outlets around the world.

When Guandique heard in prison that he was about to be arrested, he told an inmate: "Fuck, it's over. They got me now. What am I gonna do?" He told the inmate that he was "not going out alone" and vowed that when the detectives came to arrest him, he was going to cause a distraction by starting a fire with a battery and tissue, and use a key he had fashioned from toenail clippers and a piece of metal to unlock his handcuffs. He would then kill the detectives with a prison shank he had constructed from razor blades and toothbrush handles. He planned to wrap the makeshift key and the shank in plastic and conceal them in his rectum.

The inmate reported the plot to the authorities, and on February 26, 2009, Victorville prison officials removed Guandique from his cell. Inside they found an AA battery and pieces of tissue, a piece of a toenail clipper, a sharp sliver of metal, several loose razor blades, and a shank constructed of two razor blades and several pieces of plastic.

Early on the afternoon of March 3, Chief Lanier stood in a conference room inside police headquarters. She was flanked by Washington's mayor, the U.S. attorney, several top city and police officials, and the detectives who made the case: Williams and Brigidini, as well as Martinez. She announced that Guandique would be charged with first-degree murder for the death of Chandra Ann Levy. Lanier told the reporters during the standing-room-only press conference that she had spoken to Robert and Susan Levy that morning, preparing them for the announcement and the grisly details that were about to be made public in the arrest warrant affidavit, about how their daughter was raped and sodomized and stabbed to death. "There is very little that I can do or any of us can do now to offer anything to the Levys other than justice, and I hope that this offering of justice gives them some sense of peace," Lanier said. She said nothing about the department's prior focus on Condit. In fact, she never mentioned his name.

A month before the series ran, Higham and Horwitz had traveled to California to interview Condit. They met the former congressman and his son, Chad, in the Los Angeles office of his new attorney, Mark Geragos. Condit appeared gaunt. His hair was thinner and turning gray, but his eyes were clear, cobalt blue, and he retained his charismatic smile. After losing the primary in 2002, Condit had moved to Arizona with his wife, Carolyn. He ran two Baskin-Robbins ice-cream parlors before becoming mired in a franchise dispute with the company. Baskin-Robbins sued and Condit lost the ice-cream stores. He began to divide his time between California, Colorado — where his daughter lived with her family — and Arizona, where he wanted to build a house in the high desert. He had received settlements from libel suits he and his wife had filed against the *National Enquirer* and *Vanity Fair* writer Dominick Dunne, who retold the "Horse Whisperer" story on radio and television programs. Condit said he planned to do some investing and a "little bit of consulting," but offered no further specifics about his plans for the future. He later said he wanted to write a book about his experience.

During the interview with Higham and Horwitz, Condit maintained that he had never been Chandra's boyfriend, and he insisted that he didn't know her very well. He declined to discuss his feelings for Chandra, though he expressed remorse for her family — but still, he had trouble concealing his bitterness over how he had been treated by the police and the press during the summer of 2001. "I know that Chandra and her family are the victims, and I get that. But I could not even imply that I was being victimized at the same time. I felt like my reputation was being raped. That I was being assaulted physically and I could not defend myself. It was the equivalent to me of a rape. I've never been physically raped, but I've been emotionally. And my reputation has been raped. And just like probably with a physical rape, you probably never recover from those emotions or those scars. And I don't want to take anything away from Chandra and her family because I know they're the real victims. They lost someone."

After the announcement of Guandique's arrest, Condit's former attorney said his client had been vindicated; but the exoneration came at a steep price, costing his client his career and his livelihood. "While very good news, it is a tragedy that the police and media obsession with former congressman Condit delayed this result for eight years and caused needless pain and harm to the families involved," Abbe Lowell said.

On April 23, 2009, a squad of U.S. marshals led Guandique into a basement-level courtroom of the D.C. Superior Court, where reporters had gathered to catch their first glimpse of the man charged with the infamous murder. His hands and feet were shackled and he wore an orange jumpsuit, covering most of his tattoos. His stare was hardened by his time in prison, his eyes seemingly vacant. He said nothing as he stood in the well of the courtroom, his defense attorneys by his side. Ever since Guandique's arrest, his public defenders, Santha Sonenberg and Maria Hawilo, had ridiculed the government's case. "This flawed investigation, characterized by the many missteps of the Metropolitan Police Department and every federal agency that has attempted to solve this case, will not end with the simple issuance of an arrest warrant against Mr. Guandique," they said. "The public should not draw any conclusions based on speculation by the media and incomplete information."

The new prosecutors, Amanda Haines and Fernando Campoamor, have a difficult case to prove. The D.C. medical examiner never determined the cause of Chandra's death, because her remains were so badly decomposed. There were no witnesses to the crime, no physical evidence connecting Guandique to the scene, and no evidence of any accomplices. During the eight years he has been behind bars, Guandique has allegedly told so many different versions of how he supposedly murdered Chandra that it's hard to keep them straight. Several of the accounts were from jailhouse snitches whose credibility will come under intense scrutiny during the upcoming trial. Did Guandique really confess, or was he bragging to make himself seem like a tough guy in prison? Are the inmates telling the truth, or are they fabricating stories to curry favor with prosecutors to cut deals in their own cases? The conduct and the misconduct of the police department could also come under attack during the trial. So could the statements by the original prosecutor and the judge, made in open court in 2002, when they declared that they didn't believe Guandique had anything to do with the disappearance of Chandra Levy.

In the months that followed Guandique's first court appearance, Haines and Campoamor disclosed more details of their case. They said the detectives had located a new witness who claimed to have been attacked on a jogging trail by a man matching Guandique's description. The witness was stabbed in the back in a park before Chandra disappeared and remained on the ground, seriously wounded, for nearly two hours before two passersby came upon the scene. The D.C. police had never linked the stabbing to attacks in the park that summer.

In preparation for the trial, scheduled for October 4, 2010, Haines and Campoamor notified Guandique's defense attorneys that another inmate had come forward to say their client had sodomized him at knife-point. Late one night, the inmate said, Guandique pulled a knife, tied his legs up with a sheet, gagged him, raped him, and forced him to perform oral sex. During the assault, the inmate said Guandique told him "he liked to do it to women like that." The inmate also told the detectives that Guandique confessed to tying up a woman in Washington before raping and killing her.

Faced with the testimony from the jail-house informants, Guandique's defense team began to craft a strategy of their own: Another man, possibly someone connected to Condit, may have been responsible for the murder of Chandra Levy. At an October 16, 2009, court hearing, Campoamor revealed what he characterized as a mistake in evidence collection. Prosecutors disclosed that DNA from an unknown male had been detected on the black ProSpirit stretch pants found seven years earlier at the crime scene in Rock Creek Park. Campoamor said that the DNA could not be linked to Guandique, Condit, or any of the analysts who tested the stretch pants once belonging to Chandra. Prosecutors explained that the DNA most likely came from a crime scene technician, a police officer, or someone else who handled the stretch pants.

But Guandique's defense attorneys were unconvinced that it was a mistake and said the mystery DNA could be evidence of another suspect. They immediately requested permission to test about three dozen pieces of evidence in possession of the police, including items that had been seized from Condit's apartment in 2001. They said they wanted to conduct an investigation of their own, and it appeared that they wanted to determine whether the items contained DNA or other forensic evidence that might link the murder to another suspect. Prosecutors tried to prevent the defense team from gaining access to the items, calling it a "fishing expedition," but D.C. Superior Court judge Gerald I. Fisher ordered that the material be turned over.

On December 2, 2009, prosecutors unveiled what could be a possible break in their case and a window into Guandique's state of mind as he sat inside the D.C. Jail, awaiting trial. They disclosed that a grand jury had returned a fresh indictment against Guandique, alleging that he and an associate threatened to murder a jailhouse informant, identified only as "J.G." in court papers. The grand jurors found that Guandique either "wrote or caused a letter to be written" to J.G., threatening to kill the informant and the informant's family if J.G. "continued to cooperate with law enforcement." The prosecutors said Guandique also communicated the threat directly to J.G., apparently inside the D.C. Jail. He pleaded not guilty to conspiracy to obstruct justice, obstruction of justice, and threatening to injure a person, but if he is convicted, the new case could severely undercut his defense that he had nothing to do with the murder of Chandra Levy.

For Brad Garrett, the FBI agent brought in to help the D.C. police solve the murder, the Levy case is one of the few to have eluded him during the course of his storied career. He married Elisa Poteat, the former assistant U.S. attorney he worked with during the investigation. When they first started dating in 2003, she recused herself from the Chandra Levy case. Garrett retired from the bureau in 2006, starting his own private investigative firm in Alexandria, Virginia, and taking a job as a law enforcement consultant for ABC News. One morning, after he retired, Garrett drove to Rock Creek Park, pulled his car along Glover Road near Grove 17, and made his way down to the isolated spot where Philip Palmer found Chandra's skull. Garrett stood on the slope of the steep ravine and tried to visualize the violent end to Chandra's life. Did she die during the attack? Or was she alive for a while, able to see and hear the cars driving below, but too injured to move or scream for help? For Garrett, these visits had become a pilgrimage. Dozens of times during the past eight years, he had repeated this ritual and wondered where he and the other investigators and prosecutors assigned to the case might have gone wrong. With his track record as one of the most effective investigators in the FBI's modern history, Garrett should have been the one to close the case, the one to win the confession, the one to appear on the nightly news and proclaim that justice had been served.

Over time, Garrett had become more certain that the evidence pointed to a random attack by a stranger, someone like Guandique, but he couldn't be sure that it was Guandique. Garrett couldn't eliminate him as a suspect, but there was no physical evidence tying him to the crime scene. At one point, the FBI entertained the idea of sending a cooperating inmate into Guandique's cell to see if he could secure a confession, but the operation was deemed to be too dangerous. Too many people in the prison would need to know, and investigators worried that the undercover inmate could be harmed. Over the years, inmates had come forward to say that Guandique confessed the murder to them, but Garrett never thought that was enough to make an arrest. To this day, he remains concerned about the strength of the evidence.

Terrance Gainer was unconvinced that Guandique murdered Chandra. The former second in command of the D.C. police left the department shortly after Chandra's remains were found and went on to become the sergeant at arms of the U.S. Senate. Higham and Horwitz visited him in his U.S. Capitol office before Guandique's arrest and he reiterated his beliefs about Guandique; he, too, noted that there was no physical evidence connecting him to the crime. He added that his detectives had interviewed Guandique and were "very convinced that he was not the guy. You have to have faith in your detectives, and we did." A year later, after Guandique's arrest, Gainer said, "It appears we have the right person now."

Over the course of time, Jack Barrett, the chief of detectives who supervised the Chandra investigation, saw what his department and the FBI had missed. Barrett retired and became a senior analyst for an intelligence firm in Northern Virginia. The more he considered the case and ran through the various scenarios, the closer he came to the conclusion that the person who killed Chandra had been hiding in plain sight. Barrett said he tried to convince prosecutors of his changing position during the summer of 2001, and he urged them to pull Guandique from jail for an interview, but they were too focused on Condit to care. "I think Guandique did it. It was the right time frame that he was attacking these other women," Barrett said.

On December 14, 2008, hours after Shilling reenacted her attack in Rock Creek Park for the prosecutor and detectives, she met with Horwitz and Higham at Kramerbooks & Afterwords, a busy bookstore and café in Dupont Circle, not far from Chandra's apartment building. Tall, blond, and attractive, Shilling wore jeans and boots and was accompanied by her father and her sister. Over omelets and coffee, Shilling started to talk about her attack. When she saw her father's eyes fill with tears, she changed the subject. She said her life was complete with so many good things — a solid marriage, fulfilling work as a writer and a teacher, three beautiful children, grandchildren for her parents. She opened her purse, her hand shaking slightly, and pulled out a picture of the children, two boys and a girl, who were born after the attack.

Shilling knew that if she hadn't been able to fight off Guandique, these things would never have been: her career, her family. Her entire life turned on what happened inside a few seconds, on the self-defense class she took and maybe on a little luck, her fingers thrusting into Guandique's mouth at precisely the right time, striking at precisely the right angle. What if Chandra had been able to free herself? The two women had many of the same dreams and aspirations: finding their place in one of the most alluring and powerful cities in the world. Shilling tucked the picture back into her purse and said softly, "I was her."

Following Guandique's arrest, the word *closure* began to appear — in news stories, press conferences, and conversations. Robert and Susan Levy despise the word. They never use it, and they say they will never find it. Their daughter is gone and nothing can change that.

Higham and Horwitz made several trips to Modesto to meet with the Levys. Robert was still working hard at his oncology practice, and Susan was helping other parents whose children were missing or had been murdered. Their son, Adam, was trying to move forward with his life, exploring a possible career in computer animation.

The Levys say they rely on their spirituality to stay balanced. They spend time with friends and travel to exotic places such as Thailand and Vietnam, but returning home is never easy. Susan sometimes goes for days without combing her hair or putting on makeup, and there are nights when she roams from room to room, carrying a blanket, unable to sleep. "The visions," she says, "of all the horrible stuff that happened with my daughter being out there in Rock Creek Park, the skeletal remains. It is there in my mind."

Chandra's bedroom looks like a museum. Her Modesto Police Explorer uniform hangs in the closet. On the shelves are boxes stuffed with thousands of sympathy letters and cards from around the world. On the walls are photos of Chandra as a little girl, as a young woman. Susan has turned the kitchen table from her daughter's Washington apartment into a memorial and placed it in the center of the room. She covered the table with cards from Chandra's favorite sport, baseball, and wrappers from her favorite candy, Reese's Peanut Butter Cups.

"It turns your stomach, that any family, any parent would ever have to go through such terror," Susan says as she sits on her daughter's bed one afternoon. "You carry a child and nourish her, help develop her into a human being, and then to have her whole future wiped out, the carpet taken out from under her, snatched, and all that you dreamed is taken away. It's like a knife in your side. It's very painful."

Investigators and prosecutors have expressed the hope that the arrest — and ultimately the conviction — of Ingmar Guandique will help bring some solace to the Levys. But it's more complicated for them. For years, they have lived with the belief that Condit had something to do with Chandra's disappearance. It started when they first made the connection between Chandra's phone bill and Condit, and intensified when they called his home and listened to the congressman claim that he barely knew their daughter. As the truth of Condit's involvement with Chandra was gradually and excruciatingly revealed, Susan only became more convinced of his guilt, and increasingly consumed by a profound fury. She still can't let it go. In her daughter's room, surrounded by the images of

Chandra and the things she loved, Susan's eyes redden and fill with tears.

"Let me show you something," she says. Susan retrieves a piece of artwork she created soon after Chandra's disappearance, one of many she made as a form of therapy, such as a Statue of Liberty in tears. But this particular piece is composed of mixed media, paint and photographs arranged in a jarring collage. The central image is Gary Condit's head, surrounded by missiles that appear to be slamming into his skull with explosive force. From a gaping wound, blood splashes from one edge of the collage to the other. In the upper left of the painting, a shackled prisoner clad in an orange jumpsuit kneels beneath his decapitated head, a picture of Condit's face glued over it. A lovely photograph of Chandra taken in Jerusalem is off to one side, splattered with blood.

Susan puts the collage away and walks across the room. She bends slightly over the table and reaches to touch it, gently caressing the surface with her palm. Then she stands, as if filled with sudden resolve. "We have to maintain being good human beings and compassionate individuals and go on with our life because we have our son," she says. "As horrendous as this story is, I think our daughter would want us to educate people to go on living and go on enjoying life. I think that is what she would want us to do."

NOTES

CHAPTER 1:
THE BONE COLLECTOR

This chapter is based on an interview with Philip Palmer, and on confidential law enforcement documents.

On the slope of a steep ravine: D.C. police reports; interview with Philip Palmer.

Walking these woods was a ritual: Palmer interview.

Palmer's quest seemed: Ibid.

At night, children gazed: National Park Service.

Founded in 1890: Ibid.

The park also includes Fort Stevens: Ibid.

The three-story, turreted brownstone: Palmer interview.

At about 9 A.M., Palmer: D.C. police report; Palmer interview.

CHAPTER 2:
BURN IT TO THE GROUND

This chapter is based on an interview with Jeff Leen, assistant managing editor for investigations at the *Washington Post,* and the authors' notes and recollections.

CHAPTER 3:
SUDDENLY, GONE

This chapter is based on interviews with Robert and Susan Levy; Chandra's high school friends Lisa Bracken and Channaly Oum; Chandra's high school guidance counselor, Julie Danielson; Jim Figert, who managed Chandra's condominium building in Washington; law enforcement sources; David Grazman, one of Chandra's professors at the University of Southern California; and Dan Dunne, Chandra's supervisor at the Federal Bureau of Prisons. We also examined confidential law enforcement records documenting the phone calls Chandra placed and the computer searches she conducted shortly before she disappeared.

Any moment now, Robert Levy hoped: Interview with Robert Levy.

A week before, Chandra had told her father: Ibid.

Robert and Susan Levy knew: Interview with

Robert and Susan Levy.

Robert Levy tried not to panic: Robert Levy interview.

Susan Levy, a whimsical woman: Interview with Susan Levy.

"Damn it, Chandra": Interview with Jim Figert, manager of the Newport Condominium, who listened to the messages on Chandra's answering machine.

Chandra's graduation plans: Susan Levy interview.

To distract himself, Robert Levy: Robert Levy interview.

Levy understood how horror could hit: Ibid.

His wife, too, knew family tragedy: Susan Levy interview.

Robert and Susan met at a dance: Robert and Susan Levy interview.

After medical school: Ibid.

In 1870, citizens wanted to name: Historic modesto.com.

Its motto was emblazoned in 668: Historic modesto.com.

The town was also home to George Lucas: Historicmodesto.com.

The Levys moved: Robert and Susan Levy interview.

As the days passed without word: Ibid.

The Merced contained a class IV: Rafting .com.

Chandra didn't want to go: Susan Levy interview.

At Davis High School, her guidance counselor: Interview with Julie Danielson.

She began spending time in high school: Robert and Susan Levy interview.

Her pull toward a conservative: Ibid.

Danielson asked Chandra to become: Danielson interview.

Racial lines divided Davis High: Ibid.; interview with Channaly Oum.

Chandra's days working at the Modesto: Robert and Susan Levy interview; Oum interview.

She shared her interest in older men: Oum interview; interview with Lisa Bracken.

By the time Chandra arrived: Robert and Susan Levy interview.

At USC, Chandra was seen as gregarious: Interview with David Grazman.

In her first year in the school's master's: Robert and Susan Levy interview.

The statehouse is impressive: California Capitol Museum.

Chandra was hired to work in the bureau's: Interview with Dan Dunne.

In the spring of 2001, a crush: Ibid.; Oklahoma City National Memorial.

On April 28, 2001, Chandra e-mailed: Allan Lengel and Petula Dvorak, "Intern Talked of 'Boyfriend,' Landlord Says," *Washington Post,* June 21, 2001.

Chandra signed on to the Internet: Confidential law enforcement documents.

The page gave her details about: Ibid.; Friends of the Peirce Mill.

A week had passed since Chandra: Robert and Susan Levy interview.

The officer who handled the call: Confidential law enforcement documents.

Robert Levy frantically placed: Robert and Susan Levy interview.

She immediately suspected that her daughter's: Susan Levy interview.

"Lord have mercy": Ibid.; Petula Dvorak and Allan Lengel, "Minister Says Daugher, at 18, Had an Affair with Condit," *Washington Post,* July 21, 2001.

Susan grew worried: Susan Levy interview.

With Chandra's graduation day: Robert and Susan Levy interview.

Susan worried that Chandra's silence: Susan Levy interview.

Robert Levy pulled out a phone book: Robert and Susan Levy interview.

"I'm the father of Chandra Levy": Robert Levy interview.

Condit told Levy that he knew Chandra: Ibid.

She knew Condit wasn't being forthcoming: Susan Levy interview.

CHAPTER 4:
CONDIT COUNTRY

This chapter is based on interviews with Gary Condit; Robert and Susan Levy; Chandra's aunt, Linda Zamsky; Chandra's USC classmate Jennifer Baker; and law enforcement sources. We also reviewed confidential law enforcement records documenting the FBI and D.C. police interviews with Gary Condit and his wife, Carolyn.

The Rose Garden, reserved for: White House Museum.

After listening to Bush speak: Dana Milbank and Juliet Eilperin, "They Never Promised Him a Rose Garden," *Washington Post,* May 1, 2001.

The largest room in the White House: White House Museum.

Condit's seat in the East Room: Terence McHale interview with Gary Condit, *California Conversations* (Winter 2008); Juliet Eilperin and Petula Dvorak, "As a Lawmaker, Condit Is Low-Key," *Washington Post,* July 24, 2001.

Condit's past had prepared him: Interview with Gary Condit; *California Conversations* interview; Eilperin and Dvorak, "As a Lawmaker, Condit Is Low-Key."

A handsome, daredevil teenager: California

Conversations interview; Eilperin and Dvorak, "As a Lawmaker, Condit Is Low-Key."

Just one year out of high school: California *Conversations* interview; Eilperin and Dvorak, "As a Lawmaker, Condit Is Low-Key"; Jennifer Frey, "Lady of the House Back Home, One Condit's Constituency Is Stronger Than Ever," *Washington Post,* August 6, 2001.

During the day, Condit attended: California *Conversations* interview; Eilperin and Dvorak, "As a Lawmaker, Condit Is Low-Key."

In the afternoons, he worked for Norris: Kenneth T. and Eileen L. Norris Foundation.

In a liberal-leaning state: Mark Arax and Stephen Braun, "The Roots of a Scandal," *Los Angeles Times,* July 16, 2001.

In 1988, Condit and his allies: California *Conversations* interview; Arax and Braun, "The Roots of a Scandal."

"We think it's time": Willie Brown, *Basic Brown: My Life and Our Times* (New York: Simon & Schuster, 2008).

After the meeting, behind the scenes: California *Conversations* interview; Brown, *Basic Brown.*

"Look, Gary, we need to bury": California Con-

versations, interview. *Condit left the luncheon, badly beaten:* Mike Sager, "The Final Days of Gary Condit," *Esquire,* September 2002.

In 1989, Tony Coelho: Charles R. Babcock, "Coelho Campaign Listed as Junk Bonds Buyer," *The Washington Post,* April 13, 1989.

Condit flew home most weekends: Frey, "Lady of the House Back Home"; Eilperin and Dvorak, "As a Lawmaker, Condit Is Low-Key."

In Washington, Condit carved out a niche: Eilperin and Dvorak, "As a Lawmaker, Condit Is Low-Key."

In 1994, a political revolution: Andrew Glass, "Congress Runs into 'Republican Revolution,' " *Politico,* November 8, 2007.

The party had campaigned under: Heritage Foundation.

He helped to organize the "Blue Dogs": House.gov/melancon/bluedogs.com.

Two days before the White House luncheon: Confidential law enforcement records documenting the FBI's interview of Carolyn Condit.

The affair began in the fall of 2000: Confidential law enforcement records documenting the FBI's interview of Gary Condit.

She was awestruck: Interview with Chandra's USC classmate Jennifer Baker; Interview with Robert and Susan Levy.

One day that October, Chandra went: Baker interview.

Each summer, as many as twenty thousand: David Plotz, "Washington Interns, They're Not as Silly and Worthless as You Think," *Slate,* July 20, 2001.

Some were paid, many were not: James Ridgeway, "D.C.'s Political Boot Camp: An Intern's Guide to Capitol Hill," *Village Voice,* July 17, 2001.

As Condit gave the two young women: Baker interview.

A few days later: Condit FBI interview.

The affair began a few weeks later: Ibid.

The fourth-floor apartment: Lloyd Grove, "The Reliable Source," *Washington Post,* October 2, 2001.

Condit saw Chandra as savvy: Condit FBI interview.

Chandra didn't tell Baker or her friends: Baker interview; interview with Lisa Bracken; interview with Channaly Oum.

Early on, Chandra confided in just one: Interview with Linda Zamsky.

The affair carried on through the winter: Condit FBI interview.

By the time Condit received: Condit interview; Condit FBI interview.

The following day, Condit received another: Condit interview.

CHAPTER 5:
AN EXPLOSIVE CASE

This chapter is based on interviews with D.C. chief of detectives Jack Barrett and D.C. police chief Charles Ramsey. We also examined confidential law enforcement records documenting the initial phases of the police investigation.

In his nearly three decades: Interview with Jack Barrett.

Headquarters was named: Paul Duggan and Ruben Castaneda, "Four Slain at D.C. Police Headquarters," *Washington Post,* November 23, 1994; and Sari Horwitz and Debbi Wilgoren, "Slain Detective Known as Dogged Investigator," *Washington Post,* November 23, 1994.

D.C. police chief Charles H. Ramsey: Interview with Charles Ramsey; Barrett interview; Peter Perl and Cheryl W. Thompson, "Community Cop," *Washington Post,* November 22, 1998.

Barrett retired in 1999: Barrett interview.

Four years after its creation: Metropolitan Police Department.

Fifteen hundred homicides went unsolved:

Cheryl W. Thompson, Ira Chinoy, and Barbara Vobejda, "Unsolved Killings Plague District," *Washington Post,* December 3, 2000.

A few months after Ramsey's arrival: Jeff Leen, Jo Craven, David Jackson, and Sari Horwitz, "District Police Lead Nation in Shootings," *Washington Post,* November 15, 1998.

The detective reported: D.C. police incident report, May 6, 2001.

He rarely saw black officers: Sari Horwitz, "The Ghosts Are Always Around a Little Bit," *Washington Post,* June 30, 1991.

Barrett also knew that Chandra had called: Barrett interview.

Of the 535 members of Congress: "Black Americans in Congress," Office of the Clerk, U.S. Capitol.

Sergeant Wyatt turned it on: Barrett interview.

CHAPTER 6:
THE IMMIGRANT

This chapter is based on interviews with Amber Fitzgerald and Sheila Phillips Cruz. It also relies on an examination of confidential law enforcement documents, D.C. court reports, and interviews that former *Washing-*

ton Post reporter Sylvia Moreno conducted with Ingmar Guandique, his friends, and his relatives. Information about the Salvadoran Civil War came from articles by Pamela Constable in the *Washington Post.* The description of the Salvadoran community in Washington and its impact on the region came from articles by Moreno, Scott Wilson, and Philip Pan in the *Washington Post* and a survey conducted by the *Post,* the Henry J. Kaiser Family Foundation, and Harvard University.

On May 1, the day Chandra disappeared: Interview with Amber Fitzgerald; confidential law enforcement documents.

The young man: Amber Fitzgerald interview; confidential law enforcement documents, Affidavit in Support of Arrest Warrant, Superior Court, March 3, 2009.

Guandique had come to the United States: Sylvia Moreno, "Fleeing Poverty, Landing in Jail," *Washington Post,* October 6, 2002; interviews with Ingmar Guandique's family in El Salvador; prison interviews with Guandique.

More than any other major: Scott Wilson and Philip P. Pan, "A Diverse, Growing Population," *Washington Post,* January 23, 2000.

CHAPTER 7:
JANET

This chapter is based on interviews with Robert and Susan Levy; Jack Barrett; and Gary Condit's personal driver, Vince Flammini. We also examined confidential law enforcement records documenting the FBI interviews with Janet. Janet was the name she first provided to the FBI. We spoke to her at her home on the West Coast and she requested that we not publish her name, to protect her children and her family from her past. We have honored her request.

They sought help from the Carole Sund/ Carrington: Interviews with Robert and Susan Levy.

On Monday, May 14: "Vigil Rallies Help for Levy Search," *Modesto Bee,* May 16, 2001.

The Levys told one of those officials: Interview with Jack Barrett.

Across the country, in San Francisco: Confidential law enforcement documents relating to FBI interviews with "Janet."

She didn't want anyone to know: FBI interviews.

She told the agent he could call her "Janet": FBI interviews.

Janet said the news reports: FBI interviews.

Janet arrived at nine that night: Ibid.

In January 1994, as Janet: Ibid.

Janet felt that she was in a serious: Ibid.

In July 1994, Janet said Condit's daughter: Ibid.

Back on the West Coast, Janet: Ibid.

He didn't like to drive: Interview with Vince Flammini.

As the interview drew to a close: FBI interviews.

CHAPTER 8:
THE WASHINGTON LAWYERS

This chapter is based on interviews with Gary Condit; his lawyer Abbe Lowell; D.C. police executive assistant chief Terrance Gainer; Susan Levy; Levy family lawyer Billy Martin; Jack Barrett; and Levy family private investigators Dwayne Stanton and J. T. McCann.

On June 11, Cotchett took on: Martin Weil, "Lawmaker Disputes Article on Missing Intern," *Washington Post,* June 12, 2001.

Several members of the California congressional delegation: Interview with Abbe Lowell.

Near dusk on an early June night: Ibid.

The last thing Condit wanted: Ibid.

Condit drove through the streets: Ibid.

Condit had resisted the idea of hiring Lowell: Ibid.

When he turned on the television: Interview with Gary Condit.

Steve Friedman, the senior executive producer: Donna St. George and Petula Dvorak, "Missing Intern Making Uncommon Impression," *Washington Post,* May 18, 2001.

He felt that his department was under enormous: Interview with Terrance Gainer.

Another police official, Assistant Police Chief: David A. Fahrenthold and Arthur Santana, "Lots of Attention but Little News as Search for Intern Continues," *Washington Post,* May 18, 2001.

On June 14, not long after his evening: Petula Dvorak and Allan Lengel, "Missing Intern's Family Asks Condit for Help," *Washington Post,* June 15, 2001.

On Saturday, June 16, two days after: Interview with Susan Levy; Petula Dvorak and Allan Lengel, "Missing Intern's Parents Back in D.C. — With New Attorney," *Washington Post,* June 20, 2001.

At fifty-one, Martin was equally comfortable: Interview with Billy Martin; Richard Leiby, "Schooled in Scandal," *Washington Post,* July 16, 2001.

Philadelphia 76ers basketball star Allen Iverson: Ibid.; Leiby, "Schooled in Scandal."

Riddick Bowe, who had kidnapped: William

411

Gildea, "Bowe Is Sentenced to 18 Months in Prison," *Washington Post,* January 17, 2003.

The detectives had interviewed dozens: Confidential law enforcement documents.

"No theory holds any more weight": Allan Lengel and Petula Dvorak, "Intern Talked of 'Boyfriend,' Landlord Says," *Washington Post,* June 21, 2001.

To the Levys and their lawyer, Billy Martin: Interview with Robert and Susan Levy; Martin interview.

The parallel investigation: Interview with Dwayne Stanton; interview with J. T. McCann; interview with Jack Barrett; Martin interview.

On the evening of June 19: Petula Dvorak and Allan Lengel, "Condit Hires New Attorney, Meets Family," *Washington Post,* June 23, 2001.

To Barrett, the Levys' insistence: Barrett interview.

Lowell met Condit in front: Lowell interview.

Susan began to ask Condit: Susan Levy interview; Martin interview.

When Susan asked Condit: Susan Levy interview; Condit interview.

Condit was surprised: Condit interview.

CHAPTER 9:
DEAR GARY

This chapter is based on interviews with Anne Marie Smith; her lawyer, James Robinson; law enforcement sources; Vince Flammini; Jack Barrett; and Linda Zamsky. We also examined court documents, Smith's travel journal, and confidential law enforcement records documenting Smith's interviews with the FBI.

He had made so many promises: Interview with Anne Marie Smith.

She began to write the letter: Anne Marie Smith travel journal entries, May 2000– July 2001.

Smith had been with United Airlines: Smith interview.

Smith called the number Condit gave her: Ibid.

Sometimes, Condit's personal driver: Interview with Vince Flammini.

Aside from his $145,100: Michael Doyle, "Condit Office Spent on Gifts, Public Records Show," *Modesto Bee,* July 22, 2001.

On December 5, 2000: Receipt, Bella Gold Imports, December 5, 2000.

An investigation by his hometown paper: Doyle, "Condit Office Spent on Gifts."

Smith felt the rush of an emotional high:

Smith interview; Smith travel journal.

Their meetings became less frequent: Smith interview; Affidavit of Anne Marie Smith in Support of a Citizen Complaint for Criminal Indictments for Obstruction of Justice and Subornation of Perjury, filed with the Stanislaus County Grand Jury, Modesto, California, August 2001.

The same day, the Washington Post *published:* Arthur Santana, "Search Intensifies for Missing Intern," *Washington Post,* May 17, 2001.

On June 1, Smith received another: Confidential law enforcement documents relating to FBI interview with Smith on June 4, 2001.

The day after the interview: Smith interview.

She began to compose another: Smith travel journal.

Smith was reeling: Smith interview.

On June 7, the Washington Post *reported:* Allan Lengel, "Intern Spent the Night, Condit Told Police," *Washington Post,* June 7, 2001.

Like Susan and Robert Levy, Zamsky: Interview with Linda Zamsky.

The first five paragraphs of the Post *story:* Lengel, "Intern Spent the Night."

A week later, on June 13: Affidavit of Anne Marie Smith.

Smith turned to a friend of her family: Smith interview.

"I do not and have not": Affidavit of Anne Marie Smith.

Robinson notified Thornton: Interview with James Robinson.

Later that day, Smith received: Smith interview.

Smith felt utterly betrayed: Ibid.

She felt consumed by all the unanswered: Smith interview; Smith travel journal.

Smith's attorney had a plan: Smith interview; Robinson interview.

"Nuts or Sluts Defense": National Organization for Women press release, "NOW Calls on Clinton to Foreswear 'Nuts or Sluts' Defense," February 25, 1999.

In the Star *story about her affair:* Smith interview.

That June, citing sources: Fox News, June 14, 2001.

She reported that Condit told the police: Fox News, June 27, 2001.

On July 2, Cosby separated herself: Fox News interview with Anne Marie Smith, July 2, 2001.

Hurt and angry, she wrote in her journal: Smith travel journal.

This chapter is based on interviews with Halle Shilling, who was attacked by Ingmar Guandique, and U.S. Park Police detective Joe Green. We also examined criminal incident reports and court records documenting the attacks in Rock Creek Park and the arrest of Guandique.

Two months after Chandra disappeared: Supplemental Criminal Incident Record, U.S. Park Police, July 2, 2001.

Her fiancé jogged ahead: Ibid.

Wiegand tried to fight back: Ibid.

Cut, bruised, and badly shaken: Ibid.

Through the translator, Green asked Guandique: Ibid.

Green recalled another unsolved attack: Ibid.; Supplemental Criminal Incident Record, U.S. Park Police, May 14, 2001; interview with Halle Shilling.

After hitting a crest in the trail: Supplemental Criminal Incident Record, May 14, 2001; Shilling interview.

Shilling realized that she was in the worst: Shilling interview.

She went for his eyes with her fingers: Supplemental Criminal Incident Record, May 14, 2001; Shilling interview.

At the Rock Creek Hotel: Supplemental

Criminal Incident Record, July 2; interview with Joe Green.

Green posed one more question to Guandique: Green interview.

CHAPTER 11:
AN INDELICATE REQUEST

This chapter is based on interviews with Abbe Lowell, Jack Barrett, assistant U.S. attorney Barbara Kittay, Linda Zamsky, and Gary Condit. It also relies on confidential law enforcement documents.

On the afternoon of July 6: Interview with Abbe Lowell; interview with Jack Barrett.

Earlier that day: Allan Lengel and Petula Dvorak, "D.C. Police Have New Questions for Condit," *Washington Post,* July 7, 2001.

At about 3 P.M., as the interview: Lowell interview.

During the nearly hour-long interview: Confidential law enforcement documents.

Barrett asked Condit to account for his whereabouts: Ibid.

Durant pressed Condit for more: Ibid.

Before the investigators left, Condit told them: Ibid.

Now, sitting with Barrett in the Starbucks: Lowell interview.

Barrett answered directly: Barrett interview.

One was a pair of black underwear: Confidential law enforcement documents.

"Gary, Gary, Gary!": Sally Quinn, "Not a Suspect," *Washington Post,* July 8, 2001.

For nearly twenty years, the parade: Petula Dvorak, "Condit Cancels His Fourth of July Appearances," *Washington Post,* July 5, 2001.

On July 5, in an FBI office: Confidential law enforcement documents.

Carolyn Condit told the prosecutors: Ibid.

But Lowell was offended: Lowell interview.

Barrett was also displeased: Barrett interview.

Lowell was not thrilled: Lowell interview.

Kittay asked the congressman: Confidential law enforcement documents; Lowell interview; Barrett interview.

But Chandra's forty-year-old aunt: Allan Lengel and Petula Dvorak, "Aunt Details Alleged Affair," *Washington Post,* July 6, 2001; interviews with Linda Zamsky.

Chandra had confided: Donna St. George, Allan Lengel, and Petula Dvorak, "D.C. Intern Lived on Edge of Secrecy," *Washington Post,* July 8, 2001.

Condit set rules: Lengel and Dvorak, "Aunt Details Alleged Affair"; Zamsky interview.

Kittay asked Condit: Confidential law enforcement documents.

Condit said his relationship with Chandra: Ibid.

Condit acknowledged to the police: Ibid.

Kittay erupted in fury: Lowell interview; interview with Barbara Kittay; Barrett interview.

In the car on the way back: Barrett interview.

Kittay was furious: Kittay interview.

About 10 P.M. on July 9: Confidential law enforcement documents; Barrett interview; Lowell interview.

CHAPTER 12:
THE INAUGURAL BALL

This chapter is based on interviews with Jack Barrett; FBI agent Brad Garrett; Sven Jones, one of Chandra's colleagues at the Bureau of Prisons; and Robert Kurkjian. The FBI also interviewed Kurkjian and he provided law enforcement officials with detailed accounts of the time he spent with Chandra.

D.C. police and FBI agents worked: Interview with Jack Barrett; interview with Brad Garrett; confidential law enforcement documents.

They were intrigued that Chandra: Confidential law enforcement documents.

Chandra was just a friend, Jones explained: Interview with Sven Jones.

After Jones passed a polygraph exam: Ibid; confidential law enforcement documents.

Investigators were also fascinated: Confidential interviews; confidential law enforcement documents.

Robert Kurkjian was a USC graduate: Interview with Robert Kurkjian; confidential law enforcement documents.

CHAPTER 13:
THE FISH BOWL

This chapter is based on interviews with *CBS Evening News* executive producer Jim Murphy; *CBS Evening News* anchor Dan Rather; CBS News president Andrew Heyward; and Daniel Olson, who witnessed the wristwatch box incident in Northern Virginia. We also examined confidential law enforcement records documenting the watch box incident and the search of Gary Condit's Washington apartment.

As executive producer of the Evening News: Interview with Jim Murphy.

Some of the more memorable episodes: Kim Long, *The Almanac of Political Corruption, Scandals & Dirty Politics* (New York: Delta Trade Paperbacks, 2007).

One woman who had an affair: Confidential interview.

In 1974, Wilbur Mills: FindLaw: Chonology of Congressional Sex Scandals.

Two years later, California congressman Robert Leggett: Ibid.

News about Congressman Wayne Hays: Marion Clark and Rudy Maxa, "Closed-Session Romance on the Hill; Rep. Wayne Hays' $14,000-a-Year Clerk Says She's His Mistress," *Washington Post,* May 23, 1976.

In 1980, the Washington Post *magazine:* Rita Jenrette with Kathleen Maxa, "Diary of a Mad Congresswife: Thoughts and Observations Most Political Wives Only Share Among Themselves," *Washington Post,* December 7, 1980.

The senator from Colorado: Long, *The Almanac of Political Corruption.*

But rumors swirled: E. J. Dionne, "Gary Hart the Elusive Front-Runner," *New York Times,* May 3, 1987.

Reporters for the Miami Herald: Jim McGee and Tom Fiedler, "Miami Woman Is Linked to Hart," *Miami Herald,* May 3, 1987.

A Gallup poll found: "Polls: Majority Call Media Coverage of Hart Wrong, Unfair," Associated Press, May 10, 1987.

The cable stations were consumed: Howard Kurtz, "Media Defend Fascination with

Story of Missing Intern," *Washington Post,* July 10, 2001.

The National Enquirer *was wrong:* "Judge: Condit's Wife Can Pursue Libel Suit Against *National Enquirer,*" Associated Press, July 10, 2002.

The New York Post *incorrectly reported:* Joshua Micha Marshall, "Chandra's Contested Calls to Condit," *Salon,* August 1, 2001.

NBC's Andrea Mitchell: Kurtz, "Media Defend Fascination with Story of Missing Intern."

At the Evening News: Murphy interview.

Murphy went public: Kurtz, "Media Defend Fascination with Story of Missing Intern."

ABC's World News Tonight *had aired a story:* Ibid.

At 11:15 that night: Arthur Santana and Bill Miller, "Police Search Congressman's D.C. Apartment; DNA, Polygraph Also Sought from Condit," *Washington Post,* July 11, 2001.

Said Fox News commentator Bill O'Reilly: The O'Reilly Factor, Fox News Channel, July 11, 2001.

After the search, Murphy started: Murphy interview.

He thought it was a tabloid story: Interview with Dan Rather.

Early in his career: Ibid.

He wasn't about to change: Ibid.

One of Rather's bosses: Interview with Andrew Heyward.

Heyward considered the arguments: Ibid.

The case had become a cultural phenomenon: Donna St. George, "Chandra Levy Spectacle Commandeers Media Stage," *Washington Post,* July 15, 2001.

Murphy had also come to believe: Murphy interview.

In the Fish Bowl in New York: Ibid.

The next day, on July 12: Petula Dvorak and Allan Lengel, "Minister Says Daughter, at 18, Had an Affair with Condit," *Washington Post,* July 12, 2001.

On July 21, the Post *ran an article:* Allan Lengel and Petula Dvorak, "Minister Recants Story About Condit; Man Told FBI His Daughter Had Affair with Congressman," *Washington Post,* July 21, 2001.

Daniel Olson, a law firm temp: Interview with Daniel Olson.

D.C. detective Lawrence Kennedy drove: Confidential law enforcement documents.

At the Evening News *in New York:* Rather interview; Murphy interview.

Chapter 14:
A Search in the Park

This chapter is based on interviews with Abbe Lowell, Jack Barrett, Terrance Gainer, and Charles Ramsey. It also relies on confidential law enforcement records documenting the efforts to polygraph Gary Condit, the pursuit of tips about Chandra's disappearance, and the police search of Rock Creek Park.

To the public, it seemed as though: Allan Lengel and Petula Dvorak, "Abandoned Buildings Searched in Levy Probe," *Washington Post,* July 13, 2001.

One psychic said that: Confidential law enforcement documents.

One of the strangest tips of all: Ibid.

The FBI heard about the tip: Ibid.

On June 7, a month after: Confidential law enforcement sources and documents.

The news media didn't find out: Allan Lengel and Sari Horwitz, "Levy Looked Up Map of a Rock Creek Site," *Washington Post,* July 16, 2001; interview with Terrance Gainer.

She had actually been looking up: Confidential law enforcement sources and documents.

Reporters continued to besiege: Gainer interview.

The prosecutors assigned to the case: Interview with Barbara Kittay.

The new chief of detectives: Interview with Jack Barrett.

In this case — his first as a D.C. police official: Ibid.

Barrett took an unusual step: Ibid.

Behind the scenes: Interview with Abbe Lowell.

A poll of likely voters: John Lancaster and Juliet Eilperin, "Condit's Political Support Slipping," *Washington Post,* July 12, 2001.

The Levys urged the police: Petula Dvorak and Allan Lengel, "Levy Family Seeks Condit Polygraph," *Washington Post,* July 9, 2001.

Lowell didn't believe in polygraphs: Lowell interview.

They were so unreliable that Aldrich Ames: Bill Miller and Michael Isikoff, "CIA Officer Charged with Selling Secrets," *Washington Post,* February 23, 1994.

Lowell crafted another strategy: Lowell interview.

On the afternoon of July 12: Ibid.

The next day, Lowell called Barrett: Ibid.

"I think he has done what a person could do": Allan Lengel and Petula Dvorak, "At-

torney Says Condit Passed Polygraph Test," *Washington Post,* July 14, 2001.

Police Chief Charles Ramsey dismissed: Allan Lengel and Petula Dvorak, "D.C. Police Reject Condit's Polygraph," *Washington Post,* July 19, 2001; interview with Charles Ramsey.

Then he went a step further: Lowell interview.

You guys are bordering: Ibid.

Gainer lost his composure: Ibid.

He told reporters that the police: Lengel and Dvorak, "Attorney Says Condit Passed Polygraph Test."

Gainer then did: Lengel and Horwitz, "Levy Looked Up Map of a Rock Creek Site."

"It seems the congressman": Lengel and Dvorak, "Attorney Says Condit Passed Polygraph Test."

On the Sunday morning television show: Richard Leiby, "Schooled in Scandal," *Washington Post,* July 16, 2001.

On July 18, Chief Ramsey told the press: Lengel and Dvorak, "D.C. Police Reject Condit's Polygraph."

An article in the Washington Post: Allan Lengel and Bill Miller, "Box in Trash Spurs Levy Probe," *Washington Post,* July 22, 2001.

Then came stories: Allan Lengel and Petula Dvorak, "Senior Condit Aide Talks to

Investigators," *Washington Post,* July 27, 2001; Tom Squitieri and Kevin Johnson, "Top Aide to Condit Added to Probe," *USA Today,* July 26, 2001.

There was one embarrassing detail: Confidential law enforcement documents; law enforcement sources.

To Barrett, it seemed: Barrett interview.

Reporters were drilling into his past: Mark Arax and Stephen Braun, "The Roots of a Scandal," *Los Angeles Times,* July 16, 2001; Bob Dart, "The Cop, the Criminal and the Congressman," *Atlanta Journal-Constitution,* July 21, 2001.

Flammini said he constantly covered: Fox News, July 26, 2001.

With tensions between police and Condit: Ramsey interview; Lengel and Dvorak, "D.C. Police Reject Condit's Polygraph."

He tried to maintain his work routine: Interview with Gary Condit.

In typical Washington fashion: Donna St. George, "Chandra Levy Spectacle Commandeers Media Stage," *Washington Post,* July 15, 2001.

The congressman couldn't believe: Condit interview.

He was engaged in bisexual and gay: Lloyd Grove, "The Reliable Source," *Washington Post,* July 20, 2001.

At 8:58 on the morning of: Barrett interview; Ramsey interview; confidential law enforcement documents; law enforcement sources.

Ramsey thought that he had ordered: Ramsey interview; Barrett interview; confidential law enforcement documents.

Chapter 15:
The Wrong Man

This chapter is based on interviews with Brad Garrett, Abbe Lowell, Jack Barrett, Terrance Gainer, Kim Rossmo, and Jim Murphy. It also relies on confidential law enforcement documents and interviews.

FBI Agent Brad Garrett approached: Patricia Davis and Maria Glod, "CIA Shooter Kasi, Harbinger of Terror, Set to Die Tonight," *Washington Post,* November 14, 2002; interview with Brad Garrett.

The former Marine from Anderson, Indiana: Garrett interview.

The D.C. police department was technically: Ibid.

When investigators contacted Abbe Lowell: Interview with Abbe Lowell.

At the CBS Evening News *in New York:* Interview with Jim Murphy.

On the night of July 18: CBS Evening News transcript.

Lowell and Condit felt emboldened: Lowell interview.

She had helped actress Julianne Moore prepare: Ign.com.

On the evening of July 26: Garrett interview.

Garrett had already examined: Ibid.

After nearly three months of investigating: Petula Dvorak and Allan Lengel, "Leads in Levy Case Depleted, Ramsey Says," *Washington Post,* July 30, 2001.

When the interview began at 7:50 that night: Lowell interview; Garrett interview.

Condit described Chandra and provided details: Confidential law enforcement documents.

As the interview progressed, Garrett began to see: Garrett interview.

Chandra was still a teen: Richard Leiby and Petula Dvorak, "The Wait of Their Lives," *Washington Post,* August 21, 2001.

As Lowell listened to the questions: Lowell interview.

During the interview, Condit raised: Lowell interview; Garrett interview.

After the interview: Interview with Jack Barrett; interview with Terrance Gainer.

In Lafayette, Louisiana: D'Vera Cohn and Allan Lengel, "Bullets, Locations Hold Clues to Shootings, Investigators Are Using Latest Scientific Tools in Effort to

429

Solve Series of Crimes," *Washington Post,*
August 8, 2002; Lindsay Kines, "Behind
the Scenes with a Celebrity Cop: Map-
ping Evil," *Vancouver Sun,* June 19, 1999.
Rossmo had also used the program: Interview with Kim Rossmo; Arthur Santana,
"D.C. Man Convicted of Women's Slay-
ings," *Washington Post,* October 3, 2001.
Rossmo based his computer program: "Geographic Profiling," Kim Rossmo research
paper, 1998; Cohn and Lengel, "Bullets,
Locations Hold Clues"; Rossmo interview.

CHAPTER 16:
PRIME TIME

This chapter is based on interviews with
Gary Condit, Abbe Lowell, and Susan and
Robert Levy. It also relies on the transcript
of Condit's appearance on ABC's *Primetime
Thursday* with Connie Chung and a paper
Chung prepared for the Joan Shorenstein
Center on the Press, Politics, and Public
Policy at Harvard University, titled: "The
Business of Getting 'The Get': Nailing an
Exclusive Interview in Prime Time."
Abbe Lowell decided that the time had come:
Interview with Abbe Lowell.
Condit stood on the precipice: "Congressman
Has Violated the Public Trust," editorial,

Modesto Bee, August 12, 2001.

At forty-two, Dennis Cardoza: Evelyn Nieves, "Condit Loses House Race to Former Aide," *New York Times,* March 6, 2002.

Cardoza had said he would not run: Brian Melley, "Protégé Seeking Condit's Seat in Congress," Associated Press, October 23, 2001.

Deep down, Condit didn't want: Lowell interview.

Condit was sickened by the spectacle: Interview with Gary Condit.

Since her days as a local television reporter: Connie Chung biography.

She thought there was nothing wrong: Connie Chung, "The Business of Getting 'The Get': Nailing an Exclusive Interview in Prime Time," Joan Shorenstein Center on the Press, Politics, and Public Policy, April 1998.

Condit and his advisers considered: Lowell interview.

It was the biggest scoop: Virginia Heffernan, "Barbara Walters: The Exit Interview," *New York Times,* September 5, 2004.

On August 22: Condit letter to constituents, August 22, 2001.

The day of the interview: Lowell interview.

Condit was nervous when he met Chung: Howard Kurtz, "Chung on Condit: 'I Was

Incredulous' at Evasive Answers," *Washington Post,* August 25, 2001.

Nearly 24 million people: Lisa de Moraes, "Almost 24 Million Tune In to Chung-Condit," *Washington Post,* August 25, 2001.

"Congressman Condit, do you know": ABC News Transcript, *Primetime Thursday,* August 23, 2001.

Condit started to reel: Condit interview.

She wondered to herself: Kurtz, "Chung on Condit."

The cause was lost: Condit interview.

Lowell could barely watch: Lowell interview.

He told him he had done: Ibid.

Chung thought she had done her job: Kurtz, "Chung on Condit."

It was the most watched television show: Lisa de Moraes, "Chung Didn't Get Anything Out of Condit — Except High Ratings," *Washington Post,* August 29, 2001.

Chung outperformed her previous big interview: De Moraes, "Almost 24 Million Tune In to Chung-Condit."

"Why don't you just whisper it to me": Colman McCarthy, "The TV Whisper," *Washington Post,* January 7, 1995.

Condit knew he should have gone: Condit interview.

Nineteen days after the interview: Interview

with Robert and Susan Levy.

CHAPTER 17:
A SATELLITE ISSUE

This chapter is based on interviews with jailhouse informant "Ramón Alvarez"; Jack Barrett; Halle Shilling; law enforcement sources close to the case; and Karen Mosley, who was accosted by a man in Rock Creek Park. We also examined court files and hearing transcripts, along with confidential law enforcement records documenting the FBI polygraph exams of Alvarez and Ingmar Guandique. Alvarez is a pseudonym we used to protect the informant from reprisals in prison, where he is serving a life sentence for armed sexual assault.

Far from the chaos of a city: Sentencing hearing transcript, Ingmar Guandique, D.C. Superior Court, February 8, 2002.

Ament explained that there was: Ibid.

In mid-September 2001: Confidential law enforcement documents; prison interview with Ramón Alvarez.

On September 24, three days after: Confidential law enforcement documents.

Mosley heard some rustling: Interview with Karen Mosley.

On July 24, four days after: Confidential law enforcement documents.

The chief of detectives, Jack Barrett: Interview with Jack Barrett.

Now, with an explosive but unverifiable: Interviews with law enforcement sources; confidential law enforcement documents.

On November 28, Alvarez: Confidential law enforcement records documenting the FBI polygraph of Alvarez.

Nearly ten weeks later: Confidential law enforcement records documenting the FBI polygraph of Guandique.

The readings were inconclusive: Interviews with law enforcement sources.

Barrett wanted a Spanish-speaking: Barrett interview.

A presentence report noted: Pre-Sentence Report, Court Services and Offender Supervision Agency for the District of Columbia, August 6, 2001.

Equally troubling was Guandique's performance: Psychological Assessment, Forensic Health Services, Diagnostic and Reception Psychology Department, Correctional Treatment Facility, November 21, 2001.

On a Beta III exam: Pearson, Psychology and Counseling, Product Overview, Beta II Exam.

As the sentencing hearing continued: Sentencing hearing transcript.

Shilling was eight months pregnant: Interview with Halle Shilling.

"Good afternoon": Sentencing hearing transcript.

CHAPTER 18:
A GRISLY FIND

This chapter is based on interviews with Robert and Susan Levy; Park Police sergeant Dennis Bosak; D.C. medical examiner Jonathan Arden; Charles Ramsey; Dwayne Stanton; J. T. McCann; and Amy Keller, a writer for *Roll Call.* It also relies on confidential law enforcement records documenting the discovery of Chandra's remains.

Robert and Susan Levy sat side by side: Steve Twomey and Sari Horwitz, "With Levy Case Going Nowhere, Chance Stepped In," *Washington Post,* May 26, 2002.

She asked the couple whether they believed: Ibid.; interview with Robert and Susan Levy.

For Condit, the inevitable had taken place: Rene Sanchez, "Condit Loses Primary in California," *Washington Post,* March 6, 2002.

After the interview: Robert and Susan Levy interview.

Across the country: This account is based on

notes taken by Sari Horwitz; Twomey and Horwitz, "With Levy Case Going Nowhere."

At about 8:30 that morning: Robert and Susan Levy interview.

U.S. Park Police Sergeant Dennis Bosak: U.S. Park Police investigative reports; interview with Dennis Bosak.

In recent years, the religion that combines: Sylvia Moreno, "The Spirit of Santeria," *Washington Post,* January 4, 2000.

At the tree branch: Bosak interview; confidential law enforcement documents.

Bosak had another thought: Bosak interview; confidential law enforcement documents.

Does this scene remind you: Confidential law enforcement documents.

Within hours of Bosak's arrival: Horwitz notes.

The media was in a full-blown: Howard Kurtz, "The Story That Swept the Media," *Washington Post,* May 23, 2002.

He brought it back to his office: Interview with Jonathan Arden; Twomey and Horwitz, "With Levy Case Going Nowhere."

It's possible to search: Steve Twomey and Sari Horwitz, "Chandra Levy's Remains Found in Park," *Washington Post,* May 23, 2002.

On May 28, Arden called: Sari Horwitz and

Allan Lengel, "Chandra Levy Ruled a Homicide Victim," *Washington Post,* May 29, 2002.

That same day: Petula Dvorak, "At Calif. Memorial Service, a Fuller Picture of Chandra," *Washington Post,* May 29, 2002; Robert and Susan Levy interview.

Two weeks after Chandra's remains: Interviews with J. T. McCann and Dwayne Stanton.

Wearing jeans and T-shirts: Firsthand account by Horwitz; Allan Lengel and Sari Horwitz, "Police Again Scour Park in Levy Case," *Washington Post,* June 8, 2002.

Later that night, after examining: Arden interview.

Ramsey was furious: Interview with Charles Ramsey; interviews with law enforcement sources.

The detectives then turned their attention: Confidential law enforcement documents.

Washington Post *columnist Marc Fisher:* Marc Fisher, "A Thin Line Between Raking and Rakishness," *Washington Post,* June 8, 2002.

They found her heel bone: Confidential law enforcement documents.

After Chandra's remains were found: Amy Keller, "The Chandra Conspiracy," Salon.com, June 5, 2002.

Gladys Joseph had already contacted: Interview with Ingmar Guandique by *Washington Post* staff writer Sylvia Moreno.

CHAPTER 19:
A VIABLE SUSPECT

This chapter is based on interviews with Halle Shilling, Brad Garrett, Robert and Susan Levy, law enforcement sources, criminal profiler Kim Rossmo, Abbe Lowell, and Jack Barrett. We also examined confidential law enforcement records documenting the renewed search for clues in Chandra's case.

When Halle Shilling heard that Chandra's: Interview with Halle Shilling.

A few enterprising reporters: Halle Shilling, "Fight, and Live to Run Another Day: A Long-Ago Lesson in Self-Defense Saves a Woman Attacked on a D.C. Park Path," *Washington Post,* April 15, 2002.

They located Shilling and her family: Shilling interview.

Beyond the glare of the media: Confidential law enforcement documents.

The detectives decided they didn't need: Law enforcement sources.

The detectives also faced another problem: Confidential law enforcement documents.

Four weeks later: Ibid.

On August 12: Ibid.

To assist the investigation: Interview with Kim Rossmo.

Rossmo visited all three crime scenes: Ibid.

Rossmo prepared a report: Ibid.

In the mind of the FBI agent: Garrett interview.

Elisa Poteat was a young, promising: Interviews with law enforcement sources.

The daughter of a CIA science and technology officer: Biography of Gene Poteat, featured speaker, Raleigh Spy Conference, 1996; interviews with law enforcement sources.

Her chief adversaries: Interview with Jack Barrett; interview with Abbe Lowell.

Poteat viewed Guandique as the prime suspect: Interviews with law enforcement sources; confidential law enforcement documents.

While Durant and Kennedy: Confidential law enforcement documents.

During those interrogations: Ibid.

Brad Garrett joined Poteat: Ibid.

As Poteat ramped up her investigation: Washington Post Staff Writers, "Man's Friends Face Levy Case Grand Jury," *Washington Post,* October 4, 2002.

She repeated what she had told: Confidential

law enforcement documents.

Poteat subpoenaed phone records: Ibid.

Figueras and Martinez made it to Newport News: Ibid.

In early October, an unfolding rampage: Sari Horwitz and Michael E. Ruane, *Sniper: Inside the Hunt for the Killers Who Terrorized the Nation* (New York: Random House, 2003).

Poteat pressed on: Confidential law enforcement documents.

In November, Durant and Kennedy: Ibid.

As the year wound down: Ibid.

In May 2003: Interview with Robert and Susan Levy; Allan Lengel, "Chandra Levy's Remains Buried," *Washington Post,* May 28, 2003.

CHAPTER 20:
AN ARREST

This chapter is based on interviews with Charles Ramsey, Terrance Gainer, D.C. police chief Cathy Lanier, Jack Barrett, Halle Shilling, Abbe Lowell, Brad Garrett, Robert and Susan Levy, and law enforcement sources. It also relies on court documents filed in the first-degree murder case against Ingmar Guandique.

On Sunday, July 13, 2008: Sari Horwitz,

Scott Higham, and Sylvia Moreno, "Who Killed Chandra Levy?" *Washington Post,* July 13–27, 2008.

On the final day of the series: Deborah Howell, "A 13-Part Series to Love or Hate," *Washington Post,* July 27, 2008.

Far from the controversy: Confidential law enforcement sources.

At the conclusion of the series: Interview with Charles Ramsey.

The chief said she hoped the series: Interview with Cathy Lanier.

In September 2008: Affidavit in Support of an Arrest Warrant, Superior Court of the District of Columbia, March 3, 2009.

Ever since Guandique's conviction in 2002: Confidential law enforcement sources.

With a warrant in hand: Affidavit in Support of an Arrest Warrant.

At three that afternoon: Government's Consolidated Opposition to Defendant's Motions to Suppress Statements and Tangible Evidence, December 11, 2008.

In the fall of 2008, detectives: Ibid.

Guandique was specific about one of these: Ibid.

Also during the fall of 2008: Ibid.

As 2008 drew to a close: Interview with Halle Shilling.

After Shilling testified: Affidavit in Support of

an Arrest Warrant.

The Associated Press reported: Gillian Gaynair, "8-Year Mystery of Chandra Levy's Slaying May End," Associated Press, February 22, 2009.

When Guandique heard in prison: Affidavit in Support of an Arrest Warrant.

Early on the afternoon of March 3: Press conference, Metropolitan Police Department, Washington, D.C., March 3, 2009.

A month before the series ran: Interview with Gary Condit.

After the announcement: Interview with Abbe Lowell.

Ever since Guandique's arrest: Sari Horwitz and Scott Higham, "Warrant Is Issued for Suspect in Levy Killing," *Washington Post,* March 4, 2009.

In the months that followed Guandique's: "Other Crimes Evidence," attachment to letter from Assistant U.S. Attorney Amanda Haines to U.S. Public Defender Service attorney Santha Sonnenberg, June 17, 2009.

On December 2: Superior Court Grand Jury Indictment, filed December 2, 2009.

For Brad Garrett: Interview with Brad Garrett.

Terrance Gainer was unconvinced: Interview with Terrance Gainer.

Over the course of time, Jack Barrett: Interview with Jack Barrett.

On December 14, 2008: Shilling interview.

Following Guandique's arrest: Robert and Susan Levy interview.

Their son, Adam: Interview with Adam Levy.

It turns your stomach: Interview with Susan Levy.

ACKNOWLEDGMENTS

This book would not have been possible without the help and support of our many colleagues at the *Washington Post*. We must first thank Jeff Leen, Larry Roberts, and Barbara Vobejda, our editors in the *Post*'s Investigative Unit, who first conceived of the idea to examine the Chandra Levy case. They gave us a challenging assignment and allowed us to spend a year unraveling the mystery behind the police investigation into the disappearance and murder of the twenty-four-year-old Washington intern. They are superb editors — the best in the business — and good friends.

The *Washington Post* published our investigation in an experimental thirteen-part series in the paper and on washingtonpost .com. We owe our heartfelt thanks to Donald E. Graham, the chairman of the board of The Washington Post Company, and former executive editor Leonard Downie,

445

for encouraging us to take chances and supporting our investigative efforts. We also thank our publisher, Katharine Weymouth, and Boisfeuillet Jones Jr., chairman of the The Washington Post, for allowing us to leave the newsroom to continue our work and turn the series into this book.

An extremely talented group of colleagues and friends became our editors: special thanks to Tom Shroder, who guided the manuscript with a deft hand and impeccable judgment. We are also deeply indebted to Michael and Rosalie Pakenham, Caitlin Gibson, Bill Schultz, and Paulette Kessler. They provided us with invaluable advice and encouragement, and spent countless hours helping us organize our material and turn our words into prose. This is a better book because of them.

We extend our gratitude and admiration to our *Post* colleagues, especially Petula Dvorak and Allan Lengel, who first worked on this story day and night during the summer of 2001 to make sense of the convoluted, rapidly developing case. Thanks also to Michael Doyle, Washington correspondent for McClatchy Newspapers, for his fine work on the story and to Michael Isikoff, who covered the story for *Newsweek* and shared his insights with us. We are especially grateful to our former colleague Sylvia Moreno, who worked with us on the series and conducted several prison interviews with Ingmar Guandique. To this day, she is the only journalist who has interviewed the man suspected of murdering Chandra Levy. The amazing *Washington Post* researcher Meg Smith deserves special thanks for her energy, her enthusiasm, and her ability to track down anyone, anywhere, anytime. Michel duCille, Lois Raimondo, Pierre Kattar, and Alex Garcia amplified our words with their vision and powerful images. Thank you to Melissa Maltby, who found the photographs for the book, and Laura Stanton, who helped obtain the map of Rock Creek Park.

There are several people who cared enough about the truth to risk their livelihoods to help us assemble the puzzle pieces of this case. They know who they are, and we thank them for the trust they placed in us.

For providing inspiration, guidance, and unwavering support, we are grateful for our fabulous agent, Gail Ross, and her talented team, Howard Yoon and Anna Sproul. They believed in the importance of this project from the start and went far beyond the call of duty to ensure that we produced the best book possible. When we first began, we were aided by several friends and esteemed colleagues who have themselves written books and were generous with their time and advice: Rick Atkinson, Peter Eisner, Jane Mayer, Neal Thompson, and Elsa Walsh. Thank you to our friends Amy Boesky, Debbie Brown, and Jackie Meltzer, who took the time to read our manuscript, and Valerie Strauss, who urged editors at the *Post* early on to reinvestigate the Chandra Levy case.

We thank our mothers, Barbara Higham and Zella Horwitz, who have always been there for us and were incredibly supportive and loving while we worked on this investigation. Thanks also to our siblings, Derek Higham, Craig Higham, Heidi Horwitz, and Wendy Greenwald, who were understanding when we promised so many times to be more attentive "after the book is finished." Sari wishes she could share this tale with her late father, William Honor Horwitz, a wonderful storyteller who loved to write fiction and children's stories in his spare time and inspired her to become a writer. And Scott hopes that his father, Lee Higham, who always fought for the underdog, would be proud.

At Scribner, we would like to thank pub-

lisher Susan Moldow and editor-in-chief
Nan Graham for believing in this book. We
were fortunate to be in the hands of an
extraordinary editor, Beth Wareham, whose
candor, sense of humor, and creativity
guided us to the completion of our first
book together. We'd also like to thank associate editor Whitney Frick, who was
patient and kind to us on a tight deadline
schedule, production editor Laura Wise,
copyeditor Tom Pitoniak, cover designer
Rex Bonomelli, and book interior designer
Erich Hobbing.

We're grateful to Eric Lieberman, James
McLaughlin, and Amber Husbands for their
smart legal reads throughout the course of
this endeavor. The talented duo of John
Simmons and Christine Thompson of the
troupe Gross National Project spent many
hours escorting us around Washington and
sharing with us the stories behind the city's
most infamous congressional scandals.
Thanks to them for helping us understand.

We could have never written this book
without Bill Schultz and Caitlin Gibson,
who provided not only their good judgment
and advice but also their understanding and
love. We are so grateful they are in our lives.
We are also deeply thankful for our wonderful children, Jack Higham and Rachael

Honor Schultz. They bring great joy to us every day.

Finally, we thank Chandra's parents, Robert and Susan Levy, who sat with us for many emotional and painful interviews. They taught us about faith and courage and how to persevere in the face of unfathomable heartache. We hope that our work someday brings them some semblance of justice.

PHOTOGRAPH CREDITS

Associated Press.
Page 173: Photograph by Lois Raimondo, courtesy of the *Washington Post.*
Page 185: Photograph by Sari Horwitz.
Page 209: Photograph by Robert A. Reeder, courtesy of the *Washington Post.*
Page 221: Photograph by Dudley M. Brooks, courtesy of the *Washington Post.*
Page 245: Photograph by Robert A. Reeder, courtesy of the *Washington Post.*
Page 265: Photograph courtesy of the *Washington Post.*
Page 281: Photograph by American Broadcasting Companies.
Page 307: Photograph by Kevin Clark, courtesy of the *Washington Post.*
Page 327: Photograph by Gerald Martineau, courtesy of the *Washington Post.*
Page 347: Photograph by Linda Davidson, courtesy of the *Washington Post.*
Page 365: Photograph by Lois Raimondo, courtesy of the *Washington Post.*

ABOUT THE AUTHORS

Scott Higham and Sari Horwitz are reporters for the investigate unit of the *Washington Post.* They have collaborated on several projects, including an examination of the deaths of children in the D.C. foster system, which won the 2002 Pulitzer Prize for Investigative Reporting and the Robert F. Kennedy Journalism Award for reporting on the disadvantaged. Horwitz also shared in the 1999 Pulitzer for Public Service and the 2008 Pulitzer Prize for Breaking News Reporting. They both live in the Washington, D.C., area.